एकता – *Ekatā*

(Oneness among *Śiva*, *Śakti* and *Viṣṇu*)

*

Dr. Ramamurthy N

M.Sc., B.G.L., CAIIB, CCP, DSADP, CISA, PMP, CGBL, Ph.D.

*

*

Name:	एकता - ***Ekatā*** (Oneness among *Śiva, Śakti* and *Viṣṇu*)
First Edition:	2016
Author:	**Dr. Ramamurthy N,** Chennai.
Copyright ©:	With the author (No part of this book may be reproduced in any manner whatsoever without the written permission from the author).
ISBN (13):	978-93-82237-10-5
Number of pages:	278
Price:	₹.

*****

TABLE OF CONTENTS

*****

Dedication

Better Half

In Tamil there is a saying *"tāikku pin tāram"* – literally translated into "after mother it is wife".

The saying is apt in my case with my wife *Śrīmati* **Radha Ramamurthy** fitting into my mother's shoes virtually in all respects**.** Starting from adding my name into hers, she has been *with* me in all my ups and *behind* me in all my downs, as goes the saying "there is a woman behind every successful man". **S**he is the **WO**man complementing, supplementing, encouraging, nourishing, enriching and supporting me in all my endeavours. It is because of her I am what I am today.

I show my gratitude for her unrelenting dedication to the cause of the family and being a leader of Womanhood, by dedicating this book to her – It is an apt fitting instance of *Śiva-Śakti* in a single unified form.

Dr. *Ramamurthy N*

*****

Blessings

Sri Ramajayam

***Dr. R**amamurthy,* a well known renowned scholar needs no introduction. He has authored many books to inculcate spiritual and divine values of God worship. This book is unique in bringing out striking similarities and on *Ekataeness* of *Shiva, Shakthi* and *Vishnu* worship and prayers by a deep analysis and study of the thousand names of lord *Shiva, Lalithaambika* and *Vishnu* with apt comparisons from *Sahasranamas,* states that 186 names from *Shiva,* 176 names from *Lalitha* and 207 names from *Vishnu Sahasranamams* are similar and convey the same messages thus reiterating that *Shiva, Shakthi* and *Vishnu* are all one which can be understood by devotees on a prolonged state at the spiritual sphere.

He has also analysed *Sri Ruddra trishati naamaavali* and has quoted 18 comparable names.

The title of this book is quite apt, particularly in the context of present day controversies and conflicts. He has also brought out the prime source of creation to all pervading *Shakthi,* the prime divine energy, and aptly dedicated this book to his **better half** in due recognition of this pattern.

Adi Shankara's epic stotra *Soundaryalahari* starts with the first verse

शिव शक्त्या युक्तो यति भवति .... firmly declares oneness of *Shiva* and *Sakthi*.

Also *Adi Shankara* in his famous *Baja Govindam* sings मयी त्वयि अन्यत्र ऐको विष्णुः .... the same, the ***Sarva Vyaapi Vishnu*** dwells in all beings firmly declaring the oneness of *Vishnu*, *Shiva* and *Shakthi*.

Three in one Ekata ..... One in all is Ramamurthy

My blessings and best wishes to Dr **Ramamurthy** and family, and all readers of this precious book.

Nārāayaṇa Nārāayaṇa Nārāayaṇa

May 2015. ***Rāmānanda Bhārati***

*****

Introduction

ओं – Om

वक्र तुण्ड महाकाय कोटिसूर्य समप्रभ । अविघ्नं कुरु मे देव सर्व कार्येषु सर्वदा ।।

Vakratuṇḍa mahākāya koṭisūrya samaprabha | Avighnam kuru me deva sarva kāryeşu sarvadā

गुरुर्ब्रह्मा गुरुर्विष्णुर्गुरुर्देवो महेश्वरः । गुरुसाक्षात् परं ब्रह्म तस्मै श्रीगुरवे नमः ।।

Gururbrahmā gururviṣṇurgururdevo maheśvaraḥ | Gurusākshāt param Brahma tasmai śrī gurave namaḥ |

सदाशिव समारंबम् शंकराचार्य मध्यमाम् । अस्मद् आचार्य पर्यन्ताम् वन्दे गुरु परंपराम्

Sadāśiva samārambām śankarācārya madhyamām | Asmad ācārya paryantām vande guru paramparām |

वागर्थाविव सम्प्रुक्तौ वागर्थप्रतिपत्तये । जगतः पितरौ वन्दे पार्वतीपरमेश्वरौ ।।

Vāgarthāviva sampruktou vāgarthapratipattaye I Jagataḥ pitarou vande pārvatiparameśvarou

Sages have authentically confirmed that only the person who has done virtues (*puṇyas*) in previous births can learn do worship of Lords, in this birth. Actually the below verse is meant for *Śrīvidya* worship. But it is equally applicable to any worship – "*Carame janmani yadha Śrī vidyā upāsako bhaveth*". In Tamil also there is a famous saying *Avanarulāleye Avan Tāl Vananki*. Unless the Lord decides, no one can worship him nor think of him, leave alone writing books.

Earlier, couple of years back, this author was fortunate to write a book on *Śrī Lalitā Sahasranāma*, complete English translation of *Śrī Bāskararāya's bhāśyam*. With the divine blessings I also chant *Śrī Lalitā* and *Vişṇu Sahasranāmas*. Also another book called "*Samatā* – समता (An exposition of similarities in *Lalitā Sahasranāma* with *Soundaryalaharī, Saptaśatī, Viśṇu Sahasranāma* and *Śrīmad Bhagavad Gīta*)". Again just before *Śivaratri* we chant *Rudram*, 11 times a day for 11 days and also perform *Śiva Sahasranāma arcana*. At that time, when I dwelled into the names and meanings of the 1000 names in *Śiva Sahasranāma*, lot many names were common or conveyed same message as the names in *Lalitā* and *Vişṇu Sahasranāmas*. These actions lead to a kind of exploration of finding out the commonalities in these names, which stresses that the forms like *Śiva*, *Śakti* and *Vişṇu* are all just for the mental satisfaction of the devotees. The God is something above – formless (*Amūrtā* – अमूर्ता) and character/ attribute-less (*Nirguṇā* – निर्गुणा). The devotees for their own convenience, on account of illusion, like a child plays with clay, gives some form like *Ganeśa*, *Śiva*, *Vişṇu*,

Śakti, etc., and worship. Once they get maturity, they can imagine that all Lords are one and the same and understand a formless God.

In this universe the number three has been given much importance – most of the things are in triad or threesome; There are three *Devas*, three *Vedas*, three fires, three energies, three notes (*svaras*), three worlds, three abodes, three cities, three sacred lakes, three castes, etc.

- Three letters of *Praṇava mantra – a, u* and *m*.
- Three status of human beings – *jāgruth, swapna* and *śuśupti*.
- Three pairs of *mūrtis – Brahma-Sarasvathī, Viṣṇu-Lakṣmī* and *Rudra-Pārvatī*
- Three pairs of brother-sisters – *Brahma-Lakṣmī* in gold colour, *Viṣŋu-Pārvatī* in blue colour and *Śiva-Sarasvathī* in white colour.
- Three major tasks – creation, protection and destruction
- Three Gunas –*rajo* and *tamo* and *satva*.
- Three knots (*grantis*) in the path of *Kuṇḍalinī Śakti – Brahma, Viṣhŋu* and *Rudra Grantis*.
- Three *nāḍis* viz., *Susumnā, Pingalā* and *Idā* each relating to the organ *Manas, Buddhi* and *Citta*.
- Even *Bilva* or *Tulasi* leaves when used during worshipping is used in triad only. The bilva archana starts with "*Tridalam triguṇākāram trinetram, trijanma papam*". All are in threesome.

Hence the three forms of Gods – *Śiva, Śakti* and *Viṣṇu* are considered in this book and their *Sahasranāmas* compared. It is found that 186 names from *Śiva,* 176 names from *Lalitā* and 207 names from *Viṣṇu sahasranāmas* are similar and convey and the same messages. *Śrī Rudra Triśatī Nāmāvalī* is also analysed and 18 names comparable to other names are quoted. Still it is possible that this study might not have been comprehensive. But whatever has been observed, itself is an amazing evidence of oneness (*Ekatā*) among the three Gods. For ready reference, the 1000 names from *Śiva, Lalitā* and *Viṣṇu sahasranāmas* are given in annexure.

Thirumoolar has shouted loudly "*Onre Kulam oruvane Devan*" – which means there is only one religion and only one God. *Svetāśvatara Upaniṣat* indicates "there is only one *Deva*" – *devaḥ ekam*.This substantiates the subject of this entire book.

Conventions – Wherever **She** is used to indicate *Śrīdevī* it has been written in bold as **She** and similarly **he** is given in bod wherever it indicates Lord *Viṣṇu*. The transliterated Samskrutam or other language words are written in *italics*. When Samskrutam words are transliterated in English diacritical marks are used for proper pronunciation like;

ā – as in *Rama*	*ḍ* – as in mud
ḍh – as in godhood	*ḥ* – visarga in as in *Rāma*:
ī – as in peel	*ṇ* – as in pun
ṛ – as in strewn	*ś* – as in Shankar
ṣ – as in fish	*ṭ* – as in cut
ṭh – as in anthill	*ū* – as in root

My humble pranams to HH *ŚrīŚrī* ***Rāmānanda Bhārati Swāmijee***, who has blessed me and the readers with his nice introduction and some pleasantries. I am fortunate to have association with people like him. My sincere thanks are due to *Śrī* Pradeep Mittal of Originals, who arranged to print and publish this book so nicely.

My appreciation and acknowledgements are due to all those who supported in this noble cause.

The readers are requested to feel free in providing comments and feedback to the author. Let all the readers be blessed with glory of Gods.

Om Tat Sat

Chennai
March 2016

Dr. *Ramamurthy N*

*****

Śiva, Śakti and *Viṣṇu*

Śakti, meaning 'power' or 'empowerment', is the primordial cosmic energy and represents the dynamic forces that are thought to move through the entire universe. *Śakti* is the concept, or personification, of divine feminine creative power, referred to as "The Great Divine Mother". On the earthly plane, *Śakti* most actively manifests through female embodiment and creativity/ fertility, though it is also present in males in its potential, un-manifest form.

Not only *Śakti* is responsible for creation, it is also the agent of all changes. *Śakti* is cosmic existence as well as liberation, its most significant form being the *Kuṇḍalinī Śakti,* a mysterious psycho-spiritual force. *Śakti* exists in a state of *svātantrīya,* dependence on no one, being interdependent with the entire universe.

In *Śāktam* and *Śaivism, Śakti* is worshipped as the Supreme Being. *Śakti* embodies the active feminine energy of *Śiva* and is identified as *Mahādevī* or *Pārvatī.*

David Kinsley mentions the '*Śakti*' as consort of *Indra's* as *Sacidevī* (*Indrāṇī*), meaning power. *Indrāṇī* is part of a group of seven or eight mother goddesses called the *Mātrikās* (*Brahmāṇī, Vaiṣṇavī, Maheśvarī, Kumarī, Varāhī, Camuṇḍā* and *Nārasimhī*), who are considered as consorts of major gods (*Brahma, Viṣṇu, Śiva, Skanda, Varāha, Rudra* and *Narasimha* respectively).

In *Smārta Advaita* sect, *Śakti* is considered to be one of five equal bonafide personal forms of Gods in the *pancadeva* system advocated by *Śrī Ādi Śaṅkara.*

Various evidences have advised that there is no difference between *Śiva, Śakti* and *Viṣṇu.*

In *Purāṇas*, for story sake, *Śakti* is denoted as consort of *Śiva* and again **she** is mentioned as sister of *Viṣṇu*. But, in the *Śaṅkaranārāyaṇa* form the left part of *Śiva* is *Narāyaṇa*. Again in the form of *Ardhanārīśvara* the left part of *Śiva* is *Śakti*. What does this mean – there is only one left part for *Śiva*. That is *Śakti* and *Viṣṇu* are one and the same. In lot many places we have seen *Śiva* and *Śakti* are one and the same. Hence, logically, it concludes as *Śiva*, *Śakti* and *Viṣṇu* are one and only form. This has also been evidenced in various places. *Devī Mahātmīyam*, i.e. *Saptaśatī* is suppose to narrate the story of *Śrī Devī*. Ironically the first chapter narrates the story of *Viṣṇu* destroying the two demons, *Madhu* and *Kaiṭabha*. In this book, a study of three *Sahasranāmas* – *Śiva*, *Lalitā* and *Viṣṇu* has been undertaken.

The very words of *Paramācharyā* (from the book *Deivathin Kural* – Voice of God) – The beginning of *Soundaryalaharī* Verse 23 – *Tvayā hṛtvā* brands *ambā* as a thief! *Ādi Shankarā* expected, when he sought **Her** *darshan*, to have a darshan of Father and Mother in the *Ardhanārīśvara* form. But what did he see? He saw only the Mother's form, including the right side. Father is crystal white and Mother is crimson-red. But what he saw was *sakalam arunābham* – fully crimson-red. He expected to see a masculine form on the right side, but what he saw was *kucābhyām ānamram*. Hence he files an allegation on Śrī Devī that – You have already appropriated half of His body, and you were not satisfied. Now You have appropriated the other half also. The gymnastics of words is delightful. In the word *aparitruptena* there is an *apari*. This is in the first line. In the second line there is *aparam*. The latter word means other. But *apari* is the opposite of *pari*. *Paritruptena* means; by one who is fully satisfied. The *pari* stands for 'fully'. Hence *apari-truptena* means; by one who is not satisfied fully. Having taken only half the body how can **She** have a full satisfaction? **She** had only a partial satisfaction! That is what is indicated by the *apari-truptena*. It is the left side of the Lord's body that belongs to *ambā*. This is the age-old tradition. That is how *Ādi Shankarā* expected to see *ambā* when he sought **Her** *darshan*. Hence the *Āchārya* concludes – in poetic fancy, of course – that the other (right) half of *Shiva's* masculine body also has been taken over by *ambā*. It may be noted that Lord *Shiva* himself is described in the *vedas* as *taskarānām pati*: the head of all the thiefs! But *ambā* has executed a theft on Himself, by stealing the other remaining half of His body though **She** had been, with great condescension, given half of His body (the left side) already! And it is delightfully interesting to note that the poet in the *Āchārya* does not say that the other half of the body has also been captured. He dares not, even in poetic fancy, make that charge assertively against *ambā*. He only says *shangke* – I suspect. When one says "I suspect" one should give reasons. He has given two reasons. Wholly crimson red is one; the features of the chest is another. But this is not enough. To support his charge further, he gives two more, which clinches the issue. These are the two features: *trinayanam* (three eyes) and *kutila-shashichoodāla makutam* (crown that includes the half Moon in it). These two are exclusively the features of Lord *Shiva*. His name, even according to the vedas is *tryambaka*. In the preliminary *mantras* to the *rudraprashna*, the meditation verse beginning with *Āpātāla-nabhasthalāntha....* the second line describes Him as *jyoti-sphātika-linga-mouli-vilasatpoornendu...* which means that as the *shiva-linga*, He has the full Moon on His top. When the same *devatā* is figured anthropomorphically as a Person, He would have on His head, only a half Moon. Thus the three eyes and the crescent Moon belong to the Lord. But when the *Āchārya* had the *darshan* he saw both these in *ambā* **Herself**!

The Supreme Being, in the form of pure intellect has split into two due to illusion as righteousness (*dharmam*) and the person who has the righteousness (*dharmee*). Lord *Śiva* himself is *dharmee. Dharmam* has again been split into two – one male and the other female forms. The male form protects, in the form of *Viṣṇu*, the universe. The female form is mentioned as *Śakti*. All these three forms put together is the broad *Brahmam*. Thus says the *Saiva* (*Shreekanta*) religion. This has been explained in detail by *Śrī Appayya Dīksṣta* in his book called *"Ratna Traya Parīkṣa"*. He has well established this in his own commentary through various quotes and evidences. Some of the important verses from that book (Mysore publications);

Nityam Nirdoṣa Gantam Niratisaya Śukam Brahma Caitanyamekam

Proktou Dharmaprapetāvapi Nikamavatām Dharmivat Brahmakotī

Shree Bhāskararāya in his *bhāṣyam* for *Śrī Lalitā Sahasranāma*, has quoted this in many a place.

In *Lalitā Sahasranāma*, *Śrī Devī* has been addressed as *Nārāyanī, Govindarūpinī, Viṣṇurūpinī, Vaiṣnavī, Mukundā*, etc. Again, since the Supreme Being is the root cause for both of them, *Śrī Devī* has been addressed as *Padmanābha Sahodarī* treating them as brother and sister and (they have been mentioned as brother and sister in the *Prātānika Rahasya* also, which is read as part of *Saptaśatī*). Only in the names of this brother and sister, *Bhāgavatams* are written – *Śrīmad Viṣṇu Bhāgavatam* and *Śrī Devī Bhāgavatam*. One other similarity is – we have *Saptaśatī* – 700 verses, *Śrī Devī Mahātmīya* about *Śrī Devī* and *Śrīmad Bhagavad Gīta* also has same 700 verses. *Ādi Śaṅkara*, the propounder of *Advaita* philosophy, in verse 27 of his hymn, *Bhaja Govindam*, says that the *Śrīmad Bhagavad Gīta* and *Viṣṇu Sahasranāma* should be chant and the forms of Lord *Lakṣmī* and *Viṣṇu* should always be meditated on.

Further, many names of *Śrī Viṣṇu Sahasranāma* are comparable with that of the names in *Śiva* and *Lalitā Sahasranāmas* and vice versa. As far as possible this has been deliberated in this book. Thus the indifference between *Śiva, Śakti* and *Viṣṇu* has been established. This gives another perspective to *Advaita* principle, in a lighter way.

*****

Sahasranāma-s

In Samskrutam, *sahasra* means 'thousand' and *nāma* (nominative, the stem is *nāman*) means 'name'. The compound is of the *Bahuvṛthi* type and may be translated as "having a thousand names". The names provide an exhaustive catalog of the attributes, functions and major mythology associated with the figure being praised.

There are *Sahasranāma stotras* about almost all the Gods/ Goddesses like – *Gaṇapati, Subramaṇia, Lalitā, Viṣṇu, Śiva, Durgā, Lakṣmī, Sarasvatī, Śākambarī, Lakṣmīnṛsimha, Lakṣmīhayagrīva, Lakṣmīvarāha, Rāma, Hanumān, Venkateṣa, Sudarśana, Kriṣṇa, Annapūraṇī, Gāyatrī, Dakṣiṇāmūrti, Sūrya, Dharmasāstā, Mṛtyunjaya* and so on. Out of these the most famous – most used – most known are *Viṣṇu* and *Lalitā Sahasranāmas* only. In ardent religious *Śiva* temples, *Śiva Sahasranāma* is in vogue, but not much with the devotees. Again unlike other two *Sahasranāmas, Śiva Sahasranāma stotra* is not chant, but the *nāmāvalī* is used in *arcanas* in temples. The other *Sahasranāmas* are rarely used by specific group of people or in specific time periods.

The *Sahasranāmas* are generally understood as 1000 names. But the fact is that they are found in the form of verses (*Ślokas*) in different *Purāṇas*. Various commentators (*bhāśyakāras*) have split these verses into 1000 names, which are presently used for *arcanas*. One more important point to note is that these *Sahasranāma* stotras available in different *purāṇas* are all authored by a sage *Vyāsa*.

The *Viṣṇu Sahasranāma* is the most popular among laymen and a major part of prayer for devout *Vaiṣṇavas* or followers of *Viṣṇu*. While *Vaiṣṇvas* venerate other deities, they generally believe that the universe, including the other divinities such as *Śiva* and *Devī*, is ultimately a manifestation of the Supreme Lord *Viṣṇu*. Followers of *Śaivism* similarly give prominence to *Śiva*.

Śrī Śiva Sahasranāma:

There are at least eight different versions of *Śiva Sahasranāma*. The version appearing in Book 13 (*Anuśāsanaparva*) of the *Mahābhārata* is considered the kernel of this tradition (and the same is adopted in this book). The eight versions are:

1. *Mahābhārata* 13.17.30-150 (*Anuśāsana parva*)
2. *Linga Purāṇa* (1.65.54-168) is almost close to the *Mahābhārata Anuśāsana parva* version.
3. *Linga Purāṇa* (1.98.27-159) has some passages in common with the above # 2, but also with other sources
4. *Śiva Purāṇa* 4.35.1-131.
5. *Mahābhārata* (*Śānti parva* version). The critical edition of the *Mahābhārata* does not include this version, relegating it to Appendix 28 of *Śānti parva*. It does appear in the text of the *Gita* Press edition as 12.284.68-180.
6. *Vāyu Purāṇa* (1.30.179-284) is almost the same as the *Mahābhārata Śānti parva* version.
7. *Brahmāṇḍa Purāṇa* (38.1.1-100) is almost the same as the *Vāyu Purāṇa* version.
8. *Mahābhāgavata Upapurāṇa* (67.1-125) appears to be of comparatively recent origin.

In the version that occurs in this book, Kṛṣṇa recites the 1,008 names of Lord *Śiva* to *Yudhisṭira*. *Yudhisṭira* had asked *Bhīṣma* the names of *Śiva* but *Bhīṣhma* admitted his ignorance and requested him to ask *Kṛṣṇa*. Interestingly, the *Viṣṇu Sahasranāma*, also occurs in the same chapter. Some overlapping of names with the *Viṣṇu Sahasranāma* has led *Śrī Ādi Śaṅkara* to conclude that *Śiva* and *Viṣṇu* are identical, as two different aspects of one cosmic reality known as *Brahmam*. Precisely this book tries to discuss these identical names and some more matching with *Śrī Lalitā Sahasranāma* also.

***Śrī Lalitā Sahasranāma*:**

If *Īśvara* is a spiritual conception of the Absolute, *Īśvarī* or *Śakti* or *Devī* is certainly an equally valid one. And, as we generally fear our fathers and love our mothers, the concept of a mother-Goddess appeals more to our hearts than that of a father-god.

Also in the representation of a female deity, there is more scope for grace and beauty and hence for greater poetry and art.

Lalitā Sahasranāma is a text from *Brahmāṇda Purāṇa*. It is a sacred text to the worshippers of the Goddess *Lalitā Devī*, i.e. the Divine Mother, in the form, *Śakti*. *Lalitā* is the Goddess of bliss, an epithet for *Śiva*'s consort Goddess *Pārvati*. Etymologically, *'Lalita'* means "**She** Who Plays". In the root form (*vyutpatti*), the word *'Lalita'* means 'spontaneous' from which the meaning 'easy' is derived and implicitly extends to 'play'.

Lalitā, the shortened form of *Lalitāmbika,* means the playful one. *Śrī Bhāskararāyar* is the first person to write bhāşyam (commentary) for *Śrī Lalitā Sahasranāma*, called *"Sowbhāghya Bhāskaram"*. He has also written very many books, but amongst them all, *Sowbhāghya Bhāskaram* is the best. It is not only a meaning but a self-contained research paper on *Lalitā Sahasranāma*.

Bhāskararāyar himself explained 15 different types of meanings (*Artha*) for *Lalitā Sahasranāma* viz. *Artha, Bhāvārtha, Sampradāyārtha, Niharpārtha, Koulikārtha, Rahasyārtha, Mahātatvārtha, Nāmārtha, Shabdarūpārtha, Nāma Ekadeşārtha, Sākthārtha, Samarasārtha, Samasthartha, Sagunārtha* and *Mahāvākyārtha*.

The verses are organized in such a way that *Devī* is described from "Head to Toes" (*kesādhi pādham*). There are basically five tasks (pancha krtyam). They are creation (*sṛṣṭi*), protection (*stiti*), destruction (*samhāram*), hiding (*tirodhānam*) and blessing (*anugraham*). **She** has been described as "*panca kṛtya parāyanā*".

Lalitā Sahasranāma is the only *sahasranāma* that does not repeat a single name. Further, in order to maintain the meter (*candas*), sahasranāmas use fillers words like *tu, api, ca, hi,* etc., which are conjunctions that do not necessarily add to the meaning of the name except in cases of interpretation. No such fillers are used in the *Lalitā sahasranāma* and is unique in being an enumeration of holy names that meets the metrical, poetical and mystic requirements of a *sahasranāma* by their order throughout the text.

Lalitā sahasranāma is said to have been composed by eight *Vāgdevīs* upon the command of *Lalitā*. These *Vāgdevīs* are *Vaśini, Kameśvari, Aruṇa, Vimala, Jayinī, Mohinī, Sarveśvarī* and *Koulinī*. The *sahasranāma* says that "One can worship *Lalitā* only if **she** wishes us to do so".

***<u>Śrī Viṣṇu Sahasranāma</u>*:**

There used to be a hearsay story – *Ādi Śaṅkara* once desired to write

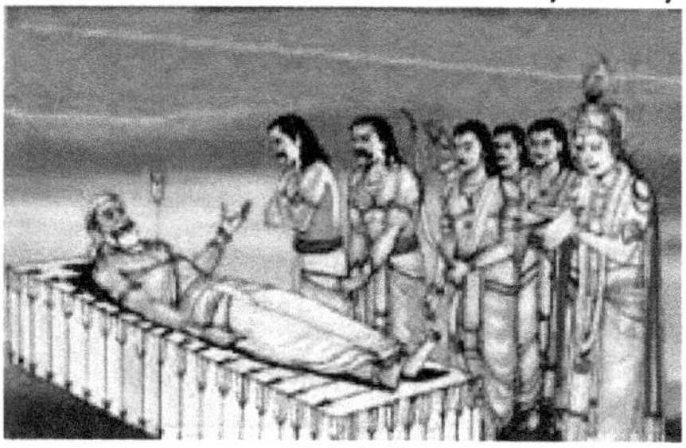

commentary (*bhāşyam – vyākyānam* – commentary) for *Śrī Lalitā Sahasranāma*. He asked one of his disciples to bring the original version for reference, but he told the disciple as "bring the *Sahasranāma*". The disciple brought the *Viṣṇu Sahasranāma*. But *Ādi Śaṅkara* returned this and kept quiet for some time. This was repeated thrice and at last asked the disciple why he brings *Viṣṇu Sahasranāma*. The disciple replied that a small girl is giving him that book and asked him to give it to his *guru*. Then he realised through his devine power that the girl was none other than *Śrī Devī* herself and got convinced that the job of writing commentary for *Lalitā Sahasranāma* is not reserved for him.

This proves that *Ādi Śaṅkara* also worships *Viṣṇu* in addition to *Śiva* and *Devī*. It is also interesting to note that this was to prove the unity between the *Śaiva* and *Vaiṣnava* cults. The *Viṣṇu sahasranāma* is a list of 1,000 names of *Viṣṇu*, the personal supreme God for *Vaiṣnavas*. It is also one of the most sacred and commonly chant *stotras*. Each name eulogies one of His countless great attributes.The *Viṣṇu sahasranāma* as found in the *Anuśāsana Parva Mahābhārata* is the most popular version of the 1000 names of *Viṣṇu*. Two more versions exist in *Padma Purāṇa* and *Matsya Purāṇa*.

The *Viṣṇu sahasranāma* has been the subject to numerous commentaries. *Ādi Śaṅkara* wrote a definitive commentary on this in the 8th century C.E., which is the oldest and has been particularly influential for many schools of Hinduism even today. *Parāsara Bhaṭṭar*, a follower of *Rāmānujar* wrote a commentary in the 12th century C.E., detailing the names of *Viṣṇu* from a *Viśiṣṭādvaita* perspective. *Madhvācarya* also wrote a commentary disclosing that each name in the *sahasranāma* has a minimum of 100 meanings. Upon being challenged by the audience, *Śrī Madhvācharaya* not only gave 100 meanings for each of the names but also expanded on each of the meanings making it a multi-fold complexity and displayed an outspoken quality to hold and explain the real and deep hidden meaning of *sahasranāma*.

According to the 149th chapter of *Anuśāsana parva* (verses 14 to 120) of *Mahābhārata*, the names were handed down to *Yudhisṭira* by *Bhīṣma*, who was on his death bed (of arrows) in the battlefield of *Kurukṣetra*.

Varāhi Tantra says that in the age of *Kali yuga*, most stotras are cursed by *Paraşurāma* and hence are ineffective. While listing the ones which are free from this curse and hence suitable for chanting during *Kali Yuga*, it is said,

"*Gīta* of the *Bhīşma Parva*, *Vişņu Sahasranāma* and *Śrī Devī Mahātmiyam* are free from all doshas and grant fruits immediately in *Kali Yuga*".

<u>*Śhiva, Lalitā* and *Vişņu Sahasranāmas*:</u>

Some interesting facts – A comparison of *Śiva, Lalitā* and *Vişŋu Sahasranāmas* – not for deciding which is superior, but an analysis is attempted:

Details	***Śiva Sahasranāma***	***Lalitā Sahasranāma***	***Vişņu Sahasranāma***
Age	Earlier	Later one	Earlier
Part of	*Mahābhārata*	*Brahmānḍa Purāņa*	*Mahābhārata*
Author	*Veda Vyās*	*Veda Vyās*	*Veda Vyās*
Composed by	Lord Kŗşņa Himself	*Vaśinyādi Aśţa Vāg Devīs*	*Sanaka*, one of the *Sanatkumaras* (eternally living Youths)
Advised by	Lord Kŗşņa to *Pāndavās* and other kings	*Hayagreeva*, an incarnation of Lord *Vişņu* to sage Agastya	*Bhīşma* to *Pāndavās* and other kings
In the presence of	*Bhīşma* and other kings	*Lalitā Devī* herself.	Lord *Krishna*, an incarnation of lord *Vişņu*
First *Bhāşyam*	Not well known	*Bhāskararāya*	*Ādi Sankarā*
Written style	Epic style	Ornate style like a *Kāvyā*	Epic style
Main characteristics	Verbal austerity.	The length of the word combinations and the abundance of various forms of *Samāsa* (compound words) and *Alankāra* (figures of speech)	Verbal austerity and lack of embellishments.

Details	***Śiva Sahasranāma***	***Lalitā Sahasranāma***	***Viṣṇu Sahasranāma***
Abodes	Does not attribute any particular abode to Lord *Śiva*. He is the Spirit in all beings and the whole cosmos.	Several abodes to the *Devī* like – *Cintāmaṇigṛha*, *Jālandharā*, *Kadambavana*, *Malayācala*, *Mahākailāśa*, *Vindhyācala*, Group of fifty *Pīṭas*, etc.	Does not attribute any particular abode to Lord *Viṣṇu*. He is the Indwelling Spirit in all beings and the whole cosmos constitutes His body.
Description of the form of the Deity	Marginal – just to show that besides being the all-pervading spirit, *Śiva* is personality too.	Very much anthropomorphic giving as it does detailed descriptions of the various parts of the body – describing the enthralling beauty of *Lalitā*	Very marginal – just to show that besides being the all-pervading spirit, *Viṣṇu* is personality too.
Description of the various exploits of the Deity.	Does not give any description of the exploits.	Like destruction of *Bhandā*, are narrated at the beginning itself	Though the incarnations are referred, never gives any description of the exploits
References to ritualistic worship	None like	Like *Śrīcakra Pūja*, the paths of *Samayā*, *Koula* and other details of mother Cult.	None like
Size	123 verses of two lines each	182.5 verses of two lines each	108 verses of two lines each
Chandas	*Anushṭup* (32 letters in each verse)	*Anushṭup* (32 letters in each verse)	*Anushṭup* (32 letters in each verse)

<table>
<tr><th>Details</th><th>Śiva Sahasranāma</th><th>Lalitā Sahasranāma</th><th>Viṣṇu Sahasranāma</th></tr>
<tr><td>Fillers to complete the meter-candas</td><td>27 fillers</td><td>Nil</td><td>15 fillers</td></tr>
<tr><td rowspan="4">Repeated Names **</td><td>45 names repeated twice</td><td rowspan="4">Nil</td><td>74 names repeated twice</td></tr>
<tr><td>11 names repeated thrice</td><td>14 names repeated thrice</td></tr>
<tr><td>4 names repeated four times</td><td rowspan="2">2 names repeated four times</td></tr>
<tr><td>1 name repeated five times</td></tr>
<tr><td>Starting of names</td><td>No such restriction</td><td>32 letters only</td><td>No such restriction</td></tr>
<tr><td>Number of names with 16 syllables</td><td rowspan="6">Not a clear research in this regard since we have lot many versions.</td><td>72</td><td>Nil</td></tr>
<tr><td>Number of names with 2 syllables</td><td>3</td><td>Nil</td></tr>
<tr><td>Number of names with 11 syllables</td><td>3</td><td>Nil</td></tr>
<tr><td>Number of names with 9 syllables</td><td>7</td><td>Nil</td></tr>
<tr><td>Number of names with 8 syllables</td><td>242</td><td>18</td></tr>
<tr><td>Number of names with 7 syllables</td><td>2</td><td>Nil</td></tr>
</table>

Details	*Śiva Sahasranāma*	*Lalitā Sahasranāma*	*Viṣṇu Sahasranāma*
Number of names with 6 syllables		34	34
Number of names with 5 syllables		122	106
Number of names with 4 syllables		278 – the largest	273
Number of names with 3 syllables		138	338 – the largest
Number of names with 2 syllables		96	228
Number of single syllable names		3	3
Total number of names	1008	1000	1000

** Though some names are mentioned as repeated twice, thrice, etc., based on the context they may convey different meanings. Hence it cannot be construed as a blunder.

*****

एकता – Oneness

Om Namaḥ Śivāya
Om Namaḥ Candikāyai
Om Namo Narāyaṇāya

Śrī Ādi Śaṅkara promulgated the *śaṇmata* philosophy – literally six opinions and in practice six religions – *Gāṇapatya, Śaiva, Śākta, Vaiṣṇava, Koumāra* and *Soura*. Hinduism in only a conglomeration of all these six religions. In addition, in practice, we call a sect called *Smārta*. *Smārta sampradāya* is a family tradition or sect composed of certain category of people who follow *śaṇmata*. The term *smārta* is used to denote a specific, specialised category who specialise in *smṛtis*, who hold the *smṛti* as the most authoritative texts. However, colloquially, *smārta – sama + arta* – treating all the religions or all the Gods as one and same. Whatever be the *puja* done, whether *Śiva* or *Gaṇapati* and so on, it is started with *ācamanīyam* as *Acutāya Namaḥ*, etc., and ended with *Śrīman Nārāyaneti samarpayāmi* – assuming no difference between any form of Gods.

In this process, there is lot of common names or names denoting the same meaning are found in the *Śiva, Lalitā* and *Viṣṇu sahasranāmas*. A humble attempt has been made in this book to compare between the three great *stotras* in praise of Lord *Śiva*, Goddess *Lalitā* and Lord *Viṣṇu* – male and female forms of the supreme self. This is not exhaustive, but only a representative sample.

Śrī Ādi Śaṅkara's *bhāṣyam* for *Viṣṇu Sahasranāma* and *Śrī Bhāskararāya*'s *bhāṣyam* for *Lalitā Sahasranāma* have been followed in this book. For *Śiva Sahasranāma*, commentaries from here and there are picked up. A *bhāṣyam* is not just a meaning. It is a commentary giving detailed meanings – as mentioned earlier – different inner meaning and *tatvas* (philosophies). The serial number of the name in the *Śiva, Lalitā* and *Viṣṇu Sahasranāmas* list appended is mentioned in each of the discussions.

The chronological order of *Śiva Sahasranāma* has been followed for convenience. When the corresponding common name is not found in *Śiva Sahasranāma*, the chronological order of *Lalitā Sahasranāma* is maintained.

1. ***Śiva*** – 3 & 21 – *Prabhuḥ* – प्रभुः – Head or leader of this entire world. Creates the world in a great grand manner. One who knows the activities of the whole world – *Īśvara, antaryāmi prakarśeṇa bhāvayati viśvam carayati, jānāti vā viśvakarttā sarvajno vā ityarttaḥ*

Lalitā – 750 – *Maheshvaree* – महेश्वरी – One who is the supreme sovereign. Leader of the universe.

Viṣṇu – 35 & 299 – *Prabhuḥ* – प्रभुः – The Almighty Lord. He who is the All-Powerful. He who has the supreme freedom to do (*Kartum*), not to do (*Akartum*), or to do quite differently from what He had already done (*Anyathā Kartum*) is considered as the *Prabhuḥ*. He is the Lord, the Master, the Owner, the proprietor. One who has all powers to do, not to do and otherwise to do is called the Great Lord.

2. ***Śiva*** – 6 & 882 – *Varadaḥ* – वरदः – One who bestows all the boons sought for by the devotees – *iṣṭapradhā*. He takes different forms to bestow compassion for his devotees –
   Varaiḥ śreṣṭaiḥ roopaiḥ dayate nāneva dārair jagatpālayatītī varadaḥ.

Lalitā – 331 – *Varadā* – वरदा – One who bestows boons. **She** grants boons to *Brahma, Viṣŋu* and other devotees. Śrī Bhāskararāya explains what is told by *Nārada* in *Matsya* and *Padma Purāŋās* – *Śrī Devī* 's uplifted hand ever confers boons. **She** will give boons to all *Devas, daityas* and ascetics.

Śrī Ādi Śaṇkara says in his commentary for the 4th verse of *Soundaryalaharī*; without even the emblem of boons in hands, *Śrī Devī* provides the boons more than expected to the devotees;

Tvadanyaḥ Pānibhyā-mabhayavarado Daivatagaŋa:
Tvamekā Naivāsi Prakatita Varābhītyabhinayā ।

Bhayāt Trātum Dātum Phalamapi Ca Vāncāsamadhikam
Śaranye Lokānām Tava Hi Caraŋāveva Nipuṇou II

Devī Purāŋa also says; **She** fulfils the desires of the *Devas* who seek boons. From the root *'Vr'* to choose, **She** is called *Varadā*, conferrer of boons, i.e. giver of the things chosen.

In the *Varāha Puranā* also in the chapter on the *Vetrāsuravadha*, *Śrī Devī* is always to be worshipped, by concentration on the ninth day of the lunar fortnight; **She** will certainly become the giver of boons to all worlds.

Viṣṇu – 330 – *Varadaḥ* – वरदः – One who blesses all true devotees and fulfils their request for boons. It can also mean "One who gives the best (*Varam*) in life to those who seek Him with perfect detachment and sharpened discrimination. *Śrī Ādi Śaṇkara* in his commentary mentions;

(i) He gives the boons desired by the devotees in their minds.

(ii) He becomes the doer of sacrificial fire and gives the boons i.e. the cow as a price. *Gourvai Vara*: is the *Veda* saying quoted for this.

3. ***Śiva*** – 10, 518 & 598 – *Sarvaḥ* – सर्वः – One who is in the form of all and everything. Omnipresent – *Gīta* (XI-40) says – *sarvam samāpnośi tatosi sarvaḥ*

Lalitā – 203 – *Sarvamayee* – सर्वमयी – One who is omnipresent and omnipotent. **She** is in the form of all things.

Viṣṇu – 26 – *Sarvaḥ* – सर्वः – He who is the all. He being the One cause from which have sprung forth all things and beings. He himself is the all. In Mahābhārata Udyoga Parva (70-12) it is mentioned as: "As He is the origin and end of all, whether existent or otherwise and as He, at all times, cognises all, He is called 'Sarva'. All waves rise from the same ocean and hence, the ocean is the very essence in all waves.

4. ***Śiva*** – 28 – *Bhagavān* – भगवान् – One who is the dwelling place of Wealth, Power, *Dharma*, Fame, Character, Knowledge and Dispassion. Or one

who knows the origin, destruction, growth, waning, intellect and ignorance of all the living beings – *Aiśvaryasya samagrasya dharmasya yaśasaḥ śriyaḥ vairāgyasya mokṣasya shaṇṇām paga idīriṇā*.

Lalitā – 117 – *Bhaktasoubhāgyadāyinī* – भक्तसौभाग्यदायिनी – One who grants all round advancement to **Her** devotees.

In the *Agni Purāṇa* the word *Bhaga* has been given various meanings like – wealth, desire, praising stories, vigor, preparation, illumination, pride, etc. Since **She** holds all these, **She** also has a name *Śubhagā*. **Her** nature is prosperity (*Soubhāgyam)*.

Also exemplary and fortune are other meanings. The one, who contemplates all these, is *Soubhāgyam.* One who grants prosperity (*Soubhāgyam*) to **Her** devotees.

Again, as per *Agni Purāṇa*, since these eight things are used in auspicious occasions – Sugar Cane, Peepul tree, sprouted cumin, coriander, cow's milk (including its variations as curd, butter, ghee, etc.), things that are in yellow colour, flowers and salt, these are called *Soubhāgyaśaṭakam* (eight auspicious things). It can also be understood as **She** offers all these to **Her** devotees.

Viṣṇu – 558 – *Bhagavān* – भगवान् – The word *Bhaga*, according to the *Viṣṇu Purāṇa* means, "One who has all the Six Great Glories – Wealth, Power, *Dharma*, Fame, Character, Knowledge and Dispassion – is called *Bhagavān*". Again, *Viṣṇu Purāṇa* says "He is named *Bhagavān* who knows

(a) the beginning and the end,
(b) the arrival and departure of beings and also
(c) *Vidyā* and *Avidyā*.

One who has all the six glorious in himself alone in *Bhagavān* and these great mighty power atomically come to Him, because his equipment is the Total-mind. *Śrī Ādi Śaṇkara,* quotes the verse with the meaning below and says that one who has all these is called *Bhagavān*. *Bhaga* means complete wealth, charity, glory, richness, relinquishment and liberation from all the bondage. It is appropriate to mean that **he** provides all these to the devotees.

5. ***Śiva*** – 33 – *Mahākarmā* – महाकर्मा – One who does very great tasks. The very big activities like creation, etc., are taken care by him –

Mahatsṛṣṭyādikam karma asyeti sṛṣṭi

In *Śrī Rudra Triśatī Nāmāvalī* also we have 127th name as *Karmārebhyaśca Namaḥ*.

Lalitā – 274 – *Panchakrutyaparāyaṇā* – पन्चकृत्यपरायणा – One who is devoted to the five functions viz., creation, protection, destruction, *Tirodhāna* (bondage) and *Anugraha* (release). **She** has much interest and involvement in all the five tasks.

It can also be interpreted that all the five functions depend on **Her**. The five functions viz. creation, protection, destruction, annihilation and causing the reappearance of the universe are that of *Brahma, Viṣṇu, Rudra, Ēśvara* and *Paramaśiva.* These five are different forms or *Śaktis* of that of *Śrī Devī* only. The officials of these five functions carry out their tasks with the permission of *Śrī Devī* only. It is **Her** order to make them do these functions. *Soundaryalaharee* says that **She** issues those orders just by twinkling Her eye-brows for a micro second;

Viṣṇu – 672 & 787 – *Mahākarmā* – महाकर्मा – One Who accompli**She**s Great Activities. To create a cosmos so scientifically precise and perfect out of the five great elements and to sustain them all with an iron hand of efficiency, all the time constantly presiding over the acts of destruction without which the world of change cannot be maintained, is, in itself, a colossal achievement of an Absolute Intelligence. He alone performs them, through Maha-Puruṣas who have surrendered themselves unto Him-those who, in total surrender, have indeed become one with the Lord in love and being.

6. ***Śiva*** – 34 – *Tapasvī* – तपस्वी – One who is the top most in doing penance. He being the boon giver to all, who does *tapas* (penance), he himself is the first among them.

Lalitā – 359 – *Tāpasārādhyā* – तापसाराध्या – One who is worshipped by ascetics. Or, *tāpa* - *samsāra* (the father of misery), *sāra* - essence (a deep), *Adhyā* - meditation, i.e. *Śrī Devī*, who is the root cause of this *samsāra* life cycle, is the essential object of meditation.

Viṣṇu – 122 – *Mahātapāḥ* – महातपाः – One of the great *Tapas*. The term *tapas* in Samskrutam has three meanings: 'Knowledge' (*Jnāna*), 'Prosperity' (*Aiśvarya*) and also 'Might' (*Pratāpa*). It is in the presence of consciousness that we come to know all our experiences. "Conscious of" a thing or an idea is the "Knowledge of" the thing or the idea. That about, which I am not conscious of, I have really no knowledge of it. All knowledges, of all bosoms, in all living creatures, everywhere, at all times, cannot be without the play of consciousness upon the respective objects of knowledge and hence this consciousness is indicated in the *Upaniṣats* as Pure Knowledge, in the light of which alone all knowledges are possible. All achievements and prosperity (*Aiśvarya*), all might and power of the living creatures can express themselves through them only when they are alive. This great truth is *Mahā Viṣṇu*. "Whose Tapas is of the nature of Knowledge" (*Munḍaka Upaniśad* 1-1-9).

7. ***Śiva*** – 35 & 634 – *Bhūtabhāvanaḥ* – भूतभावनः – One who creates all the five elements. Just by desire he creates ether, fire, air, water and earth.

Tasmātvā etasmātātman ākāśa: sambhūtaḥ
Ākāśāt ..... Sa tapas taptvā itam sarvamasṛjata

He created all these by his penance. He protects all that is created –

Bhūtāni pāvayati janatati varddayatīti bhū pāvanaḥ

Lalitā – 949 – *Panjcabhūteśī* – पञ्चभूतेशी – One who is head of five elements (earth, etc.). Since *Śrī Devī* is in the form of essence of all the five basic elements, it can be said that **She** is the head of them. This can further be read in *Pancadashī* and *Pancabūta Viveka* by *Śrī Vidyāraŋya*.

Viṣṇu – 9 – *Bhūtabhāvanaḥ* – भूतभावनः – He originates and develops all Elements.

8. ***Śiva*** – 44 & 95 – *Viśvarūpaḥ* – विश्वरूप: – Omnipresent. We know the story of *Lingotbhava* – Lord *Śiva* taking a *Viśvarūpa* and Lord Brahma took the form of a swan and flew in search of his head. Lord *Viṣṇu* took the form of a tortoise (*Kūrma*) pierced through the earth in search of his feet.

In *Śrī Rudra Triśatī Nāmāvalī* also we have 106th name as *Viśvarūpebhyaśca Namaḥ*.

Lalitā – 256 – *Vishvarūpā* – विश्वरूपा – One who is in the form of the world or *Viṣvam*. Since *Śrī Devī* (*Brahmam*) thought "I will take various forms", this world was formed. Hence *Śrī Devī* is in the form of this world itself. The soul is also called as *Paśu*. *Sva* means dog, the lowest kind of form, comparable to that of a dog. Since the soul worships *Śrī Devī* it is released from *svarūpa.* The *rūpā* becomes *vikaṭham*, *Śrī Devī* is called as *Viśvarūpa.*

Viṣṇu – 717 – *Viśvamūrtiḥ* – विश्वमूर्ति: – Of the form of the entire universe. Lord as the total – created, so his form is called Viśvarūpa. The total gross form of the universe to be gather represents his gross-form-divine.

Śrī Ādi Śaṇkara in his commentary says – He is this world and its form since everything is himself. First name *Viśvā* can also be compared – this has been interpreted elaborately. Some of the main points are;

- Since he is the cause for this world called *Viṣvam*, *Brahmam* is called *Viṣvam*.
- This *Viṣvam* is not something different from *Paramapuruṣa.* Hence *Brahmam* is called as *Viṣvam*.
- Since it pierces in, *Brahmam* is called as *Viṣvam*.
- The word *Viṣvam* indicates '*Om*'.

9. ***Śiva*** – 50 & 847 – *Pavitram* – पवित्रम् – Complete purity. One who protects from the thunder called *samsara* – *bhaveḥ samsāravajrapādāt drāyata iti pavitram*.

Lalitā – While lot many names talk about purity there is no specific name denoting *Pavitram*.

Viṣṇu – 62 – *Pavitram* – पवित्रम् – One who gives purity to the heart. To the seekers who are meditating upon Him, He gives inner purity and hence He is known as *Pavitram*.

10. ***Śiva*** – 51, 116 & 824 – *Mahān* – महान् – With very great embellishment. He is great because he is always sparkling and omnipresent. One who is worshipable. One who is in the form of the philosophy (*tatva*) called *Mahat*.

Lalitā – 774 – *Kartā* – कर्ता – *Mahatī* – महती – One who is very big. **She** is the biggest – i.e. bigger than very big. *Mahā Nārāyaṇa Upaniṣat* (I-1) says; *Mahato Mahīyān*.

The other things can be measured only with this. Thus says *Śākapūrṇī* –
Mahān Kasmān Manenānyān Jahāti.
The meaning of this name according to *Yāskar's Nirukta* is – one that is to be worshipped; *Mahanīyo Bhavati*.

The name of the Veena instrument in the hands of *Nārada* is called *Mahatī*. **She** is in that form also.

Viṣṇu – 841 – *Mahān* – महान् – The Great; the Glorious; the Mighty. One who is not conditioned by the five Elements – nor by Time and Space. Quite on the other hand, it is He Who is the very Existence in everything.

11. ***Śiva*** – 52 – *Niyamaḥ* – नियमः – One who is in the form of controlling authority (*niyama*). *Yoga Sūtra* (2-32) says *couca santośa tapaḥ svāddhyāya īshvara praṇitānāni niyamāḥ*

Viṣṇu – 161 – *Niyamaḥ* – नियमः – The Appointing Authority. It is He, who orders all the mighty forces of nature and prescribes for each the Laws of their conduct, the ways of their behaviour and the methods of their functions. The Sun, Moon, Air, Water, Dik-Bālakas, Lord of Death, etc. are all appointed and ordered by the Lord.

12. ***Śiva*** – 56 & 528 – *Ādayaḥ* – आदय: & *Ādyaḥ* – आद्य:– The beginning of everything in this world. *Mahānārāyaṇa Upaniṣat* (23.3.2) says *"Yo devānām pratamam purastāt viśvādiyo rudro maharṣi:"* – *Rudra* is the first known among the Devas, Ṛśis and others. He is beyond all.

He is prior to the beginning of this universe – *Samsārāt parācīna śuddhaḥ* – Tamil Thiruvenmbavai by Manikavācakar says;

Munnaippazham porutku munnaippazham porule.

Lalitā – 615 – *Ādiśakti*: – आदिशक्ति: – One who is the primordial power. **She** does the three main tasks of creation, protection and destruction of the entire universe and pervades everything in the form of root cause energy (*Śakti*).

Viṣṇu – 67 – *Jyeṣṭhaḥ* – ज्येष्ठ: – The eldest of all, since there is nothing prior to him.

13. ***Śiva*** – 60 – *Viśālākṣaya* – विशालाक्ष: – One who has broad eyes, which can see distant objects also. In Samskrutam, normally the word *Akṣa* means any organ – *vipulāni akṣāṇi indriyāṇī yasya saḥ*. But in practice the word *Akṣa* indicates eyes – for instance Mīnākṣī, Viśālākṣī, etc.

Lalitā – 292 – *Vishālākṣī* – विशालाक्षी – One who has long and large eyes. The eyes leading upto the ears will be beautiful.

In *Soundaryalaharee* there are many verses describing the beauty and greatness of eyes of *Śrī Devī*. Specifically these verses may be referred; 52 to 57 – *Gate Karnābhyarnam, Vibhakta Traivarŋyam, Pavitrīkartum Na:, Nimeshon Meshābhyām, Tavāparne Karne* and *Drushā Dragheeyasyā*

In this *Lalitā Sahasranāma* itself there are very many names describing the beauty of the eyes of *Śrī Devī*; 18 – *Vaktralakshmī Parīvāhacalanmīnābhalocanā*, 332 – *Vāmanayanā*, 561 – *Mrugākṣī* and 601 – *Darāndolitadīrghākṣī*.

In *Lalitā Trishatī* also **She** is addressed as *Kamalākshī* (7th name). That is, her eyes are like blossomed Lotus.

14. **Śiva** – 61 – *Somaḥ* – सोमः – One who is in unison with *Umādevī* – *sa* + *uma* = *Soma*. We have heard of *Somāskanda*, which means alongwith *Uma* and *Skanda* – *Sa* + *Uma* + *Skanda*.

In *Śrī Rudra Triśatī Nāmāvalī* also we have 233rd name as *Namaḥ Somāyaca Namaḥ*.

Lalitā – 910 – *Somyā* – सोम्या – (In some schools this is mentioned as *Soumyā* – सौम्या) – One who is fit to be adored in the *Soma* sacrifice. The word *Soma* means moon or camphor. Hence *Soumyā* means one that pleases the mind like Moon.

Viṣṇu – 505 – *Somaḥ* – सोमः – One who in the form of the moon-light (*Soma*) nourishes all the plant kingdom with their respective essential sap. It is very well known that the moonlight is the one, which enriches the food value in the fruits and grains. In *Gīta*, *Bhagavān* says – I in the form of the moon light, enrich all the plant kingdom.

15. **Śiva** – 64 – *Sūryaḥ* – सूर्यः – One who is in the form of Sun.

Lalitā – 275 – *Bhānumaṇḍalamadhyasthā* – भानुमन्डलमध्यस्था – One who is in the midst of the solar orbit. It is one of the methods of worshipping *Śrī Devī* meditating upon **Her** in the Sun's disc.

Sūrya Maṇḍala Madyastthām Devīm Tripurasundarīm I
Pāsāngucadhanurbānān Tārāyantīm Śivām Bhaje II

It is said that the golden man seen within the Sun etc., is the supreme Lord *Parameśvarā; Ya Īśo Antarāditye Hiraṇmayaḥ Puruṣo Rudtāte*. It is also described that *Bhānumaṇḍala* is the *Anāhata cakra*. *Śrī Devī* is in the form of *Kunḍalinee* there.

Viṣṇu – 881 & 883 – *Raviḥ* – रविः & *Sūryaḥ* – सूर्यः – One Who absorbs the vapour (*Rasa*) from everything. As *Sūrya Nārāyaṇa*, He dries up everything in the universe. The term etymologically means the One Source from which all things have been born or out of which they have been delivered. The Lord as the First Cause is the Womb of the Universe. On the surface of the world it is the Sun that nurtures and nourishes all living creatures. It must be noted that many of the Lord's names indicate or are associated with the Sun – as he is like the Sun in the solar System: the Centre around which the entire system revolves and by Whose benign rays, as the "Orb-of-all Energies", He thrilling to life the infinitude of creatures.

16. ***Śiva*** – 73 – *Anaghaḥ* – अनघः – To whom no sin can approach. Even though he destroyed the *yajna* of Daksha, he does not get any sin – *yajnanopi niṣpāpas-tejīyastvāt-svatantratvācca*.

Lalitā – 987 – *Anaghā* - अनघा – One who is without any *Agham* (sorrow or sin).

Viṣṇu – 146 & 831 – *Anaghaḥ* – अनघः – One who is sinless. *Cāndokya Upaniṣat* (8.7.1) says *apahatā pāpmā* – he is without sin. He is without sorrow.

17. ***Śiva*** – 79, 103, 427 & 768 – *Mantraḥ* – मन्त्रः, *Mantravit* – मन्त्रवित्, *Mantrakāraḥ* – मन्त्रकारः, & *Mantraḥ* – मन्त्रः – One who is in the form of all *mantras* starting with the *Praṇava* (Om). One who knows all the *mantras*. One who created the *Vedas*. One who is in the form *Mṛtasanjīvinī mantra*, which is used to give re-birth to the dead.

Lalitā – 846 – *Mantrasārā* – मन्त्रसारा – One who is the essence of all *mantras*. *Sāstra* indicates *Vedas*. Thus explains the *Brahma Sūtra* (I-1-3); *Shāstra Yonitvāt*. Those who follow *tantras* also accept *sāstra* as it defines the rules. The word *mantra* indicates *Veda* also. Again the *mantras* included in the *tantras* also indicate the same *tantras*. **She** is the essence of all these.

Viṣṇu – 280 – *Mantraḥ* – मन्त्रः – One who is of the nature of the *mantras* of the *Vedas*. The declarations of the *Vedas*, the *mantras* are the vehicles that will take us straight into an experience of the Transcendental. The vehicles are often called by the name of their destination. *Mantra* means that which can save us on being properly meditated upon. Only through the *mantras* of the *Upaniṣats* we ever come to experience the Supreme Nature of the Lord and hence this name *Mantraḥ*. *Gīta* (XV-15) says "I am the one who prepared the Vedas and one who knows the Vedas" – *vedāntakṛt vedavideva cāham*

18. ***Śiva*** – 80 – *Pramāṇaḥ* – प्रमाण: – One who is in the form of logical intellect.

Viṣṇu – 428 & 959 – *Pramāṇam* – प्रमाणम् – The proof. He is the underlying principle of all intellectual arguments and for all scientific methodology, since He is the very Consciousness behind all discussions. Lord Nārāyaṇa is the very authority behind all *Dharmas* and hence He becomes the essential Reality behind all (*pramāṇa*). He whose very form is the Vedas, which are the only 'proof' for the Eternal Reality. Or, it can be construed as, He who is pure Infinite Consciousness (*Prajnānam*) as we have it in the great Commandment, "Consciousness is the Infinite Reality".

19. ***Śiva*** – 82 – *Yogiḥ* – योगि: – One who is in *Yoganiṣṭa*.

Lalitā – 653 – *Yoginī* – योगिनी – One who has a *Yoga* form. *Yoga* means union (based on the root *Yuj*). Hence **She** is called as *Yoginī*.

Viṣṇu – 849 – *Yogī* – योगी – One Who can be realised through Yoga. One who is the greatest *Yogī*. The term *Yoga* is defined in Śastras as "stopping all thought flows". One who has no thought agitations –who has totally conquered the mind (Māyā) and lives in His own Effulgent Self-nature is the greatest *Yogī*.

20. ***Śiva*** – 86 & 761 – *Mahābalaḥ* – महाबल: – One who has a very great strength. *Rudram* says *Balavikaraṇāya namo, balāya namo, balapramatanāya namaḥ sarvabhūtatamanāya namaḥ*

Lalitā – 222 – *Mahābalā* – महाबला – One who has great might. The word *balā* means – army, strength, fragrance, taste, form, soul, etc. *Śrī Devī* has all these in abundance. The word *balā also* means a crow. Great *yogins* like *Bhusundā* worshipped *Śrī Devī* in the form a crow and got great strengths. Hence *Mahābala.* This has been addressed in *Yogavāsiṣṭha*.

Viṣṇu – 172 – *Mahābalaḥ* – महाबलः – One who has Supreme Strength. He, being Omnipotent, is the Source of all Strength that we see in each individual organism in life. His Vitality reflected in each of us, is our individual strength; naturally He is the Infinitely Strong.

21. ***Śiva*** – 92 – *Animiṣaḥ* – अनिमिषः – One who does not blink his eyes.

Lalitā – 281 – *Unmeshanimishotpannavipannabhuvanāvalee* – उन्मेषनिमिषोत्पन्न –विपन्नभुवनावली – One who makes this world arise and disappear with the opening and shutting of **Her** eyes.

Is it correct to say opening and closing of eyes relating to *Śrī Devī*, since *Devas* do not blink their eyes? *Śrī Devī* cannot be treated as belonging one race called *Devas*. Hence, the expression "opening and shutting" refer to the influence of the destiny of beings.

The expression also means, **She** does the task of creation with so much ease, just by blinking **Her** eyes. *Śrī Ādi Śaṇkara,* in his *Soundaryalaharī* (55th verse), describes the same meaning with different interpretation as; if *Śrī Devī* closes **Her** eyes the entire world will be destroyed and hence **She** never closes **Her** eyes –

Nimeṡonmeṣabhyām Pralayamudhayam Yāti Jagati
Tavetyāhūssantodharaṇidhara Rājanyatanaye I
*Tvatunbheshājjātam Jagadidam**She**ṣam Pralayata*:
Paritrātum Sanke Parihṛta Nimeṣāstavadrca: II

Viṣṇu – 215 – *Animiṣaḥ* – अनिमिषः – One who is ever awake. Or one who is not winking as fish – in His Fish incarnation (*Matsyāvatār*) or as Ātman.

22. ***Śiva*** – 94 & 877 – *Umāpatiḥ* – उमापतिः – Husband of *Umā*. *Umā* has the form of that *Brahmavidyā* itself. He is **her** *pati;*

Umāyāḥ brahmavidyātma ṡarīrāyāḥ patiḥ

Lalitā – 633 – *Umā* – उमा – One who has the great name *Umā*. *Śrī Devī* was born as daughter of *Himavān* and his wife *Menā* and had the name *Pārvatī.*

She started to do ardent penance at the age of 5 aiming to marry *Parameśvara*. Hence *Menā* became anxious and wanted to prevent *Pārvatī* from doing penance. I.e. **She** called *Pārvatī* as *'U'* and said *Mā* (not to do). Hence the name *Umā*.

The letter *'U'* relates to *Śiva, Mā* means *Lakshmī* (auspicious). Hence *Umā* means the auspiciousness of *Śiva*. The word *Śiva* itself means auspiciousness. **She** limits (*Mā*) *Śiva* (*'U'*). The word *Umā* has several meanings *Umā, Adasī, Haimavatī, Haridhra, Kīrti* and *Kāntiśu*. **She** is all these forms; *Yā Devī Sarvabhūteşu Kāntirūpeṇa Samstitā.*

In *Linga Purāŋa, Śiva* says to *Devī*, "In my *Praŋava* there are letters *A-U-M* (*UMA*) in the form of *Vişŋu, Śiva* and *Brahma*. These letters are in the order in the *Praŋava*, with the three notes (*mātrās*) and with the highest pluta";

Ukāram Ca Makāram Ca Akāram Ca Krameritam
Tvadīyam Praŋavam Vitdhitrimātram Plutamuttamam.

The *Mahāvāśişţa* says, "Uma is so called because it contains the essence of the *Praŋava* "; *Omkāra Sāra Śaktitvāt Umetiparikīrttitā*

In the heart of all beings, whether asleep or awake there is a cavity whence arises the sound being produced without contrast, which is *Śabdabrahmam*, the *Praŋava*, without the letters *A*, etc. The cavity is *Śiva* and in his head there is an *Indukalā* (crescent), which is the form of *bindu*. According to the *Shiva Sūtra* (I-13) *Umā* means the *Icchā Śakti* of *Yoginis* – The young *Umā* is called the *Iccha Śakti*.

Vişṇu – 505 – *Somaḥ* – सोमः – Earlier we discussed this name as alongwith *Umā*. This name and the meaning is very apt for Lord *Śiva*. When this name occurs in *Vişṇu Sahasranāma*, then this clearly indicates Lords *Śiva* and *Vişṇu* are one and the same.

23. ***Śiva*** – 102 – *Kāmaḥ* – कामः – One who is be keen on by all.

Lalitā – There are at least 10 names in *Lalitā* Sahasranāma conveying the same sense. They have lot many inner philosophical (*tatva*) meanings. Those who are particularly interested can read the book mentioned in the bibliography section by the same author.

Viṣṇu – 297 – *Kāmaḥ* – कामः – One who is the beloved. Not only He is the beloved of the devotees, but every activity of all living creatures is an attempt at courting and winning bliss and happiness. The Blissful Self is the goal of all creatures in life. Even insignificant unicellular organisms revolt against pain and they too seek happiness. Humans are no exception. The Infinite Bliss which is experienced only on transcending the body, mind and intellect, is that which is constantly demanded by every organism that breathes in this universe. In the ignorance of this All Satisfying Goal, the world suffers. That Lord is the beloved of all devotees and in fact, He is also the beloved of even those who deny Him and run after the sense objects. The theist seeks Him through devotion or meditation. The atheist too seeks Him only in and through all his diligent pursuits of the sense-stimuli.

24. ***Śiva*** – 128 – *Kṛṣṇaḥ* – कृष्णः – One who is always blissfully happy. The word *Kṛṣ* denotes the Existence (*Sattā*) status *'sat'* and the word *'ṇa'* means *Bliss* (*ānanda*). Hence *Krishna means* "Existence with Bliss" *(Satānanda).)* Thus, the very name divine, 'Krishna', represents the Supreme Paramātman. So said in Mahābhārata, Udyoga Parva (70-5).

Kṛṣirpūvācakaḥ śabdo, ṇacca nirvṛti vācakaḥ
Tayoraikyam param brahma kṛṣṇa ityabideeyate

Lalitā – Normally *Śrī Devī* is mentioned as reddish in colour. This has been mentioned in lot many places in *Lalitā Sahasranāma*. However, **She** has a name as Śyāmalā, which means black in colour. Śrī Devī , being a sister of Lord *Viṣṇu*, it is quiet natural that **She** is also of same colour as *Kṛṣṇa*.

Viṣṇu – 57 & 550 – *Kṛṣṇaḥ* – कृष्णः – The word *Kṛṣṇa in Samskrutam* means 'the dark'. The Truth that is intellectually appreciated, but spiritually not apprehended, is considered as "veiled behind some darkness".

Or, because of His dark-blue complexion He is called as *Kṛṣṇaḥ*. *Mahābhārata Śanti Parva* 343 says, "As My colour is dark-blue, I am called *Kṛṣṇaḥ*, Oh *Arjuna*!".

In *Mahābhārata*, we find *Kṛṣṇaḥ* explaining Himself to Arjuna when the earth becomes **She**lled in by its hard crux I shall turn myself into an iron ploughshare and shall plough the earth. One who incarnated in the Yādava tribe as the son of Vasudeva and Devakī. It is commented upon as "one who served the Hindu Spiritual World in the form of *Kṛṣṇa Dvaipāyana*", which is the full name of *Vyāsa*, the author of most of the *Purāṇas*. However, *Kṛṣṇaḥ* also means "The Dark"; the one great Infinite Consciousness that plays in us constantly, because of which we are aware of our experiences and yet, never can we directly apprehend this Source of All-life within ourselves. The *Kṛṣṇaḥ* is the "unknown factor" that expresses through us-whose manifestations are all our physical, mental and intellectual capabilities. He is, therefore, called as the 'Unknown', the 'Dark' – *Kṛṣṇaḥ*.

Apart from the above meaning *Kṛṣṇaḥ also means the* Enchanter of all His devotees (*ākarśaṇa*). Truth is the one, which irresistibly attracts everybody towards itself. The commentators have interpreted this significance in a more attractive context. They conclude that *Kṛṣṇaḥ* means "One who sweeps away the sins in the heart of those who meditate upon Him". Truth has got a magnetism to attract to itself all the ego and ego-centric passions of the individuals. Viewed in this sense, *Kṛṣṇaḥ* is not considered as a deity of the farmyard in the agricultural estates. The Lord ploughs the hard stupidities in us and prepares the heart-field, weeding out all the poisonous growths of sin and cultivates therein-pure Bliss which is of the nature of Reality.

25. ***Śiva*** – 130 & 995 – *Siddhārthaḥ* – सिद्धार्थः – One who has obtained whatever he wanted. He already has everything in this world. He has nothing more to obtain;

Siddha eva na tu sādhyā arttā arttanīyā patārtāyaśca.

Lalitā – Though there are many names conveying this meaning there is no specific name to compare in this regard.

Viṣṇu – 252 – *Siddhārthaḥ* – सिद्धार्थः – One who has gained all that has to be gained and achieved all that has to be achieved. That which has to be achieved in life during an individual's existence have all been classified under four heads and they are called as the four "aims of life" (*Puruśārtha*). They are Righteousness, (*Dharma*), Wealth and Possession (*Artha*), desires & ambitions (*Kāma*) and liberation from imperfections (*Mokṣa*). One who has gained all these 'four' have nothing more to gain as there cannot be any sense of imperfection in Him. One who has gained (*Siddhaḥ*) all that has to be gained (*Arthaḥ*) is *Siddhārtha*, i.e., Lord *Vişṇu*.

As a coincidence, it can be reminded that the original name of Goutama Bhuddha is also *Siddhārtha*.

26. ***Śiva*** – 133 – *Ajaḥ* – अजः – One who does not have birth. *Svetasvata Upanişat* (4.21) says; *Ajāta ityenam kaccit bhīru: prapatyate | Rudra yatte dakşiṇa mukham tenamām pāhi nityam ||*

Lalitā – 866 – *Ajā* – अजा – One who is unborn. The same message is conveyed in 136th name *Nityā* – **She** is eternal and in 174th name *Nirbhavā* - without origin. The *Svetashvatara Upanişat* (IV-5) – "The one, unborn; was not born, will not be born";

Ajāmekām Lohita Shukla Krushnām Bahvee: *Prajā*: *Srujamānām Saūā*: I
Ajo Hyoko JushamānonuShete Jahātyenām Bhuktabho Gamajonya: II

In another *Sruti* we read as – unborn and will not be born again;

Najāto Najanishyate.

In *Devī Upanişat* also (26th *ṛg*) we read as;

*Yasyā Anto Na Vidyāte Tasmāduchyatenantā*II
Yasyā Jananam Nopalabyate Tasmātuchyatojā II

The *Mahābhārata* also the same meaning is conveyed: "I was not, am not and will not be born at any time, I am the *Kşetrajna* of all beings and hence I am called as *Aja*";

Na Hi Jāto na Jāyeham Najanishye Kadāchana I
Kşetragna: *Sarvabhūtānām Tasmadahamajaḥ Smrutaḥ* II

Gīta (II-27) says, "Death is certain of that which is born; birth is certain of that which is dead. You should not therefore lament over the inevitable;

Jātasya Hi Dṛvo Mṛtyuḥ Dṛvam Janma Mṛtasya Ca I
Tasmādaparihāryerte Na Tvam Śocitumarhasi II

When there is no birth, there is no death also.

Viṣṇu – 95, 204 & 521 – *Ajaḥ* – अजः – Unborn. Birth implies a modification; birth cannot be without the death of its previous condition. Since the Eternal and the Infinite, is ever Changeless there can be in It neither birth nor death. That which is born must necessarily die (*Śrīmad Bhagavad Geeta* II-27) and so, that which is unborn should be deathless (*Amṛtaḥ*).

Ajaḥ is also a term denoting the Creator, Brahma; He who, in the form of *Hiraṇyagarbha*, apparently creates the delusory world of plurality is *Viṣṇu*.

890th name *Naikajaḥ* – नैकजः – is also worth comparing here – *Na*-not; *Eka*-once; *Ja*-born. One who is born not only once, but many times, in many Forms, to serve the devotees in His different Incarnations. In fact, all births are all His manifestations alone as he is the Spark-of-Existence in the Universe of inert matter. Through all equipments He alone is the One Consciousness that dances Its Infinite Glories

As the changeless and deathless reality, he has neither birth nor any decay, 'Unborn' in philosophy means undying; therefore, Eternal, Changeless, "Born to Lord *Viṣṇu*" is yet another meaning and according to this interpretation, the term can suggest *'Pradyumna'*, son of *Viṣṇu*, who is considered to be in our *Purāṇas* as an incarnation of the Lord of Love.

27. ***Śiva*** – 134 – *Bahurūpaḥ* – बहुरूपः – One who is many forms. *Śruti* says, *Rudra* has billions of forms. *Śrī Rudram* verses evidence this;

Asankhyātāḥ Sahasrānai Ye Rudra Atibhūmyām.

Lalitā – 824 – *Bahurūpā* – बहुरूपा – One who has many forms. *Devī Bhāgavatam* says – Though **She** is in the form of the Supreme Being, **She** takes the form of *kriyā śakti* (action energy) for killing the demons *Bhanḍāsura* and others; *Arūpāparabhāvatvād Bahurūpā Kṛyātmika*

Devī Purāŋa also says **Her** forms are many types (moving or static) – *Devas*, human beings and animals – hence **She** is *Bahurūpa.*
Vāmana Purāŋa says;

Vishvam Bahuvidham Gneyam Sā Chā Sarvatra Vartate

Tasmātsā Bahurūpatvādbahurūpā Shivā Matā

Ambāstavam of *Śrī Kālidāsā* (8th verse) says;

Dākṣāyanīti Kutiledi Kuhāriṇīti Kātyāyanīti Kamaleti Kamalāvatīti I
Ekā Satī Bhagavatī Paramārtatopi Sandṛśyase Bahuvidhā Nanu Nartakīva I I

Viṣṇu – 721, 723 & 765 – *Anekamūrtiḥ* – अनेकमूर्तिः, *Śatamūrtiḥ* – शतमूर्तिः & *Caturmūrtiḥ* – चतुर्मूर्तिः – Since he takes many a forms in the self-imposed incarnations to help the human beings he is *Anekamūrtiḥ*. On account of various alternatives various forms are created from a single knowledge matter and hence *Śatamūrtiḥ*. He has four forms viz., *Virāt* (imperishable), *Sūtram* (formulae), *Avyākrutam* (unmanifested) and *Turīyam* (fourth) and hence he is *Caturmūrtiḥ*. Or since he has four different colour forms as white, red, yellow and black.

28. ***Śiva*** – 143 – *Rudraḥ* – रुद्रः – One who removes all sorrows. *Ṛt – rodhana hetur dhuḥkkham tat drāvayati vināśayati iti rudraḥ* – *Ṛt* means dreadful distress. He removes those type of sorrows. Or during the period of great dissolution (*pralaya*) he makes every living being cry. Or he is in the form of *prāṇa* to everyone – *prāṇā vāva rudraḥ*.

Sun is also called as *Rudra*. During great dissolution Sun rises and burns the entire world. On account of this, torridly rains and world submerges in the waters.

To start with he originated from the forehead of Brahma. He wept loudly and fearfully; because he wept, he is called the weeper (*Rudra*).

In *Śrī Rudra Triśatī Nāmāvalī* also we have 233rd name as *Rudrāyaca Namaḥ*.

Lalitā – 269 – *Rudrarūpā* – रुद्ररूपा – One who is the in the form of *Rudra*. The form of *Śrī Devī* when the *tamas* quality dominates is called *Rudra*. In this form **She** destroys the world. *Rudra*, who drives away sorrow; because of the *samsārā* cycle. *Rujam* – sorrow, *Drāvayati* – removes, *Rotayati* – make other cry. The separation on account of destruction makes others cry. Hence *Rudra*.

Viṣṇu – 114 – *Rudraḥ* – रुद्रः – One who makes all people weep, at the time of death or during the total dissolution. One who makes all weep is *Rudraḥ*. From a devotee's standpoint the same term is interpreted as the one who liquidated all sorrows is *Rudraḥ*. Bhagavān declares Himself to be "Among the *Rudras*, I am *Śaṅkara* – (*Gīta* X-23). According to purāṇas there are 11 *Rudras*; the eleventh *'Rudra'* is called as *Śaṅkaraḥ* – *Sam karoti iti* = *Śaṅkaraḥ* – One who blesses all with Auspiciousness (*Sam*) is *Śaṅkara*. In the normal sense (colloquially) the word *Rudra* will mean lord *Śiva*. But here it specifies Lord *Viṣṇu* – indicating the oneness.

29. ***Śiva*** – 151 – *Daitrayagnaḥ* – दैत्र्यज्ञः – Slayer of demons.

Lalitā – 318, 599 & 696 – *Rākṣasaghnī* – राक्षसघ्नी, *Daityahantrī* – दैत्यहन्त्री & *Daityaśamanī* – दैत्यशमनी – One who is the slayer of demons *Bhanḍāsura* and others.

One who quells the demons/ evil forces. **She** killed demons like *Bhanḍan, Mahishan, Sumbhan, Nisumbhan* and many others. The word *Shama* means to control. **She** controls the evil thoughts arising in the minds of **Her** devotees. **She** is the slayer of demons. *Saptaśatī* (XI-55) also says;

Ithdam Yadā Yadā Bādā Dānavotthā Bhaviśyati.

Viṣṇu – 73 – *Madhusūdanaḥ* – मधुसूदनः – One who destroyed the great demon Madhu. The story of *Viṣṇu* destroying the two demons, Madhu and Kaiṭabha, is a story of secret suggestions in *Mahābhārata*. Madhu also means honey in Veda as the fruits of actions (*Karma-phala*). Actions leave impressions and these sensuous Vāsanās are destroyed by meditations on the Reality and hence the Supreme gathers to itself the name Madhusūdanaḥ – the Destroyer of *Vāsanās*.

The stories of Lord *Viṣṇu* killing the demons are available in almost all the *purāṇās*. For this purpose only he has taken lot many incarnations. In *Gīta* (IV-8) he says – *Paritrānāya Sadūnām Vināśāya Ca Duṣkṛtām*

30. ***Śiva*** – 152, 370, 384 & 533 – *Kālaḥ* – काल: – One who is in the form of time. Or one who conducts everything in this world.

One who is in the form of all arts – *kalānām catuḥśaṣṭi sammitānām nivāsa*. One who maintains the accounts of virtues and sins in the form Citragupta – *kalayati sarveśām puṇya pāpātikam tattat phalapradānārttam sankhyātīti kālaḥ*. One who creates the birth and death cycle;

janma maraṇa pravāham kālayati samvalayatīti

Lalitā – 557 – *Kālahantree* – कालहन्त्री – One who is the destroyer of time (*Mṛtyu*). *Svetāsvatara Upaniṣat* (VI-2) says, omniscient, time of time, possessed of all qualities, all knowing – *Brahmam* is the *Kāla* (death) for *Yama* (god of death) himself; *Gnaḥ Kālakālo Guŋī Sarva Vidyā*:

Viṣṇu – 418 – *Kālaḥ* – काल: – One who measures the merits and defects in each individual and who doles out the appropriate results. *Gīta* says, "I am the Time of counting". *Kālaḥ* is another the name of Yama, the Lord of Death and in this sense, it can mean "the Lord, who is Death or Annihilation-personified to all His enemies".

31. ***Śiva*** – 159 – *Sarvakāmaḥ* – सर्वकाम: – He himself is all desires. *Chāndokya Upaniṣat* (3.14.12) says *Sarvakarmā, sarvakāmaḥ sarvakandaḥ sarvarasaḥ* – all actions, all needs, all flavours. The same *Upaniṣat* (3.19.3) says *asmin sarve kāmāḥ samāhitāḥ*

Lalitā – 63 – *Kāmadāyinī* – कामदायिनी – One who fulfills **Her** devotees desires. *Dāyinī* – one who gives to **Her** devotees, *Kāma* – *Kāmeśvara*, that is, one who leads **Her** devotees to *Kāmeśvara* and becomes one with **Him**.

Kāmada means *Śiva* – that is one who destroyed Cupid. *Ayinī* means auspiciously united. *Kāmadayinī* means, one who is auspiciously united with the destroyer of *Kāma*.

Hereditary property is called *Dāyam*. *Śrī Devī* has *Kāma* as *Dāyam*. Her association with *Kāma* is timeless.

Viṣṇu – 851 – *Sarvakāmadaḥ* – सर्वकामदः – One Who fulfils all desires of all true devotees. Such devotees have no further desire but to reach, meet and merge in Him. In this way the term would also indicate that He destroys the chances of fulfilment of all unholy, sensuous and lusty desires in the faithless.

32. ***Śiva*** – 164 – *Maheśvaraḥ* – महेश्वरः – The *Īśvar* above every one. In practice we *prabandak* = manager. *Mahāprabandak* = General Manager. In that sense *Maheśvara* should mean General *Īśvar*. *Svetāvastara Upansiśad* says – *māyām tu prakṛtim vidyān māyinam tu maheśvaram* – it has to be understood that the nature is illusion (*māyā*) and one who make others act is *Parameśvara*.

Lalitā – 208 & 750 – *Kartā* – कर्ता – *Māheśvarī* – माहेश्वरी & *Maheśvarī* – महेश्वरी – One who is the supreme sovereign. One who is the consort of Lord *Maheśvara* (*Paramaśivā*).

Earlier it has been mentioned that there is no duplication of names in *Lalitā Sahasranāma*. These two names 208 and 750 differ by a letter. On account of long and short nature of *Ma*, it can be taken that the names are not duplicated.

Viṣṇu – 96 – *Sarveśvaraḥ* – सर्वेश्वरः – God of all gods or the Supreme Controller of all. In a sense it means the Almighty, the All-powerful. "He is the Lord of all," says *Bṛhadāraṇyaka Upaniṣat* (6-4-2).

33. ***Śiva*** – 170, 171 & 172 – *Nṛtyapriyaḥ* – नृत्यप्रियः, *Nityanartaḥ* – नित्यनर्तः & *Nartakaḥ* – नर्तकः – One who is always fond of dance. *Tāṇḍaveśvara Chidambara Mūrtiḥ* – The head of dancers in the city of Chidambara.

In *Śrī Rudra Triśatī Nāmāvalī* also we have 87th name as *Sabhāpatibhyaśca Namaḥ*. Though this was meant to mean head of a *Sabhā*. The presiding deity of Chidambaram temple is also called as *Sabhāpati*.

One who is always dancing. One who controls everything.

Lalitā – 734 & 738 – *Naţeshvaree* – नटेश्वरी & *Lāsyapriyā* – लास्यप्रिया – One who is the consort of *Naţesa*. This means that **She** is the consort of *Naţarāja*, dancing in *Chidambara*. The word *Chidambara* can be taken in two meanings – the place *Chidambara* or the ether of heart. Both are befitting meanings.

One who is fond of dancing. **She** is pleased by seeing dance of others. In general ordinary people also are pleased with songs and dance. It has been practiced for long wherein artists perform in front of kings and get rewarded. In the court of the empress *Śrī Devī* also dance and music performances are given. It is clear that these performances are made in temples also.

For the 184th name in *Lalitā Triśatī – Lāsya Darśana Santuṣṭā*, the commentary of *Śrī Ādi Śaṇkara* is as follows; A king, who has got satisfied with all his desires, without attaining any fruits, enjoys hunting, games of children, etc. In the same way *Śrī Devī* also enjoys the dance showing four-fold - desirable, undesirable, mixed and abuse and the resultant happiness and sorrow and the consequent facial expressions, the shaking of legs, hands and other organs. Thus enjoyed *Śrī Devī* bestows the results of the actions of devotees without any partiality; *Nā Datte Kshyachipāpam Na Chaiva Sukrutam Vibhuḥ*.

She is pleased with the dance according to the tune and drums performed by *Ramba, Ūrvaśi* and other *Devata* ladies.

172nd name of *Lalitā Triśatī – Hallīsa Lāsya Santuṣṭā* also indicates that **She** is pleased to see the dance of ladies. **She** is also happy to see a type of dance called *Kolāţţam* performed by ladies.

She dances alongwith *Naţesa*. The dance of these two has been mentioned in 41st verse of *Soundaryalaharee*;

Tavādhāre Mūle Saha Samayayā Lāsyaparayā
Navātmāna Manye Navarasa Mahātāndava Naţam I

The dance by men is called *tāṇḍavā* and that of women is *lāsya.* It has been mentioned that when *Maheśvara* did the *Tāṇḍavā, Śrī Devī* also did the *Lāsya.* When both are dancing, at the request of *Śrī Devī*, both started the fifth task called *Anugrahā* by re-creating the entire universe with most compassion.

Viṣṇu – 801 – *Akṣobhyaḥ* – अक्षोभ्यः – One Who is ever unruffled. Ordinarily an individual gets disturbed, subjectively, by the presence of desires, anger, passions, etc., and objectively an average man is constantly stormed by the enchanting dance of beautiful sense-objects all around him. Lord, the Self, is a state of existence wherein neither the subjective disturbances of the mind, nor the objective persecutions of the sense-organs can ever reach to ruffle the quietude and peaceful grace of His perfection. In describing the state of the *Stitaprajna*, *Bhagavān* says in *Gīta* that such a one will be *Akşobhya* like the ocean: "He attains Peace into whom all desires enter as waters enter the ocean, which filled from all sides, remains unmoved; but not the desirer-of-desires".

34. ***Śiva*** – 181 – *Vijayaḥ* – विजयः – One who is in the form of success. *Kenopanişat* (4.1) says – the result of success always belongs *Brahmam* – *brahmaṇo vā etatvijaye mahīyatvamiti*.

Lalitā – 346 – *Vijayā* – विजया – One who is ever with special victories. The consort of *Sudarśana Cakra* of *Viṣṇu* is *Vijayalakshmī*. **She** is the conceptual form. The differentiated feeling of '**I**'.

According to the *Devī Purāṇa*, *Vijayan* is the *Śiva* form in Kashmir, which is one of the sixty-eight sacred places. Since **She** is in that form, **She** is called as *Vijaya*.

Again as per *Devī Purāṇa*, after conquering the king of demons named *Padman*, **She** is known in the three worlds by the epithet *Vijaya* (ever victorious) and *Aparājitā* (unconquerable).
In *Śilpa Śāstra* (sculpture science) a type of building is called *Vijayam*. **She** is in that form of and hence *Vijaya*.

According to the *Cintāmaṇi*, *Vijaya* is an auspicious hour – in the month of *Āśvin*, in the tenth day of the bright fortnight, when the stars appear, that time is known as *Vijaya*, giving success to all undertakings started during this time. In the *Ratnakośa*, we read, the time, just after the dusk (twilight - *Sandhyā*) when the stars begin to shine, is called *Vijaya*, favourable to all undertakings. The eleventh *muhūrta* (eight hours and forty-eight minutes after midday) is named *Vijaya*. A journey should begun at this time by all who desire success. *Śrī Devī* is in this time form.

In *Devī Upaniṣat* **She** is indicated as;

Tāpāhariṇīm Devīm Bhuktimuktipradāyinīm
Anantām Vijayām Sūtthām Ṡaranyām Ṡivadām Ṡivām.

Viṣṇu – 147 – *Vijayaḥ* – विजयः – The Victorious. One who realises the Self can thereafter stand apart from the thraldom of matter, Victorious over the tyrannies of the flesh, feelings or facts. Thus, the Seat of Self is the Seat of Victory over matter. The Peace and harmony of the Self can never be assailed by the noisy hordes of the world of plurality. *Vijaya* is one of the names of *Arjuna* and the Lord Himself says, "Among the *Pāndavas*, I am Arjuna" – *Gīta* (X-37).

35. ***Ṡiva*** – 186, 209, 216 & 529 – *Yagnaḥ* – यज्ञः – One who is in the form of sacred *homa* or *yagna*. He destroys the *yagnas* done with evil intention.

One who is in the form of *yagna*, called *yoga* merging the *jīva* and *Īśvar*;

jīveśayoḥ sankatikaraṇa rūpo yogaḥ.

Lalitā – 769 – *Yagyarūpā* – यज्ञयरूपा – One who is the embodiment of sacrifices. Five types of sacrifices are prescribed for a human being – **She** is in the form of all these *yagnas*;

(i) *Deva Yagnam* – praying to *Devatas*.
(ii) *Pitṛ Yagnam* – praying to *antecedents* (father, grandfather, etc.) of the family race.
(iii) *Brahma Yagnam* – chanting of *Vedas*, teaching it to others and paying gratitude to the teachers and sages.
(iv) *Manuśya Yagnam* – offerings to fellow human beings, especially satisfying the unexpected visitors by offering them food etc., building of

temples, construction of tanks – service to the society.

(v) *Bhūta Yagnam* – helping the trees, plants, animals, birds, etc., in a proper way.

Offering the knowledge and experience got through the senses of the body is called *Gnāna Yagnam*. **She** is in that form also. This has been described in *Mukyāmnāya Rahasya* as;

Indriya Dvārasamgṛhyaigandhādyairātima Devatām I
Svabhāvena Samārādhyā Gnātuḥsoyam Mahāmakha: II

All the *yagnās* are the form of *Īśvara*. This has been described in detail in *Harivamsam* and *Padma Purāŋa*.

Viṣṇu – 445 & 971 – *Yagnaḥ* – यज्ञ: – One who is of the nature of *yajna*. All sacrifices are His own forms. He exists as sacrifice in order to satisfy human beings and gods.

One whose very nature is *yagna*. The term *yagna* means "work undertaken with a pure spirit of total dedication in complete co-operative endeavor with total selflessness, there is *Śrī Nārāyaṇa* in action through His creatures.

Śrī Ādi Śaṇkara in his commentary mentions; He is in the form of all the *yagnas* or He gives satisfaction to all *Devas* and offers the fruits of *yagnās*. *Veda* says; *Yagno Vai Viṣŋuḥ* (*Taitreeya Samhita*).

Gīta (X-25) says that the Lord is in the form of *Japa Yagnam* also; *Yagnānām Japayagnūsmi*.

36. ***Śiva*** – 190 – *Madhyamaḥ* – मध्यम: – One who looks everying from the middle and does not have any partiality.

In *Śrī Rudra Triśatī Nāmāvalī* also we have 275th name as *Madhyamāyaca Namaḥ*.

Lalitā – 370 – *Madhyamā* – मध्यमा – One who is in the form of *Madhyamā* – speech in the middle stage of its external expressions. There are four stages of speech – from origination till it comes out of the mouth – *Paśyantī, Parā, Madhyamā and Vaikharī.*

This speech, which is neither like *pashyanti*, stopping immediately after rising, nor like *Vaikharee* with articulation fully developed, it is called *Madhyamā* – intermediate stage between the two;

Pashyantīva na Kevalam Uttīrnā Nāpi Vaikharīva Bhahiḥ I
Sphutatara Nikhilāvayavā Vāgrūpā Madhyamā Tayorasmāt II

Viṣṇu – 793 – *Ratnanābhaḥ* – रत्ननाभः – Of beautiful navel like a jewel (*ratna*). Text books of Bhakti-cult advise devotees that they should meditate upon the Lord's navel-point, as a flashy, brilliant jewel (*Ratna*). This point of concentration is not without significance. Psychologists confess that they have no other knowledge beyond the obvious fact that thoughts express themselves as actions. But deeply meditative mystic enquirers delved deeper to detect and chart the story of actions.

It has been discovered that in seed form all thoughts are with the Infinite (*Parā*) before manifestation. From this womb they become manifest and an individual becomes dimly aware of thoughts in their embryo form-vague and still incompletely un-formed (*Paśyantī*). Thereafter, the thoughts get translated into expressions (*Madhyamā*) and in their last full stage of manifestation they come to express themselves as actions in the outer world (*Vaikharī*).

In this chain of processes when thoughts become manifest for the thinker, it is said the seat of *Paśyantī* stage is the navel region. This brilliant seat of nascent manifestation of all thoughts is indicated here as "the jewel of his navel".

Depending on the dominant stage of speech, it is called as base voice, head voice, chest voice, stomach voice, etc.

37. ***Śiva*** – 195, 496 & 613 – *Ajitaḥ* – अजितः – One who was never conquered by anyone. One who cannot be conquered by anybody. One who cannot be conquered by the three *guṇas* – *Guṇātītaḥ*

Lalitā – 346 – *Vijayā* – विजया – One who is ever with victories. As per *Devī Purāṇa*, after conquering the king of demons named *Padman*, **She** is known in the three worlds by the epithet *Vijaya* (ever victorious) and *Aparājitā* (unconquerable).

Viṣṇu – 549 – *Ajitaḥ* – अजित: – One who is vanqui**She**d by none. Unconquered and hence, the unconquerable in any of His incarnations. We never meet Him as vanqui**She**d in any of his confrontations with mighty evil.

38. ***Śiva*** – 198 – *Gambhīraḥ* – गंभीर: – One whose depth cannot be found. Who cannot be identified by any sense. Tamil saying goes *Adimudi kāṇa mudiyāthattu* – neither the feet nor the head can be seen. Taitrīya *Upaniṣat* says; *Yato vāco nivarttante aprāpya manasā saha*

Lalitā – 854 – *Gambhīrā* – गम्भीरा – One who is fathomless or one whose depth cannot be measured. Her limits cannot be identified.

Gam is the *Gaṇapati bīja*, *bhī* - fear, *ra* - drives out. One school says, since **She** removes fear of *Gaṇapati*, **She** is *Gambhīra.*It seems, it can be said that **She** removes the fear by worshipping *Gaṇapati*. The first step in worshipping *Śrī Vidyā* is *Gaṇapati* worship. Through this any obstruction or fear during the worship is removed.

Viṣṇu – 543 – *Gabhīraḥ* – गभीर: – The Unfathomable. *Upaniṣat*s also declare that He is unknown. The limited human intellect cannot apprehend or visualise, or plumb the depth of, or unravel the mystery of His Wisdom, Power, Strength or Purity. He is so gigantic with his knowledge, wealth, strength, vigor, etc.; *Gnānaiṣvaryabalavīryādibhirgambhīro Gambhīraḥ*.

39. ***Śiva*** – 207 – *Viṣvaksenaḥ* – विष्वक्सेन: – One who rescinds the army of demons; *vishvak viśu sarvataḥ anjanti phalāyantī yasya prayānoyeke daityānām senā iti*

Viṣṇu – 125 – *Viṣvaksenaḥ* – विष्वक्सेन: – He, while facing whom, even the mighty army of the gods retreat and scatter away, is called *Viṣvaksenaḥ*. He is the Almighty and All-Powerful and no army can stand in front of Him.

Before start of any auspicious activity, *Śaivas* or *Smārtas* worship *Gaṇapati* and then start the main rite. Similarly it is the practice of some groups of *Vaiṣṇavites* to worship *Viṣvaksena* and then start the major activity.

40. ***Śiva*** – 208, 377, 712 & 753 – *Hariḥ* – हरि: – One who destroys everything – *sarvasamharttā* – or one who controls everything.

One who is in the form of Ānjaneya – *Hanumān Rāmarūpasya Viṣṇoḥ sahāyaḥ* – it has been mentioned in various purāṇās that Ānjaneya is an incarnation of Lord *Śiva*.

One who removes all the sorrows of devotees – *harati bhaktānām duḥkkhamiti hariḥ* – or one who removes the birth and death alongwith their causes.

One who holds a triad as a weapon – *hantītī hā sūlastamrāti ādatte sa haraḥ*
In *Śrī Rudra Triśatī Nāmāvalī* also we have the following names:

- 5th & 246th names as *Harikeśebhyo Namaḥ*.
- 12th name as *Harikeśāya Namaḥ*
- 283rd name as *Harityāya Namaḥ*

Viṣṇu – 650 – *Hariḥ* – हरि: – The Lord is called "The Destroyer". He, who destroys the false values and the inner conflicts created by human beings in their own life and in their consequent discordant contact with the world around them. These confusions and sorrows created by human beings, for themselves in life, due to their own ignorance of their own divine nature, is called *Samsāra*. Lord Nārāyaṇa is the Destroyer of this Samsāra sorrows if His devotees. That he destroys the entanglement in the cycle of birth and death alongwith ignorances and causes.

41. ***Śiva*** – 236 & 621 – *Vaiṣṇavīḥ* – वैष्णवी: & *Viṣŋuḥ* – विष्णु: – One who is in the form of *Viṣŋu*. The very name implies the oneness among the Lord

Śiva and *Vişŋu*. Earlier we discussed a name as *Rudra* for Lord *Vişŋu*. These evidence us that only the name or the form differs. But in essence they are one and the same.

Lalitā – 339 & 892 – *Vişŋumāyā* – विष्णुमाया & *Vaishŋavee* – वैष्णवी – One who is the power of *Vişŋu.* One who is *Vişŋu Māyā Śakti*. *Vişŋu* is all-pervading, unlimited by place, time, *Brahmam,* in the form of inner self in all souls, etc. In *Saptashatee* also we read as;

Yā Devī Sarvabhūteśu Vişŋu Māyeti Samstitā I
Namastasyai Namastasyai Namastasyai Namo Namaḥ II (V-14)

The *Kālikā Purāŋā* also says *Vişŋumāyā* is that which differentiates, everything, into manifested and un-manifested according to the *tamas, rajas* and *satva* qualities.

Vişṇu – 2 – *Vişŋuḥ* – विष्णुः – The term *Vişŋu* is dissolved as *Veveşti Vyāpnoti iti Vişŋuḥ* – That pervades everywhere is *Vişŋuḥ.* That has the nature of pervasiveness is *Vişŋuḥ*. He is the one who pervades all and nothing ever pervades Him. *Īsāvāsyam Idam Sarvam* – All this is indwelt, pervaded by the Lord. This very same idea is described in the typical style of the *Purāṇas*, in the incarnation of the Lord as *Vāmana*, who, with His feet, measured the entire universe. Because of this act, the Lord got the name *Vişŋuḥ*, says *Mahābhārata*. *Vişŋuḥ* Purāṇa (3-1) says: The root *Viş* means "to enter". The entire world of things and beings is pervaded by Him and the *Upanişat* emphatically insists in its mantra "whatever that is there is the world of change". Hence it means that "He is not limited by space (*Desa*), time (*Kāla*) or substance (*Vastu*)". *Śrī Ādi Śaṇkara*'s in his commentary says **he** is the *Māyā* of Universal Absolute. The *Śakti*, which limits this Absolute is illusion. *Gīta* (VII–14) says – *Daiveehyeshā Guŋamayee Mama Māyā Duratyayā* – this is my divine illusion, consisting of *Guŋas* is hard to surmount.

As he pervades everything he is called as *Vişŋu*. The term *Vişŋu* is derived from the root *Viş* (indicating the presence everywhere) combined with the suffix *nuk*.

42. ***Śiva*** – 245 – *Prajāpatiḥ* – प्रजापतिः – One who is head of all living beings (*prajās*).

Lalitā – 823 – *Jananī* – जननी – One who is the mother of the entire universe. While *Śiva* and *Viṣṇu* are called as father of this universe, it is quiet natural that Śrī Devī is called as mother of this universe. We find some more names also conveying the same meaning, which we have discussed elsewhere.

Viṣṇu – 69 & 197 – *Prajāpatiḥ* – प्रजापतिः – The Lord (*Pati*) of all living creatures (*Prajā*). The term *Praja* means 'Children'. Hence *Prajāpati* means the Great Father, to whom all beings in the living kingdom are His own children. In this sense, the term connotes One, who, as the Creator, creates all creatures. Since every creature has emerged from Him, the living creatures are His folks (*Prajā*) and He is their *Pati*. The term *Pati* has a direct meaning – 'father'. Thus *Viṣṇu*, as the only source from which all creatures have emerged out, is called as *Prajāpatiḥ*.

43. ***Śiva*** – 248 – *Sarvagaḥ* – सर्वगः – Omnipresent. Or one who does everything – *samaṣṭi kāryarūpaḥ*

Lalitā – 702 – *Sarvagā* – सर्वगा – One who is omnipresent. The message that **She** is present everywhere conveyed in the previous name is again stressed here. This can be compared to the saying in Tamil that he is available in a pillar and even a dust particle – *Tūṇilum Iruppān, Turumbilum Iruppān*.

The *Varāha Purāṇa* says, when *Śrī Devī* in the form of the creative *Śakti*, was performing penance in the *Sveta* mountain, *Brahma* said, "You amy ask a boon". *Śrī Devī* replied, "Oh holy one! I cannot bear to remain in one place, hence I beg you to grant me the boon of omnipresence. Thus asked, *Brahma* then replied to the creative *Śrī Devī*, Oh thou of all forms, thou shall become omnipresent".

The same message is conveyed in *Devī Purāṇa* also as also; "Oh great wise one, this is the true established doctrine about *Śrī Devī*, **She** is certainly the *Vedas*, sacrifices, heaven; all this universe, animate and inanimate, is pervaded by *Śrī Devī*. **She** is sacrificed to and **She** is worshipped, **She** is food and drink. Everywhere *Śrī Devī* is present in different forms and names as in the trees, in the earth, wind, ether, water, fire. Thus, this *Śrī Devī* is ever to be worshipped according to the rules; one who thus known here, will be absorbed into **Her**".

Viṣṇu – 123 – *Sarvagaḥ* – सर्वग: – He who is present everywhere, meaning "One who pervades everything". The cause pervades its effect: gold in all ornaments; ocean in all waves; cotton in all cloth. The Infinite Consciousness Itself expresses as both world-of-matter (*Kşetra*) and the Knower-of-the-field (*Kşetrajna*). *Viṣṇu*, the Infinite is beyond these two (*Uttamaḥ Puruṣaḥ*) in whom there is no expression of matter and hence, no 'Knower'-hood. He is the All-Pervading Self, *Viṣṇu*.

44. ***Śiva*** – 256 – *Stutāyaḥ* – स्तुताय: – Omnicient. Or one who is worshipped by all.

Lalitā – 928 – *Stutimatī* – स्तुतिमती – One in about whom lots of praises have been sung. There are lots of praises about her – both *Vaidhīka* and *Loukīka* and hence *Stutimatī*. Among the *Loukīka* praises, the top ones are – *Lalitā Stavaratnam* by *Śrī Durvāsa*, *Mūka Pancaśatī* by *Śrī Mūka* and *Soundaryalaharī* by *Śrī Ādi Śaṇkara*.

Viṣṇu – 682 – *Stutiḥ* – स्तुति: – The act of praise. The very noble, divine "act of invoking the lord" is only by his grace. "*Avanarulāleye Avan Tāl Vaṇangi*" – to worship his feet with his own blessings – a famous Tamil saying.

45. ***Śiva*** – 259 – *Vyālarūpaḥ* – व्यालरूप: – One who is in the form of a snake. We may be wondering how Lord *Śiva* is in the form a snake. It has different interpretations:

- He is *Ādiśeşa*.
- He is the *Kunḍalinī* energy, which is in the form of a snake.
- He wears snake as an ornament.

Lalitā – 110 – *Kunḍalinī* – कुन्डलिनी – One who is in the form of *Kunḍalinī* energy. This energy is in the form of a snake coiled anti-clockwise in 3.5 rounds. The three rounds respectively represent the letters *A, Ū* and *Ma*. The half round is the half scale. That implies *Kunḍalinī* corresponds to *Om* – the *Praŋavamantra*.

She is breathing like the snake sleeping in *Mūlādhāra*. The breath of this *Kunḍalinī,* the energy of the soul, is the vital life (*prāŋan*). One can hear the sound of this breath by completely closing the ears. If it is not heard, it is told that death is nearing.

The form of *Kunḍalinī* is explained in detail in the 10th *verse* of *Soundaryalaharī.*

Viṣṇu – 92 & 907 – *Vyālaḥ* – व्याल: & *Kuṇdalī* – कुण्डली – One who is unapproachable. *Vyāla* also means 'Serpent'; to those who have no devotion or understanding, God or Truth is as horrible and terrible as a 'serpent'. Moreover, it is so difficult to grasp in our understanding that it is like a serpent: ever eluding, always slippery.

One Who wears the famous ear-ring called the *Makara-Kuṇḍala*. The term *Kuṇḍalī* also signifies the 'Serpent' – hence the *Kuṇḍalinī Śakti* – the 'Serpent-Power' – the coiled mystic-glory lying now inert, uninvoked at the base of the back-bone in the deep pelvic region. Here the 'Serpent' may be taken as the thousand - tongued *Ananta* on whom *Śrī Nārāyaṇa* is described as ever reclining in His *Yoga*-rest.

In all religions, 'Serpent,' it seems, symbolises the 'mind'. In Hinduism it is true. Whether it is in Kṛṣṇa's dance on the Kāliyan-Serpent, or *Śiva* wearing as ornaments the Serpents (*Bhūṡaṇa*), or *Śrī Hari* resting upon Ananta – the idea is always the conquest of the mind, the poisonous serpent.

Śrī Ādi Śaṇkara mentions; *Viṣŋu* is in the form of *Ādi Sesha* – a snake. Or *Viṣŋu* wears the earrings similar to the Sun's galaxy. Or *Samkya* and *Yoga* are the two earrings in the form of fish.

46. ***Śiva*** – 260 – *Guhāvāsī* – गुहावासी – One who resides in the cave of the heart. Taitrīya *Upanișat* (2.1) says *Nihitam guhāyām paramevyoman* – the *Paramātma* lives in the *Paramākāśa* of the heart.

Lalitā – 706 – *Guhāmbā* – गुहाम्बा – One who dwells in a cave. Following the Samskrutam grammar; *Madyama Pada Lopī, Śrī Bhāskararāya* explains this name. From the phrase; *Guhāyām Sthitā Ambā*, the middle word is removed and this name *Guhāmbā* is obtained. It means that **She** is in the form of a shadow. There are two people shadow and light in the cavity viz., the heart.

The *Kaţopanishad* (III-1) says;

Rutam Pantou Sukrutasya Loke Guhām Pravişţou Parame Parardhe I
Cāyātapou Brahmavido Vadanti pancāgnayo Ye ca Trināciketā: II

There are the two, drinking their reward in the world of their own works, entered into the cave of the heart dwelling on the highest summit (the ether in the heart). Those who know *Brahmam* call them shade and light. The meaning is that as both, shadow and light, enter the cavity of the heart and both contradict each other; hence duality is sanctioned by the scriptures.

Vişņu – 111 – *Puņdarīkākşaḥ* – पुण्डरीकाक्षः – One who can be contacted and fully experienced in the Heart Space (*Punḍarīkam*). In the *Nārāyaṇa Upanişat* (10) the same term is employed – In the core of the body, in the Heart Space, dwells the Supreme. In the 'Heart', the meditator can experience the Reality more readily and very clearly and hence the All-Pervading Reality is described as "dwelling in the Heart-cave".

47. ***Śiva*** – 270 & 278 – *Durvāsaḥ* – दुर्वासः – One who is in the form of *Durvāsa* in the incarnation of *Amsa*. Since he is omnipresent, it is very difficult to provide him any attire – *durlabham vāso yasya ananta bhāradvaat*. He is limitless – how can he be provided with any dress – *nirmalasya kutaḥ snānam vastram viśvodarasya caḥ*. Or when he wears the skin of a tiger or elephant how can we provide him any other dress.

Vişņu – 780 – *Durāvāsaḥ* – दुरावासः – He whom the Yogis bring to reside in their hearts, with very great difficulty. He is not easy to lodge – within the heart steadily for even great seekers who are diligent in their consistent pursuit. To withdraw the mind from the objects of pleasure and to steadily contemplate upon the great seat of Life is not an easy accomplishment. Therefore, even yogins, in their persevering meditation, find it not easy to contemplate steadily upon Śrī Nārāyaṇa, hence this name. "This Yoga of equanimity, taught by Thee, O slayer of *Madhu*, I see not its enduring continuity, because of the restlessness (of the mind)," cries Arjuna in the *Gīta*. Bhagavān also adds that the meditation should be "As a lamp placed in a windless place does not flicker".

48. ***Śiva*** – 274 – *Atulyaḥ* – अतुल्यः – One who does not have anyone else to compare. *Svetāvāstara Upaniṣat* (4.19) says – there is none equal to *Paramātmā* whose name is most glorious –

Na tasya pratimāsti yasya nāma mahadyashaḥ

Lalitā – 184 – *Nistulā* – निस्तुला – One who is incomparable/ unequal/ peerless. There is nothing to compare with **Her** and hence *Nistula.* We cannot weigh **Her** comparing with anything else. *Tripura Upaniṣat* (82) says *Hetu Dṛśtānta Varjitam* – without cause or comparison.

Viṣṇu – 355 – *Atulaḥ* – अतुलः – One who cannot be compared to anything else. *Gīta* (XI-43) says – there is none equal to Thee, not to speak of any one greater – *Na tvat samosty abhyadhikaḥ kutonyaḥ*

49. ***Śiva*** – 284 – *Sarvadhārī* – सर्वधारी – One who bears or supports everything.

Lalitā – 659 – *Sarvādhārā* – सर्वाधारा – One who is the supporter of all. **She** has all the supports as **Her** form. *Sarvā*, the whole world, *dhārā*, gradation, i.e., **She** is one with created things. It is called as *Parampara* (race), since everything originates one after another from the previous one.

Viṣṇu – 104 – *Vasuḥ* – वसुः – The One who is the very support of all elements and the One who Himself is the very Essence of the elements. This is something like a dream made up of our own mind; and the very same dream-world plays itself out, all the time sustained in the very same mind. Similarly, the Self indwells all and all dwell in the Self. In *Gīta* (X-23) we are told by the

Lord, "I am among the *Vasus* the *Pāvakaḥ*". Therefore, the Self exists like air-allowing everything to remain in it and sustaining everything by it.

50. ***Śiva*** – 291 – *Nigrahaḥ* – निग्रह: – One who punishes the evil or wicked people.

Lalitā – 696 – *Daityaśamanī* – दैत्यशमनी – One who quells the evil forces/ demons. The word *śama* means to control. **She** controls the evil thoughts arising in the minds of **Her** devotees.

Viṣṇu – 761 – *Nigrahaḥ* – निग्रह: – The killer. An uninitiated student may get shocked when he finds that the Lord is invoked as a murderer! But it is true. The only difference is that He is only the destroyer of the ego-just as a doctor is a 'murderer' of diseases; just as the Sun is the destroyer of the night; as summer is the annihilator of winter. Similarly, the Lord is the destroyer of ego and ego-centric limitations in the devotee. In Samskrutam this word also indicates "One who absorbs the devotee unto Himself". Once an individual withdraws himself even an iota from his total pre-occupation with the world and turns his attention to the spiritual centre in himself, the Lord fascinates and enchants the seeker's attention more and more to His own Infinite Glory and ultimately absorbs (*Nigrahaḥ*) the individual totally into the state of Pure-Consciousness.

51. ***Śiva*** – 292 – *Kartā* – कर्ता – One who creates and protects everything.

Lalitā – This has been mentioned in many a place, in *Lalitā* Sahasranāma. For instance 264 – *Sṛṣṭikartrī* – सृष्टिकर्त्री and 882 – *Yajnakartrī* – यज्ञकर्त्री can be quoted.

Viṣṇu – 380 – *Kartā* – कर्ता – The Doer. He is the One in whose presence alone all activities are possible and hence by a transferred epithet, though the doings all belong to the equipments, the Self is called as 'Doer'. One who can freely perform all the functions of creation, sustenance and destruction, is the 'Doer'. One who is free and hence he is his own master.

52. ***Śiva*** – 311 – *Ādityaḥ* – आदित्यः – One who is in the form of Sun. *Utainam Viśvābhūtāni sadṛṣṭo mṛḍāyāti naḥ* – The living beings see the Rudra, who is visible in the form of Sun. Let him make all of us happy.

Lalitā – 596 – *Raviprakhyā* – रविप्रख्या – One who has brightness like the Sun. In the heart there is a solar disc that is the second division of the *Panchadaśī mantra*. Hence *Śrī Devī* is called as *Raviprakhya.*

The *Āryā Śatakam* (verse 50) of *Mūka Pancaśatī* indicates the same message;

Madhye Hṛdayam Madhye Nitilam Madhye Shiro'pi Vāstavyām
Canḍakara Cakra Kārmuka Candra Samābhām Namāmi Kāmākṣīm

Viṣṇu – 39 – *Ādityaḥ* – आदित्यः & 563 – *Ādityaḥ* – आदित्यः – The golden-hued person in the Sun's orbit. In *Śrīmad Bhagavad Gīta* (10.21) it is mentioned *Ādityānām aham Viṣṇu* – among the *Ādityas* I am *Viṣṇu*. There are twelve Ādityas and *Viṣṇu* is one of them. Or it may imply the meaning that just as one Sun reflects as many in water receptacles, it is the one Spirit that is reflecting as many *Jīvas* in numerous body-minds.

One who was born of *Aditi* in His incarnation as *Vāmana*.

53. ***Śiva*** – 323 – *Ātmanirālokaḥ* – आत्मनिरालोकः – One who takes complete care of *Jīvātma*. *Gīta* XIII-22 says:

Upatraśṭānumantā ca barttā bhoktā maheśvaraḥ
Paramātmeti cāpyukto dehesmin puruṣa: paraḥ

That *parama puruṣ*, called *Maheśvara*, who sees from above, thinks, supports and enjoys from behind, dwells in this body.

Lalitā – 617 – *Atmā* – आत्मा – One who is in the form of *Ātman* or *Jīva* (soul). This name indicates *Jīvātmā.* The word *Ātmā* has several meanings – body, mind, *Brahmam*, nature, firmness and intelligence. Since *Śrī Devī* is in these forms this name is very much apt for **Her**. *Ātmā* word can be taken to mean *Paramātmā* (the Supreme Being). The *Ātmā* indicates body. Hence all bodies of embodied souls are the forms of *Śrī Devī* only.

Viṣṇu – 84 – *Ātmavān* – आत्मवान् – One established in his own greatness, i.e. requiring no other support than Himself. Chaandokya *Upaniṣat* (7.24.1) says – what is that in which, Oh! Bhagavan – that is established? –

Sa bhagavaḥ kasmin pratiṣṭhita iti, sve mahimni

54. ***Śiva*** – 333 – *Aśvatthaḥ* – अश्वत्थः – One who is in the form of *Aśvattha* tree.

In *Śrī Rudra Triśatī Nāmāvalī* also we have 87th & 138th and 88th & 139th names as *Aśvebhyo Namaḥ* and *Aśvapatibhyaśca Namaḥ*.

Lalitā – 325 – *Jagateekandā* – जगतीकन्दा – One who is the root cause of this universe. The word *Kandā* has lot of meanings like to fill, root of the plants, cloud, etc. The root of the plants supports the entire plant. It provides the required strength. Same way **She** supports and provides strength to this whole world.

Viṣṇu – 824 – *Aśvatthaḥ* – अश्वत्थः – That which does not last even for the next day. *Kathopaniṣat* (2.3.1) says *Ūrdhvamūlovāk śākha eśoṣvatthaḥ sanātanaḥ* - this is the eternal *Aśvattha* (Pipal tree) with roots above and branches downward.

The *Gītā* (XV-1) says with roots above and branches below, the *Aśvattha* tree is spoken of as indestructible;

Ūrdhvamūlam adhaḥ śākham aśvattham prāhur avyayam

55. ***Śiva*** – 336 – *Vamadevaḥ* – वामदेवः – The Lord who gives the fruits according to the actions (*karmas*) done by the souls. *Svetāsvāstara Upaniṣat* says *Vāmānām karma phalānām deva iva devo rājā vibājakaḥ Karmādhyakṣaḥ sarva bhūtātivāsaḥ*.

Lalitā – 469 – *Vāmadevī* – वामदेवी – The consort of *Vāmadeva*. There are five forms (faces) for Lord *Śiva*. viz., *Īsāna, Tatpuruṣa, Agora, Vāmadeva* and *Satyojāta*. In that **She** is the consort of *Vāmadeva*.

In *Śiva Purāṇa, Śiva* has been described as "Of beautiful appearance, red as the red paste (*kunkuma*), the north face of the Lord called *Vāma* is firmly established";

Kumkumakşoḍa Sankāśam Vāmāgyam Vanaveśdṛt I
Vaktramuttaram Īśvasya Pratistāyām Pratiṣṭitam II

Vāma - to be worshipped, *deva* - the deity. The *Aitreya Sruti* says, "The *Devas* addressed him; he indeed is to be worshipped by all of us, hence he is called *Vāmadeva*";

Tam Devā Abruvan Ayam Vai Na: *Sarveśām Vāma Iti Tasmādvāmadevaḥ*

Vāma – the left side, *Deva* - he shines, i.e. *Ardhanārīśvara* (half body is *Śiva* and the other half is *Devī*) is called *Vāmadeva*.

Vāma – fair; beautiful *Devī*. *Vāma* - the fruits of actions, Devī, the presiding deity of them.

The *Devī Purāṇa* says, *Vāma* means opposite or inverted; as *Śrī Devī* gives bliss through that path **She** is called *Vāmadevī*.

Vāmam Viruddharūpam Tu Viparītam Ca Gīyate I
Vāmena Sukhadā Devī Vāma Devī Tata: *Smrutā* II

56. ***Śiva*** – 340 – *Vāmanaḥ* – वामनः – One, in the form of *Viṣṇu*, who suppressed Bali, taking the incarnation *Vāmana*.

In *Śrī Rudra Triśatī Nāmāvalī* also we have 156th name as *Vāmanāyaca Namaḥ*.

Lalitā – 945 – *Vāmakeśvaree* – वामकेश्वरी – One who is in the form of *Vāmakeśvara tantra*.

Those who follow the left path are called *Vāmakās*. They do not perform the five sacrifices viz., *Pancayajnās*. They do not repay the credits to *Devas*, sages (*rishis*) and *pitṛs* (ancestors). **She** is head of them – i.e. **She** is worshipped by them.

Vāmana indicates creation. *Dakşa* and other *Prajāpatis* who create the world are called *Vāmakās*. **She** is head of them.

Viṣṇu – 152 – *Vāmanaḥ* – वामनः – Of the ten great incarnations, the fifth one is Vāmana and the very name indicates "One who has a small body". It was in the form of a child (*vatuḥ* = A child student in a *gurukula*) that *Vāmana* approached the divinely righteous Emperor *Mahābali* to beg of him a little land, of the length of his tiny three steps and the Lord measured His three steps all the three worlds and thus conquered *Mahābali*. He checked (*Vāmayati*) the rising pride of possession in *Bali*, hence He, in that incarnation as a *Vatu*, is called *Vāmana*.

The term *Vāmana* also means 'worshipful': "Him, the Dwarf, sitting in the middle of the heart, all gods adore", so we read in the *Kaṭopaniśad* (5-3).

57. ***Śiva*** – 349 & 974 – *Avyayaḥ* – अव्यय & *Avyayaḥ* – अव्यय – One who does not change.

Viṣṇu – 13 – *Avyayaḥ* – अव्ययः – One for whom there is no decay. *Śruti* says – *ajaromarovyayaḥ* – un-aging, undying and un-decaying.

58. ***Śiva*** – 368 – *Īśānaḥ* – ईशानः – One who undertakes every task with utmost care. One who influences everything, by being within as *antaryāmi*, to act – *Īṣṭe iti īsāno niyantā antaryāmītyarttaḥ*. Lord *Śiva* is said to have five faces – *Sadyojāta, Vāmadeva, Aghora, Tatpuruṣa* and *Īśāna*. This name can also be construed to mention about the one of the faces *Īśāna*.

Viṣṇu – 64 – *Īśānaḥ* – ईशानः – The Controller of all the five Great Elements. When this term is used, *Īśvara* becomes the Administrator of His own Law in the phenomenal world of plurality. The executive function of His Infinite Will, when manifested through Him, the Lord *Īśvara*, is said to function as *Īśānaḥ*. Or, the term can also mean one who is the Supreme *Īśvara* – the *Parameśvara*.

59. ***Śiva*** – 359 – *Madhuḥ* – मधुः – One who is in the form of *Vasanta ṛtu* (spring season). Vasanta ṛtu is as sweet as honey (madhu) and since Lord *Śiva* does all the good requirements of the living this as sweet as honey, this name is apt for him.

Lalitā – 292 – *Madhumatee* – मधुमती – The word *Madhu* means honey or alcohol. Alcohol also was one of the offerings during worship. Those who worship in religious manner offer honey, others offer alcohol itself.

In *Saptashatee* also it has been mentioned that *Śrī Devī* consumes alcohol. *Veda* says that the form of *Śrī Devī* herself is like a honey;

Mahtyai Vā Etaddevatāyai Rūpam Yanmadhu.

Cāndokya Upaniṣat says that the honey of *Devas* is Sun. **She** is in that form.

Āditya Vai Devamadhu.

Viṣṇu – 168 – *Madhuḥ* – मधुः – The term *Madhu* familiarly stands for 'honey'. It also indicates 'nectar'. One who generates Nectarine Bliss in the hearts of the devotees is called *Madhu*. The spring season in India is called as Madhumāsa since spring is the season of flowers; full of honey for the bees and joy for the human beings. The month called Madhu (March-April) is the *Chaitra* month, which is especially considered as auspicious for prayers and meditation. One who is of the nature of the *Mādhava-māsa*, the month of *Mādhava* (April-May) can also be the suggestion in this term. *Vaiśākha* (April-May) is considered as the most auspicious time of the year for the worship of *Viṣṇu*.

60. ***Śiva*** – 361 – *Vācaspatiḥ* – वाचस्पतिः – One who is in the form of *Bṛhaspati*, the *Guru* of *Devas*.

Lalitā – 704 – *Sarasvatī* – सरस्वती – One who is in the form of *Sarasvatī*, the presiding deity of knowledge.

The knowledge is surrounded by ignorance. This has been explained in *Gīta* (V-15) also as; *Agnānenāvṛtam Gnānam Tena Muhyanti Jantavaḥ* – The omnipresent does not take note of the merit or demerit of any. Knowledge is veiled by ignorance; mortals are thereby deluded (pot and picture instance). Knowledge is covered by nescience hence people are bewildered and it is necessary to confuse sinful men because they are devoid of divine grace; to conceal from them the knowledge of non-duality which is the highest human desires and which removes all sorrow. Once he becomes knowledgeable the non-dual thought is highlighted. The salvation also will be reached.

Viṣṇu – 573 – *Vācaspatirayonijaḥ* – वाचस्पतिरयोनिजः – One who is a master of all knowledge (*Vidyas*) or who is unborn through a mother's womb. He is *Vācaspati*, since he is the master of all learnings.

61. ***Śiva*** – 369 – *Īśvaraḥ* – ईश्वरः – One who is omnipotent. Or one who enjoys everything – *aśnoti vyāpnoti Īśvara:*

Lalitā – 271 – *Īśvarī* – ईश्वरी – One who is in the form of *Īśvar*. One who does the fourth task called *Tirodhāna* is *Īśvar*, completely in the form *satva* quality. *Śrī Devī* is in this form.

The quality of *Īśvara* is Lordship, activity, independence, consciousness, etc. Since *Śrī Devī* is with all these qualities, **She** is *Īśvarī*.

Viṣṇu – 36 & 74 – *Īśvaraḥ* – ईश्वरः – One who is Omnipotent and hence has all powers in Him to the full. The manifested powers of Life express themselves in every intelligent man as the power of action in the body (*Kṛyā Śakti*), the power of desire in the mind (*Icchā Śakti*) and the power of knowledge in the intellect (*Jnāna Śakti*). All these three powers are manifestations of Him and since He is the One everywhere, He is the total mighty power-the Great *Viṣṇu*.

One who has the ability to do anything without the help of other beings or things is called *Īśvara*. Śrī Ādi Śaṇkara in his commentary mentions; one who has all the wealth without being affected by any type of sorrows (natural rule).

62. ***Śiva*** – 379 – *Nandanaḥ* – नन्दनः – One who is also in the form *Nandi*, his own vehicle.

Lalitā – 450 – *Nandinī* – नन्दिनी – Daughter of *Nandagopa*. It has been mentioned in *Bhāgavatam* (X *Skanda*) that *Śrī Devī* was (*Mahāmāyā*) born as daughter of *Nandagopa*.

Since **She** bestows delight **She** is *Nandinī.*

Nandinī, a certain cow born in the family of the celestial cow *Kāmadhenu.* It has been indicated in *Raghuvamsa* by *Kalidāsā* that *Nandinī* did services to the emperor *Dilīpa* and got a baby.

Viṣṇu – 527 – *Nandanaḥ* – नन्दनः – One who makes others blissful. Since the Lord is the very source of the happiness of the devotees who reach the divine plane of Pure Consciousness, it is in Him they get themselves intoxicated with the endless drunkenness of thus unceasing Bliss.

63. ***Śiva*** – 387 – *Caturmukhaḥ* – चतुर्मुखः – One who has four faces. Normally Lord *Śiva* is said to have five faces. Here, since he is mentioned to have four faces, he can be considered to be in the form of *Brahma,* who has four faces.

Lalitā – 505 – *Caturvaktramanoharā* – चतुर्वक्त्रमनोहरा – One who is fascinating with **Her** four faces. *Svādiṣṭāna* is the place of water. Hence starting from ether until water the four primary elements represent the four faces of *Śrī Devī* . The 14th verse of *Soundaryalaharī* also conveys the same differently mentioning that *Svādiṣṭāna* as the place of fire and *Maŋipūraka* as the place of water.

Viṣṇu – 765 – *Caturmūrtiḥ* – चतुर्मूर्तिः – Four-Formed. The Lord, is considered as having four forms-meaning that He, in His manifestations in the world, takes these four forms. The *Purāṇas* have declared that the incarnations of the Lord in the various *yugas,* were of different colours: white in *Kṛta Yuga,* red in *Tretā Yuga,* yellow in *Dvāpara Yuga* and dark (black) in the *Kali Yuga.* But according to *Vedānta,* the Lord, the Self, has four distinct expressions in the subjective life of each individual: the Waker, the Dreamer, the Deep-sleeper and the Pure-Self. In the microcosm these are called as *Virāṭa, Taijasa, Prajnā* and *Turīya* and in the macrocosm, the Lord's complete expression, in the total gross, subtle and causal bodies, is called as *Virāṭ, Hiranyagarbha,* Īśvara and, beyond all bodies as the Eternal Paramātma. These four are mentioned as *Virāṭ* (imperishable), *Sūtrātmā* (formulae), *Avyākṛta* (unmanifested) and *Turīya* (fourth) by different schools.

64. ***Śiva*** – 392 – *Yogādhyakṣaḥ* – योगाध्यक्ष: – Head of all *yogas*. Having all the organs under self-control is called *yoga* –

Tām yogamiti manyante stirāmindriya – dhāraṇām

Lalitā – 654, 655 & 656 – *Yogadā* – योगदा, *Yogyā* – योग्या & *Yogānandā* – योगानन्दा – One who bestows *Yoga* to votaries. One who can be reached through *Yogas*. The *yoga* bestowed by **Her** is the route to reach **Her**. *Yoga* is the assumption of union. Since **She** is in that form and since **She** bestows that to the devotees, **She** is in the form known by the same.

Yoga has four parts – *mantra, laya, hata* and *rāja. Rājayoga* has three parts – *Sānkya, Tāraka* and *Amanska*. These details are to be learnt from *Yoga sāstra*. Similarly in Astronomy also there are *devatas* starting from *Mangala* till *Sankata.* Since **She** is in all these forms, **She** is *Yoginee*.

One who is in the form of bliss got through *Yoga*. The unison of *Shiva* and *Śakti* is called *Yoga*. The bliss got through this is *Yogānandam*. The thought of external world is forgotten during sleep. This is also *Yogānandam* only. *Śrī Devī* is in this self-bliss form. **She** is in the form of *Yoganarasimhar* called as *Yogānandar*.

Viṣṇu – 18 & 19 – *Yogaḥ* – योग: & *Yogavidāmnetraḥ* – योगविदांनेत्र: – The one who can be known or realised only through *yogas*. By withdrawing the sense organs from their objects of preoccupation, when the mind of the seeker becomes quietened, he is lifted to a higher plane-of-consciousness, wherein he attains '*yoga*', meaning wherein he realises the Reality. At such moments of equanimity and mental quiet 'yoga' is gained – *Gīta* (II-48) says – *Samatvam yoga ucyate*. Since **He** is experienced through Yoga He is known as *Yogaḥ*.

One who guides (*neta*) all the activities of all men "who knows *yoga*" (*Yogavitis*). To all men of realisation, He who is the Ideal, is the Supreme Lord. Just as our activities are today ordered by our selfishness and individuality, the Ideal that commands and orders all activities in the bosom of a Man of Realisation is his God-Consciousness. This realm of experience is *Viṣṇu*. In the *Gīta* also all the chapters are called as *yogas*.

65. ***Śiva*** – 412 – *Akṣaraḥ* – अक्षर: – One who does not have any annihilation. *Akṣarapuruş – jīvasākşi* – one who dwells in the hearts of the people.

Vişṇu – 17 & 481 – *Akṣaraḥ* – अक्षर: & *Akṣaram* – अक्षरम – He who is without destruction i.e. the Supreme Spirit. The word *Akṣara* is formed by suffixing '*sara*' to the root '*aś*'. The changeless one. *Gīta* (XV-16) says all beings are changing and the *kūṭasta* is changeless –

Kṣaraḥ sarvāṇi bhūtāni kūṭastho kşara ucyate.

66. ***Śiva*** – 413 & 1002 – *Parabrahmaḥ* – परब्रह्म: & *Brahmaḥ* – ब्रह्म: – He is that *Brahmam* which cannot be compared with anything else. *Akşaram Parabbrahmam – sā kāşṭā sā parāngatiḥ* – that is the limit, the highest refuge.

The biggest that cannot be measured by any of the units like time, length, weight, etc. *Deśataḥ kālato vastuścca paricceta śūnyam.*

Lalitā – 822 – *Brahma* – ब्रह्म – One who herself is *Brahmam.* The one got in salvation and the knowledge that it is no different from the self-soul is called *Brahmam*. *Vişṇu Purāṇa* (VI-7-53) explains the character of *Brahmam* as – the *Brahmam* is the knowledge which is got by destroying the duality, beyond speech, least in quality and identified only within the self-soul;

Pratyastamita Bhedam Yatsattā Mātra Gocāram I
Vacasāmātma Samvedyam Tajgnānam Brahma Samjitam II

Vişṇu – 663 & 664 – *Brahmā* – ब्रह्मा & *Brahma* – ब्रह्म – One who creates everything as the creator *Brahmā*. Being big and expanding, the Lord, who is known from indications like *Satya* (truth), is called *Brahma*. Taitrīya *Upanişat* (2.1) says *satyam jnānam anantam brahma* – Brahma is truth, knowledge and infinity.

Vişṇu Purāṇa (6.7.55) says – That knowledge is *Brahmam*, which is without any kind of difference, which is pure existence, which is beyond the power of words to express and which self-knowing.

Pratyastamita-bhedam yat sattāmātram agocaram
Vacasām ātma-samvedyam tat jnānam brahma-sanjnitam

67. ***Śiva*** – 418 – *Śuddhaḥ* – शुद्धः – One whose mind is crystal pure.

In *Śrī Rudra Triśatī Nāmāvalī* also we have 208th name as *Iṣudhimateca Namaḥ*.

Lalitā – 765 – *Śuddhā* - शुद्धा – One who is ever pure. That is, **She** is without the dirt called ignorance. Actual meaning is that **She** is in the form of knowledge.

Viṣṇu – 155 – *Śuciḥ* – शुचिः – One who is spotlessly 'clean' and hence, ever-Pure. Impurities in a substance are things other than itself; when dust is on the cloth, the cloth is impure, unclean. Since the Self, the *ātman*, is the Non-Dual Reality, having nothing other than itself in it, ever-pure alone must it always be. And *Śuciḥ* is one who gives this purity to those who contemplate upon Him constantly.

68. ***Śiva*** – 420 – *Mānyaḥ* – मान्यः – One who is worthy of worship.

Lalitā – 213 – *Mahāpūjyā* – महापूज्या – One who is most worship-able. **She** is worshipped even by *Brahma, Viṣŋu* and *Rudra*, who themselves are worshiped by the devotess.

Greater than the great people and hence *Mahatī*. Since **She** is worshipped by *Brahma, Viṣŋu* and *Śiva*, **She** is *Pūjya.* Hence as *Mahatī* and *Pūjyā*, **She** is *Mahāpūjya.*

It has been mentioned in *Padma Purāŋa* and *Devī Bhāgavatam* as; each of the *devas* worship *Śrī Devī* in different forms and/ or *yantras* – out of these *Agni, Sukra* and *Sūrya* worship *Śrī Devī* in an idol form made of ruby;

Śiva Brahma Viṣŋu Kubera Viśvedeva Vāyu Vasu Varuŋa
Agni Śukra Soma Sūrya Graha Rākṣasa Piśāca
Matrugaŋāti Pedhena Tattatpūjanīya Devī Mūrti Bedho
Mantre Cailendra Nīla Svarŋa Roubhya Pittala Kāmasya
Spatika Mānikya Muktāpala Pravāla Vaiḍūrya Tripusīsa Vajya Loha

The *Brahmānḍa Purāŋa* says that the expiation for all the sins, knowingly or unknowingly done, is just remembering the lotus feet of *Śrī Devī*. Hence *Mahāpūjya.*

Viṣṇu – 749 – *Mānyaḥ* – मान्य: – One Who is to be honoured. He is the most worshipful as He is the very material Cause for the world of plurality. The very words of *Ādi* Śaṅkara – If he, who has realised the Supreme, is so blessed and to be honoured in this world, how much more worshipful is the Lord who is the very substratum and support of the whole universe and by whom all are blessed and inspired to gain their experiences in the world of things and beings.

69. ***Śiva*** – 438 & 609 – *Haviḥ* – हवि: – One who is in the form of stuffs that are offered in a sacrificial fire – *homa* – *Brahmārpaṇam brahma haviḥ*. What is offered is Brahmam and the process of offering is also Brahmam. One who is in the form of food offered in the *homa*.

Lalitā – 536 – *Svadhā* – स्वधा – One who is in the form of *Svadhā.* The words *Svāhā* and *Svadhā* are used when oblations are offered to gods in the sacrificial fire. *Devī Bhāgavatam* (IX-43-7) says – the word *Svāhā* is uttered when the sacrificial fire is about gods and the word *Svadhā* is used when it is about *pitṛs* (predecessors in the family race);

Svāhā Devī Havirdāne Pṛśastā Sarvakarmasu I
Pitṛ Dāne Svadhā Şastā Dakşiṇā Sarvato Varā II

The *Mārkaṇḍeya Purāṇa* says - there are seven words which are used in the *Homa* (sacrificial fire), in the oblation and in the cooking. By repeating (or uttering) your name only, Oh *Devī*! the merit of repeating these names are obtained by *Brahmavādins*;

Somasamsthā Haviḥ Samsthaḥ Bāgasamsthāśca Sapta Yāḥ I
Tāstvaducchāranād Devī Kriyante Brahmavādibhiḥ II

The *Linga Purāṇa* says – the consort of *Śiva* in the form of fire is said to be *Svāha.*

Şuşţu – well, *Am* – *Viṣṇu* or self, *Dadhāti* – nourishes or protect. Hence *Svadhā.*

According to the *Taitrīya Sruti* – your own (*sva*) speech (*Āhā*) – means one's own speech.

The *Sāmaveda Brāhmanam* and the *Yāskara's Nirukta* also explain *Svāha* thus; *Su* – well, *Āhā* – speech; or *Sva* – Self, *Āhā* – to speak.

- *Su* – good, *Āhā* – to be given as an oblation.
- *Sva* – one's own people, *Āhā* – to recognise – i.e. **She** recognises the people as her own self.
- *Su* - well, *A* - *Brahma*, *Ha* – to go – i.e. to take along to *Brahma*.

Viṣṇu – 698 – *Haviḥ* – हविः – The Oblation. That which we offer unto Him is also permeated by Him – there is nothing other than He, Himself, the same everywhere, in all places, at all times. In *Gīta* (IV-24), Lord insists that the 'oblations' are nothing but Brahmam.

70. ***Śiva*** – 445 & 971 – *Śobhanaḥ* – शोभनः – One who is in the form of auspicious.

Lalitā – 116 & 462 – *Bhadramūrtiḥ* – भद्रमूर्त्तिः & *Śobhanā* – शोभना – One who has an auspicious form. *Viṣṇu Purāṇa* says *Brahmam* is the only one that is auspicious – *Brahma Tanmangalam Viduḥ*. One who is all radiant with beauty. The 972nd name *Āśobhanā* is worth cross referring here.

Viṣṇu – 374, 801 & 999 – *Kṣobhaṇaḥ* – क्षोभणः, *Akṣobhyaḥ* – अक्षोभ्यः – The Agitator. If the Self were not in the equipments, the equipments will not get agitated – will not pursue their functions The Atman, the Pure Consciousness is that which thrills and agitates both the matter (*Prakṛti*) and energy (*Puruśa*) and causes the manifestation of the living entities (lives), who, with their actions, constitute the dynamic aspect of the world. If the Self is not there, there can be no movement or expression of life; everything would have remained completely inert and insentient. He is the Lord who thrills the world and makes it so beautifully palpitating with life. Hence, He is called as the Agitator (*Kṣobhanaḥ*). One who is ever unruffled. Ordinarily an individual gets disturbed, subjectively, by the presence of desires, anger, passions, etc. and objectively an average man is constantly stormed by the enchanting dance of beautiful sense-objects all around him. Lord, the Self, is a state of existence wherein neither the subjective disturbances of the mind, nor the objective persecutions of the sense-organs can ever reach to ruffle the quietude and peaceful grace of His perfection. In describing the state of the *Stitaprajna*, *Bhagavān* says in the *Gīta* that such a one will be *Akşobhya* like the ocean: "He attains Peace into whom all desires enter as waters enter the ocean, which filled from all sides, remains unmoved; but not the 'desirer-of-desires". One who cannot be exasperated by anyone, by any act or acts, however blasphemous they may be. One whose peace and calm cannot be stormed out by any happening in his outer world; Ever-peaceful. The term suggests Infinite patience, love and kindness towards man and his frailties.

In the initial part of *Vişŋu Sahasranāma,* it is mentioned as *Mangalanām ca mangalam*. *Śrī Ādi Śaṇkara,* in his commentary says – *Mangalam* means felicity, its tool and to instruct the same; some thing above auspicious and hence *Mangalanām ca mangalam*.

71. ***Śiva*** – 447 – *Svastidaḥ* – स्वस्तिदः – One who bestows auspiciousness.

Lalitā – 448 – *Svastimatī* – स्वस्तिमती – One who is in the form of eternal truth. One who is in the form of benediction.

Suşţu – properly or beautifully. *Sattha* – existence/ the state of existence. One who has this is called *Svastimatī*. (The learned frequently use the phrase *Asti Bhāti Priyam* – the same *Asti* is used here. The word *Sattha* is used in the same sense as in the phrase *Sat Cit Ānandam*.

Since it is immortal, in the spiritual parlance it is used as *Sattha.* (The learned speak of *Saththā* in three different ways – *Pratipāsika* [relating to fate], *Vyāvahārika* [relating to worldly business] and *Pāramartika* [spiritual knowledge]). Explaining all these here may not be possible and are to be learned from *Vedānta* books.

Svasti, according to the *Ratna* dictionary, means - benediction, benevolence, sinless, holy and auspiciousness.

Vişṇu – 901 – *Svastidaḥ* – स्वस्तिदः – One Who gives *Svasti* to all His sincere devotees. A true devotee is one who has discovered his fulfilment in seeking and gaining the Infinite Bliss that is *Śrī Hari*. Naturally, he comes to turn away from the realms of inauspiciousness. To the extent he is able to move into the *Hari*-Consciousness, he is to that degree in the Bliss-Experience. Therefore, the Lord is termed as the "Giver-of- Auspiciousness".

72. ***Śiva*** – 480 – *Mahāmāyaḥ* – महामाय: – He is a *māyā* (illusion) to his devotees. *Mahatī brahmātibirabi ajayyā māyaā yasya saḥ – Svetāvāstara Upaniṣat* (4.10) says – Even *Brahma* and other Devas cannot win over his *māyā – Māyām tu prakṛtim vidyān māyinām tu maheśvaram.*

Lalitā – 215 – *Mahāmāyā* – महामाया – **She** is in the form of great illusion (*Mahāmāyārūpiṇī*), (since **She** creates lust to all *devas* starting from *Brahma*). *Durgā Saptashatee* says;

Gnānināmapi Chetāmsi Devī Bhagavatīhisā I
Balādākruśya Mohāya Mahāmāyā Prāyacchati II

The name of the *Śakti* seed letter (*bījākśara*) *Hrīm* is *Māyā* or *Śakti*. The complete power of *Śrī Devī* is hidden in this. This *Hrīm* seed is a knot like for all the three *kūṭās* of *Pancadaśākṣarī mantra*. **She** is in the form of that *Hrīm* seed letter as *Mahāmāya.* This seed letter *Hrīm* has four splits as - '*H*' + '*R*' + '*E*' + '*M*' – it is similar to different parts (organs) of a tree are subtly hidden within a seed. Hence *Mahāmāya.*

The *Kālikā Purāṇā* says; **She** who always makes him devoid of knowledge, the being who possessed knowledge (of his real nature)] whilst in the womb, compelled him to take birth by means of the winds of delivery and leads him by reason of the *samskāra* of previous births to desire of food etc.; thence into confusion egotism, doubt, subsequently leading him again and again to undergo (the stages of) anger, distress and greediness and then leads him into (sensual) desire causing anxiety day in and day out, producing sometimes pleasures and sometimes pain, is called the *Mahāmāyā* (great illusion).

According to one lexicon dictionary *māyā* means compassion; hence *Mahāmāyā* means full of compassion.

Viṣṇu – 170 – *Mahāmāyaḥ* – महामायः – One who is the Supreme Master of all Māyā. He is the very Substratum upon which all the plurality spring up and play their infinite enchantments, constantly basking in the Light of the Supreme Consciousness. *Ātman*, the Self, is untouched by the play of Māyā and yet the *Māyā*-play is sustained only by the exuberant warmth of His Divine presence. The Sun is the Master of all clouds, inasmuch as, in its presence, borrowing its heat, water by its own nature gets evaporated and the water, vapour again, because of its own nature of a lesser density than the atmospheric air, rises to the higher altitudes and gathers there as clouds. It is, again, the nature of the atmosphere that at higher altitudes it is cooler and the water-vapour so cooled becomes water again and due to the higher density of water it descends as rain. In this example the Sun can be called as the 'Creator' of all clouds and the "Cause for the rams," and consequently the sun is also the "Master of the Seasons". And yet, the Sun is uncontaminated by all these phenomena that are happening in its presence.

In the same fashion the Infinite Reality, *Viṣṇu*, is indicated here as the Great Magician, who has the magic of Māyā at His command. Krishna Himself confesses in the *Gīta* (VII-14) – Very difficult indeed it is to cross over My *Māyā*.

73. ***Śiva*** – 492 – *Pratyayaḥ* – प्रत्ययः – One who is in the form of knowledge (*jnāna*).

Lalitā – 981 – *Jnānajneyasvarūpiṇī* – ज्ञानज्ञेयस्वरूपिणी – One who is in the form of knowledge and the object of knowledge.

Gīta (XIII-17) says – *Jnānam Jneyam Jnānagamyam Gṛḍi Sarvasya Viśṭitam* – I am in the form of the knowledge, the knowable and the goal of knowledge, seated in the hearts of all.

This is called as the object and the sight. (There is a book by name *Drik Driśyam Vivekam*, the author of which is not clearly known. Somewhere it has been mentioned that this is written by *Śrī Ādi Śaṇkara*).

It can also be mentioned that **She** is reachable only through knowledge.

Viṣṇu – 93 – *Pratyayaḥ* – प्रत्ययः – One whose very nature is Knowledge. That the Supreme is Knowledge Absolute is very well known. It is in the light of Consciousness that all 'knowledges' are possible. "Knowledge of a thing" is the awareness of its nature. Awareness is Knowledge. Since the Supreme is the One Awareness everywhere, all 'Knowledge' spring from the Self. Hence, He is called "the Pure Knowledge". "Consciousness is *Brahmam*" says *Mahāvākya*.

74. ***Śiva*** – 500, 589 & 642 – *Analaḥ* – अनलः – Always inadequate or insufficient. How much ever we enjoy, we do not feel like adequate.

The word *anila* indicates fire. He is in the form of fire. He has endless power.

Viṣṇu – 293 & 711 – *Analaḥ* – अनलः – The *jīvātmā* is called *Anala* because it recognizes *Ana* or *Prāṇa* as himself. As *'nal'* is root of *'anala'* it denotes smell. Hence accordingly to the vedic sentence *agandham arasam* – the *paramātmā* is without smell – *anala*. Or since *paramātmā* is without *'alam'*, that is, end. He is *anala*.

One whose wealth or power has no limits.

75. ***Śiva*** – 501 – *Vāyuvāhanaḥ* – वायुवाहनः – One who uses air (*vāyu*) as his vehicle. Or one who controls air. *Vāyurvahati yat bītyā iti vāyuvāhanaḥ*. *Taitrīya Upaniṣat* (2.8) says *bīśāsmāt vātaḥ bhavate*.

Viṣṇu – 331 – *Vāyuvāhanaḥ* – वायुवाहनः – The One who controls, regulates and moves the great winds. In Samskrutam literatures, the movement of air in the atmosphere has been classified under seven types and they are called the *"Sapta Marutaḥ"*.

In short, the inconceivable might and power of the winds and their life-sustaining abilities are all lent out to the air by His own munificence and hence He is called as *Vāyuvāhanaḥ*.

76. ***Śiva*** – 509 – *Guhyaḥ* – गुह्यः – One who is hidden. One who is in the form of *Upaniṣats*, which have hidden meanings. The very next name – 510 –

Prakhāśaḥ – प्रकाश: – seems to be contradicting to this name – one who is visible to all. One who is in the form of Karma kāṇḍa which is shining. Śrī Rudram says – *Utainam viśvā bhūtāni sa dṛṣṭo mṛḍayāti naḥ* – all living beings see this Rudran. Let, he in the form of Āditya, make us all happy.

In *Śrī Rudra Triśatī Nāmāvalī* also we have 263rd name as *Guhyāyaca Namaḥ*.

Lalitā – 624 – *Guhyā* – गुह्या – One who is most secretive both in form and meanings. *Guhyā* also means one who dwells in a cave, i.e. heart. **She** is secretive and dwelling in our heart. Hence **She** can be identified only by inward search.

The word *Guhyā* can be considered to mean *Jīvātma* (soul), *Paramātmā* (supreme) and the union of both. The presiding deity who can bestow these results is called *Guhya.*

649th name *Adṛśyā* – अदृश्या is also worth comparable here – One who is Invisible. Not to be perceived by eyes and other senses or organs. *Dṛśyā* means one who is seen. It is not to be felt by mere sight, but to be recognised/ understood. Hence not perceived by any senses.

The *Brahādāraŋya Upanişat* (III-4-2) says, "You do not see the seer of sight".

The *Devī Bhāgavatam* (book III) says, "Your unqualified form is not an object of visual perception. *Śakti* is without quality, difficult or approach. The Supreme Person also is without qualities".
Vişṇu – 542 – *Guhyaḥ* – गुह्य: – One who can be understood by the secret *Upanişats* or one who dwells in the secret cavity viz., heart. 545th name – *Gupta*: – गुप्त is also comparable here – He is beyond speech and mind.

77. ***Śiva*** – 510 – *Prakhāśaḥ* – प्रकाश: – One who is in the form of shining *karmakāṇḍa*. Or he shines so that he is visible to all – *Śrī Rudram* says – *udainam viśvā bhūtāni sa dhṛśṭo mṛḍayāti naḥ* – all living beings see this *Rudra*. Let that *Rudra*, who is in the form of shining Sun make all of us cheerful.

Immediately previous name 509 is *Guhyaḥ* – which means he is in secret. In many other places, it has been mentioned that one has to struggle and do very hard penance to see the Lord. These are deceptively contradicting. The apparent meaning should not be taken. The inner *tatva* displayed has to be understood.

Lalitā – 414 – *Svaprakāshā* – स्वप्रकाशा – One who is self-luminous. **She** has luminary powers, which is nothing different from **Her**. Only through her luster, the other objects get light. There is no object luminating **Her**. **She** is self-luminous and self-splendour;

Brahadāraŋya Upanişat (IV-3-9) says, here this person becomes self-luminous; *Atrāyam Puruşaḥ Svayam Jyotiḥ;*
Na Tatra Sūryo Bhāti Na Candra Tārakam Nemāvidyutobhāntikutoyamagniḥ I
Tameva Bhāntamanubhāti Sarvam Tasya Bhāsā Sarvamidam Vibhāti II

Su - much, *ap* - water, *prakāśa* – manifested. Hence this can also be interpreted as **She** shines much brighter in water.

Vişṇu – 274 – *Prakāṣanaḥ* – प्रकाषनः – The one who illuminates everything; expressing himself as the all-pervading consciousness in every equipment. He is the knower, knowing everything in each bosom (*Sarvavit*) and knowing all things that are happening in the universe at one and the same time in His omniscient (*Sarvajnaḥ*). He is the Illuminator of all experiences. Just as the one Sun illumines everything in the world the Reality illumines both the fields of experiences and the knower-of- the-field.

78. ***Śiva*** – 515 – *Sudarśanaḥ* – सुदर्शनः – One who has pleasing or auspicious sight. Or one who is easily accessible by all.

Lalitā – 683 – *Śobhanā Sulabhā Gatiḥ* – शोभना सुलभा गतिः – One whose path is lustrous and easy to traverse. The word *gati* has many a meaning – the targeted place to reach, goal, way, destiny, knowledge, etc.

The word *Śobhanā* means great auspicious. *Sulabhā* means easily attainable. *Gati* means salvation. This name is a combination of all these three words. To reach the salvation easily, **She** can be worshipped comfortably.

Viṣṇu – 417 – *Sudarśanaḥ* – सुदर्शन: – One who is easy to be perceived if the seeker has sufficient devotion. Or he whose meeting is auspicious inasmuch as it removes the seeker's worldly worries.

79. ***Śiva*** – 521 – *Nābhiḥ* – नाभि: – One who is the supporting body for the entire universe. The naval button is called *Nābhi*. It is the centre of gravity of the body. Similarly Lord Shiva is the centre of gravity of the universe.

Lalitā – 34 – *Nābhyālavālaromālilatāphalakuchadvayī* – नाभ्यालवालरोमालि लताफलकुचद्वयी – *Śrī Devī*'s two breasts are like fruits in a creeper (line of hair) climbing from the trench (the naval).

The deep naval is like a trench. The narrow line of hair grown upwards from the naval is like a creeper. The two breasts appear as if they are hanging from the creeper (an excellent metaphor).

78th *verse* of *Soundaryalaharī* may also be referred;

Stanamukula Romāvalilata.

Viṣṇu – 48 – *Padmanābhaḥ* – पद्मनाभ: – One from whose navel (*nābhi*) springs the Lotus (*padma*), which is the seat of the four-faced Creator, *Brahma*.

Lotus represents Truth or any of its manifested powers. The creative faculties in man flow from the navel area (*nābhi*) and manifests as the four-faced inner equipment (*Antaḥkaraṇa*) constituted of the mind, intellect, chit and ego.

In the *Yoga-śastras*, we find a lot of details regarding this concept. According to them every 'idea' springs from Him (*Parā*) and then at the navel area, each of them comes to be 'perceived' (*Paśyantī*).

Thereafter they play in the bosom as thoughts (*Madhyamā*) and at last they are expressed (*Vaikharī*) in the outer fields-of–activity. This has been discussed in other places also as four different stages of speech.

In this discussion-upon the evolutionary stages through which every 'idea' becomes an 'action' – we gather a clearer insight into the meaning of the symbolism of "the Creator seated on the lotus", which springs forth from the navel of the Lord, the Supreme *Viṣṇu*.

80. ***Śiva*** – 524 – *Puṣkaraḥ* – पुषकर: – One who provides nourishment to all. Or one who created the *Brahmāṇḍam*, which is in the form of a Lotus – *puśkarasya brahmāṇḍasya stapatiḥ*

Lalitā – 804 – *Puṣkarā* – पुष्करा – One who gives nourishment (bliss or completeness) to all. In Samskrutam the letter *ra* and *la* are not much differentiated. Hence it can be taken as *Puṣkalā* – i.e. omnipresent.

In one of the books it is stated that **She** is one of the consorts of *Sāstā* – *Pūrŋā* and *Puṣkala.* Both the names mean fullness.

According to *Devī Bhāgavatam* (VII-38-19) the place of *Gāyatrī* is called as *Śrīmadpuṣkaram*.

Viṣṇu – 40 & 556 – *Puṣkarākṣaḥ* – पुष्कराक्ष: – One who has eyes (*akṣaḥ*) as beautiful as the lotus (*puṣkara*); the descriptive epithet: 'Lotus-eyed'. Joy and Peace in the bosom of an individual are expressed in the world outside at no other point so vividly as in the eyes. The One, whose inner peace and joy, beaming out through His eyes, bring into the devoted hearts all the aesthetic beauty and romantic thrills of seeing a lotus dancing in the breeze, In short, the term indicates the Lord who with His beautiful looks, magically lifts all the sorrows in the devotee's heart and fills it with Peace, Joy and Perfection. The Samskrutam word *Puṣkara* also means the Universal-Space, thus, it also has the interpretation, "one who is ever pervading all space".

81. ***Śiva*** – 545 – *Alokāḥ* – अलोका – One who is beyond all these worlds.

Lalitā – 960 – *Lokātītā* – लोकातीता – One who transcends the worlds – **She** is beyond all the worlds. After crossing all the worlds from *Indra* to *Viṣŋu*, *Mahākailāsa*, the world of *Paramaśiva* can be seen. **She** resides in this world. The *Śivadharmottara* says that the world of *Paramaśiva* transcends all other worlds. It has been mentioned that those who reach here do not have re-birth.

It can also be considered as that **She** is beyond all worlds or souls (the souls originate from her only).

Viṣṇu – 133 – *Lokādhyakṣaḥ* – लोकाध्यक्ष: – One who presides over all fields of experiences - all *lokas*. President is one who is responsible for the conduct of the assembly; he guides the discussion in a disciplined manner and ultimately at the end of it all, he dissolves the meeting. All through the discussions he never interferes with the freedom of speech and action of the members, if they act within the agenda of the day. Similarly, the Lord presides over all the fields of activities, never interfering with the freedom of the individuals to act. "The Supreme *Puruṣa* in this body is also called the spectator, one who gives the permission, the supporter, the enjoyer, the great Lord and the Supreme Self". From the Purāṇic standpoint the Lord in His *Vāmana* manifestation was installed as the king of the three worlds and therefore, this name, say the *Pourāṇikas*.

82. ***Śiva*** – 551 & 999 – *Śucaḥ* – शुच: & *Śuciḥ* – शुचि: – One who is spotlessly clean. Or he cleans the minds of his true devotees. One who does not have any type of bondage with the world.

Lalitā – 148 – *Nityaśuddhā* – नित्यशुद्धा – One who is eternally pure. **She** is beyond any impurity in all the three times (tenses); hence this name.
Veda says; *Asparśasca Mahān Śuciḥ* – **She** does not touch anything, elder to all and always pure.

Another verse of *Veda* says; The body is untidy, but the person inside is clean;
Atyanta Malino Deho Dehī Cātyanta Nirmalaḥ

Viṣṇu – 155 & 251 – *Śuciḥ* – शुचि: – One who is spotlessly 'clean' and therefore, Ever-Pure. Impurities in a substance are things other than itself; when dust is on the cloth, the cloth is impure, unclean. Since the Self, the *ātman*, is the Non-Dual Reality, having nothing other than itself in it, Ever-pure alone must it always be. And *Śuciḥ* is one who gives this purity to those who contemplate upon Him constantly. The immaculate Reality which is never contaminated by the *Māyā* and its by-products is *Mahāviṣṇu*. When dirt (*Mala*) exists upon anything, it becomes unclean. In the Absolute Oneness there can be nothing other than itself and therefore the Fourth-plane-of-Consciousness (*Turīyam*) is indicated in our Scriptures as the Transcendental Ever-Pure Self, *Śrī Hari*.

83. ***Śiva*** – 553 – *Āśramasthaḥ* – आश्रमस्थः – One who in that corresponding form of *dharma* in all the four *Aśramas*.

Lalitā – 286 – *Varŋāshramavidhāyinī* – वर्णाश्रमविधायिनी – One who established the social divisions and castes. After creating all from *Brahma* to worms, **She** created the *Vedas*, which are her own commands, in order to lead the created beings into the right path. The *Vedas* are divided into two parts, the *Karmakāṇḍa* and *Gnanakāṇḍa*; as according to the rule, the *Devas* and lower animals have no share in the *Karmakāṇḍa*, the (divine) mother established righteousness (*dharma*) through *karmakāṇḍa* after dividing human beings into four castes and four orders.

Viṣṇu – 852 – *Āśramaḥ* – आश्रमः – One who is the bestower of rest on all who are wandering through all the *āśramas* in the forest of *samsāra*.

84. ***Śiva*** – 555 – *Viśvakarmaḥ* – विश्वकर्मः – One who knows all the actions happening in this world. Or he is in the form of *Viśvakarma*, the chief architect of *Devas*.

Viṣṇu – 50 – *Viśvakarmaḥ* – विश्वकर्मः – The very creator of the world-of-objects, of all equipments of experiences and of all experiences in all bosom - is called the *Viśvakarma*. Herein the Infinite Lord is but a Witness of all that is happening and though the experienced world is sustained in Him, He is not involved in the imperfections or mortality, that are happening all around at all times in the Viśvam. Bhagavān in *Gīta* says – "They are in Me, I am not in them".

85. ***Śiva*** – 557 – *Viśālaśākhaḥ* – विशालशाखः – One who has broad hands –
dhīrgga bāhuśākhāpakşāntare bāhou iti metinee.

Viṣṇu – 316 – *Viśvabāhuḥ* – विश्वबाहुः – One who has number of hands; whose hands are everywhere doing all activities in the universe. The life in the bosom as long as it exists, so long alone the hands and the legs function. The hands can lift and do its job only when it is in contact with life. Life expressing through the hand is its function. All hands that are doing variegated activities all over the world are all His hands in-as- much as, where He is not, that lifeless hand can perform no more any activity. Since He is thus the dynamic One Principle that functions through all hands at work, He is called a *Viśvabāhuḥ*.

86. ***Śiva*** – 565, 566 & 1001 – *Paraḥ* – परः & *Aparaḥ* – अपरः – He is oldest of all or earliest to all. He is prior to the beginning of this universe – *Samsārāt parācīna śuddhaḥ* – Tamil Thiruvenmbavai by Manikavācakar says;

"Munnaippazham porutku munnaippazham porule".

Aparaḥ means he is the latest to all. Tamil poem goies – *Pinnai putumaikkym peerttum apperriyane*? Since he does not have an origin neither an end, he is the oldest and the earliest. *Śrī Rudram* says *Namo jyeśṭāyaca kaniśṭṭhāya ca namaḥ pūrvajāya cāparajāya ca*.

In *Śrī Rudra Triśatī Nāmāvalī* also we have 173rd and 174th name as *Namaḥ Pūrvajāyaca Namaḥ* and *Aparajāyaca Namaḥ*.

Lalitā – 790 – *Parāparā* – परापरा – One who is in the form of *Brahmam* called *Parā* (absolute), *Aparā* (relative) and *Parāparā* (both absolute and relative). *Parā* – the other person, *Aparā* – dependent on self, i.e., it respectively means an enemy and a friend. *Śreemad Bhagavad Geeta* (IX-29) says that the *Brahmam* is of these two types; *Na Me Dveshyosti Na Priyaḥ* – I have neither foe nor friend.

Parā – superior and *Aparā* – inferior. *Sruti* says, "*Brahmam* is the servant. *Brahmam* is ferry-men; and Brahmam is these gamblers";

Brahmadāsā Brahmadāshā Brahmameme Kitavā Uta.

Parā - he who is far off, *Aparā* he who is near. *Gīta* (XIII-15) – "I am far and near".

These different meanings are based on the *Vihsva* dictionary;

Parāḥ Syāt Uttama Anātma Vairi Dūreśu Kevale II

In general the *Brahmam* is said to be two types viz., pure form and an adulterated form. *Parāparam* is of third type.

The *Praśno Upaniṣat* (V-2) says - "This is indeed, Oh *Satyakāma*! *para* and *apara*"; *Etadvai Satyakāma Param Cāparam Ca*. The *Smruti* also says, "Two *Brahmams* are to be known, one is *Parā* and the other is *Aparā*";

Dve Brahmāŋī Veditavye Param Cāparameva Ca.

Parā – posterior; *Aparā* – anterior. *Śiva* with the unified form of *Śakti* is *Parāparam or Parabrahmam*. **She** is in that form. To give such meanings for the words *Parā* or *Aparā* there are enough evidences in *Vedas*; *Yuje Vām Brahma Pūrvyam Namobhiḥ* or *Ēśo Uśā Apūrvyā Vyacchati Priyā Divaḥ* II

Parā and *Aparā* are the twofold ether. *Sivānandalaharī* has explained this in detail.

The twofold knowledge, as described in the *Muŋḍaka Upaniṣat* (I-1-4) *Parā Vidyā* and *Aparā Vidya.* The *Linga Purāŋa* also says, two kinds of knowledge should be known, *parā* and *aparā*; the *Vedas* are *Para* and the *Vedāngās* are *Apara*.

Skanḍa Purāŋa (*Yagna Vaibhava Kānḍa*, 6th chapter) says two types of the *Praŋava* are; *Parā* and *Aparā. Parā* has the qualities of *Sacitānanda* and *Aparā* is pure form, in the form of sound. Since it prays *Parabrahmam,* it is called as *Praŋava* (the word *nava* has such a meaning). Since it is a tool to reach *Parabrahmam,* it is called as *Praŋavam*.

There itself, the interpretation of *Vedas* is of two types – the Supreme Being is *Param* and the tool to reach it is called *Aparam*.

In the *Yoga Śāstra* also knowledge is divided into three – *Parā*, *Aparā* and *Parāpara.* For it is said, "Knowledge is said to be threefold by the division of *para, apara* and *parāpara.* Of these, the first is the supreme knowledge and is the cause of cognizing the Lord, the bondage and the Self. The second, *aparā* knowledge, is simply the cause of cognising the bondage. The *parāparā* knowledge is, just as the change of the sight between a man and cat in the night, it does not distinguish the marks *vilakşaŋā*".

Nityā Şoḍaśikārnava (8th chapter, 2nd verse onwards) explains that *Śrī Devī*'s *pūja* is of three types – *Parā, Aparā and Parāpara. Para* is worshipping with non-duality in mind (however it is done). *Apara* is worshipping *Śrī Chakra. Parāpara* is worshipping different types of idols.

The speech is of two types – *Parā* and *Apara. Aparā* includes *Paśyantī, Madhyamā* and *Vaikharī.*

Para is the fourth state. *Aparā* is the three states awaken (*Jāgrath*), dream (*Swapna*) and deep sleep (*Śuśupti*).

The *homa* (sacrificial fire) is of two types *Parā* and *Apara.* The *Parā* is the state after the destruction of all dualistic interpretations respecting the known, the knower and knowledge. The *Parā homa* is said to be that which being absorbed, does not arise again, in the blaze of the great eternal fire of own self, which burns forever without fuel. This is done in an imaginative way.

The *apara homa* is again two-fold, gross and subtle. The gross form offering the articles in the form directly. The subtle form is done in the fire in the *Mūlādhāra* i.e. *Prāṇāgnihotra.* In the *Sāmayika Pūja,* which is part of *Navāvarana Pūja* in the *Bindu Tarpaŋa,* there is a verse stating that – in the fire called *Samvit,* which burns without any fuel, all the 36 *tatvas* (from *Shiva* onwards till earth) are offered. By chanting this verse, after getting permission from the teacher the special *argya* from the self-vessel is consumed. That verse is as follows;

Antar Nirantara Nirindhanamedhamāne Mohāndhakāra Paripantini Samvidagnou
Kasmincdatbhuta Marīci Vikāśa Bhūmou Viśvam Juhomi Vasudhādi Śivāvasānam II

Varāha Purāŋa says when speaking about the *Trimūrtis* - The creative energy is said to be *Para* which is the white colour. *Vaishnavī,* which is red and long-eyed is *Apara.* The *Roudri* energy is called *parāpara.*

87. ***Śiva*** – 561 – *Kapilaḥ* – कपिल: – One who is in a *kapila* or red-like colour.

Viṣṇu – 898 – *Kapilaḥ* – कपिल: – The Lord Himself, manifested as the great sage Kapila, propounded the Sānkhya philosophy. In *Gīta, Bhagavān* declaring His own Glory, describes Himself: "I am Kapila among the great ones".

88. ***Śiva*** – 573 & 938 – *Devaḥ* – देव: – One who has passion towards success - *Vijikiśu*. One who plays through his activities like creation, etc. Or one who causes the entire universe to act. One who shines as *Ātma* in all living beings.

In *Śrī Rudra Triśatī Nāmāvalī* also we have 296th name as *Devānāgm Hṛdayebhyo Namaḥ*.

Lalitā – 955 – *Deveśī* – देवेशी – One who is the head of all divine forces like *Brahma, Viṣṇu, Śiva* and others.

Viṣṇu – 375 – *Devaḥ* – देव: – One who revels is *Deva*. This term *'Dīvyati'* in Samskrutam also means "to conquer", "to shine" and "to praise". Therefore, Lord *Viṣṇu* is rightly called as *Devaḥ* because He sports through His play – the great Creation-Sustenance-Destruction, He functions in all Beings as He shines as the Universal Consciousness; and He is praised by all the devotees. *Svetasratara Upaniṣat* indicates "there is only one *Deva*" – *devaḥ ekam*.

89. ***Śiva*** – 580 – *Ugraḥ* – उग्र: – One who swallows everything during the great dissolution – *utkarśeṇa krasatītugraḥ*.

In *Śrī Rudra Triśatī Nāmāvalī* also we have 239th name as *Namaugrāyaca Namaḥ*.

Lalitā – 571 – *Mahāpralayasākṣiṇī* – महाप्रलयसाक्षिणी – One who is the witness of the great dissolution. As the entire universe perish at the time of the great dissolution. *Brahma* and *Viṣṇu* also merge with *Śrī Devī*. However, *Śiva* does not perish just because of the pride of your earrings only, says *Śrī Ādi Śaṇkara,* in his *Soundaryalaharī* 26th verse; *Virinciḥ Pancatvam Vrajati...*

A witness is that person who does not participate in the action, is not affected by the fruit of it and completes seeing the action. **She** is such a witness to the great dissolution.

Viṣṇu – 421 – *Ugraḥ* – उग्रः – The Terrible. The one who gives fear to those who are diabolically evil, or, as the *Upaniṣat* declares, "For fear of Him the fire burns; for fear of Him shines the sun; For fear of Him *Indra, Vāyu* and Death proceed with their respective functions," – hence He is the Terrible.

90. ***Śiva*** – 586 – *Māyāvīḥ* – मायावीः – One who creates the world through his *māyā* (illusion). *Dakṣināmūrti Stotra* says – *māyā kalpite deśa kāla kalanā vacitria citrīkṛtam māyāvīva vijrumbayatyapi mahā yogīva yaḥ svaccayā* – the place created through māyā has changed a lot on account of place and time. Hence he created this universe with different levels, through his own wish, as a *māyāvī* or *mahāyogī.*

Lalitā – 716 – *Māyā* – माया – One who is in the form of illusion. The power which obscures what is plain is *māyā* or illusion. Or to make plain what is not available. Both these are the acts of *māya.*

In addition the acts of dream or supernatural powers are all due to *māya.* The *Devī Purāṇa* says, "It is called *māyā* because it is the instrument of marvelous actions, producing unheard of results, like dreams or jugglery";

Vicitra Kārya Karanā Acintita Balapradā I
Svapnedrajālavalloke Māyā Tene Prakeertitā II

The same is set forth at length in the *Varāha Purāṇa* (in 37 verses), where *Viṣṇu* says to the Earth; "The cloud sends forth rain and water is collected. Next the quarters become clear. This is my *māyā,* Oh! Beloved one, even the Moon wanes, again waxes and on the new moon day it is invisible. This is my power of illusion, by it I remain in the water. I create *Prajāpatis* as well as I destroy them".

The *Sāṇḍilya Sūtra* (86) says, "His (the lord's) energy is *māya*".

Śrī Muthuswami Dīkşata also has sung addressing *Śrī Devī* as '*Māye*'.

The *Śākta Praŋava*, also called as *Bhuvaneśwarī Bīja* or *Hṛllekā*, is called as *Māyā Bīja*.

According to the non-duality advised by *Śrī Ādi Śaṇkara*, only when the illusion is removed the knowledge of *Brahmam* can be obtained. (Many a type of practice is mentioned here – like the darkness is removed once lit or once the knowledge is obtained the ignorance and illusion are removed). According to *Śrīvidyā* practice illusion is the energy (*śakti*) of *Brahmam* only. *Śrī Kānci Kāmakoṭi Paramācārya*'s talk in this regard is (The book *Deivathin Kural*, 6th Volume, Pages 686 to 689); the question, that why and how the illusion happened, does not arise according to non-duality principle. *Śākta Sāstra* says that *Cit Śakti* only plays a game by reflecting the illusion in many forms. The soul, in the as is form – having the senses as tools, has to unite with the eternal *Brahmam*. The *Brahmam* only seems as soul due to illusion. The non-duality principle says that, if the illusion is removed through knowledge then the soul will become the *Brahmam*. Basically the soul and *Shiva* are one and the same. Again it is same at the end of salvation also. This has been clearly accepted in *Śākta* more particularly in *Śrīvidyā tantra*. The difference between the two is the creative duality. No difference about salvation. It has to be simply ignored that it is only illusion which seem to be dual.

Vişṇu – 170 – *Mahāmāyaḥ* – महामाय: – One who is the Supreme Master of all *Māyā*. He is the very Substratum upon which all the plurality spring up and play their infinite enchantments, constantly basking in the Light of the Supreme Consciousness. *Ātman*, the Self, is untouched by the play of *Māyā* and yet the *Māyā*-play is sustained only by the exuberant warmth of His Divine presence. The Sun is the Master of all clouds, inasmuch as, in its presence, borrowing its heat, water by its own nature gets evaporated and the water, vapour again, because of its own nature of a lesser density than the atmospheric air, rises to the higher altitudes and gathers there as clouds. It is, again, the nature of the atmosphere that at higher altitudes it is cooler and the water-vapour so cooled becomes water again and due to the higher density of water it descends as rain. In this example the Sun can be called as the 'Creator' of all clouds and the "Cause for the rams," and consequently the sun is also the "Master of the Seasons". And yet, the Sun is uncontaminated by all these phenomena that are happening in its presence.

In *Gīta* (VII-14) also, in the same fashion the Infinite Reality, *Viṣṇu,* is indicated here as the Great Magician, who has the magic of *Māyā* at His command. Kṛṣṇa Himself confesses: "Very difficult indeed it is to cross over My *Māyā*" the divine illusion is made up of qualities, is hard to surmount; but those who take refuge in *Śrī Kriṣŋa* alone, can cross over it;

Daivī Hi Ēśā Guŋamayī mama Māyā Durātyayā I
Māmeva Ye Prapadyante Māyāmetām Taranti Te II

91. ***Śiva*** – 587 – *Suhṛdaḥ* – सुहृद: – One who has a noble heart.

Lalitā – It has been mentioned that there are twenty-eight kinds of obstructions for the adoration of *Śrī Devī*. One method to cross-over the same is, by having friendship with those who has understood *Śrī Devī*'s philosophy (*tatva*). That is *Suhṛda*. By gaining good friends, the devotee attains *arthasiddhi*.

Viṣṇu – 460 – *Suhṛt* – सुहृत् – The friend of all living creatures. A true friend is one who gives all that he possesses without expecting any return.

92. ***Śiva*** – 588 & 641 – *Anilaḥ* – अनिल: – One who is in the form of air. Since everything merges with him he does not have a place to merge with – *anāhatāt anilaḥ – annātvā anilaḥ*.

One who does not have anyone to control. Or one who he is always awake without any sleep. Or one who is easily accessible by the devotees.

Viṣṇu – 234 & 812 – *Anilaḥ* – अनिल: – One who has no fixed residence – *Anilayaḥ*. Or one who is always moving. Or one who is without a beginning. *Illana* means inducement. One who is without any inducement is *anila*. *Illana* also means sleep. Hence one who is ever awake is *anila*. Or the Lord is not *nila*, difficult to understand. He is easily accessible to the devotees.

93. ***Śiva*** – 603 – *Mahādevaḥ* – महादेव: – Head of all devas or greatest deva. Since he is worshipped by all other devas and since he is very big in his form he is called *Mahādeva*.

Pūjyate yaḥ suraiḥ sarvar mahāmccaiva pramāṇataḥ |
Maheti dātuḥ pūjāyām mahādevastataḥ smrutaḥ ||

Earlier itself it was mentioned that when *Mahā* is prefixed it a manager becomes General Manager. Similarly *Mahādeva* is General of *Devas*.

Lalitā – 209 – *Mahādevee* – महादेवी – *Mahatī* means one who has immense and immeasurably big body. *Śiva Purāŋā* says;

Bṛhadasya Sarīram Yat Aprameyam Pramāŋataḥ I
Dhātur Mahetipūjāyām Mahādevītataḥ Smṛtā II

Śiva in his eighth form, is known as *Mahādevā*; his consort is *Mahādevī*. *Mahādevī* is the presiding deity at the *Sāligrāma Cakratīrta* on the banks of *Ganḍakī* River in Nepal.

She has got entire energy of all *devas*. **She** is the greatest of all the *Devīs*. Hence *Mahādevee*.

Viṣṇu – 491 – *Mahādevaḥ* – महादेव: – The Great Deity, He is the Source of all Consciousness and from Him have risen all further deities and beings, therefore, it is right to consider Him as the Supreme Lord.

In the lay-man language, *Mahādeva* indicates Lord *Śiva* only. But here we see that it indicates *Viṣṇu* also. Again evidencing oneness.

94. ***Śiva*** – 614 – *Śivaḥ* – शिव: – Blemish-less pure and auspicious form –
Śuddhaḥ nirūpātiridyarttaḥ | *Viśuddhiḥ śivatā svataḥ iti vāyusam hitāyām* ||

The *pancākṣara mantra*, as popularly known, is the holy five syllables/ letters that is the supreme *mantra* of all devotees of Lord *Śiva*. This great *mantra* is **Om *Namaḥ Śivāya***. The five syllables in this mantra are *na - maḥ - śi - vā – ya* (*Om* is *praṇava* prefixed to any mantra and not accounted for).

This mantra is the heart of *Vedas*. It is the core of the very famous chapter of Vedas that stands in the middle of the Vedas - the *Śata rudrīyam*. This great *mantra* of *Veda samhita* while hailing the God as the Lord of everything of the worlds, salutes the God as *namaḥśivāya ca śivatarāya ca*.

The meaning of this matchless *mantra* is abound. The *purāṇas* and the philosophical texts talk in a very detailed and elaborate manner its meaning and significance and hail its ultimate-ness. For instance, the word *Śiva* means auspiciousness and perfection. It refers to the God, who is Perfect without any kind of dependency on anything external to make It complete. Naturally because of this self-perfection, it is completely blissful and ever auspicious. (All other auspicious things are in one way or the other dependent on the external circumstances etc.)

The subtle meaning of this very holy *mantra* is – *namama* – not mine; *Śivāya* – belongs to *Śiva*. It is negating the *ahankāa* (ego) and realising everything to belong to Lord *Śiva* only.

The statement in the *Vedas* – *Yāte Rudra Sivāthanūḥ* may be referred in this place.

In *Śrī Rudra Triśatī Nāmāvalī* also we have 252nd name as *Namaḥ Śivāyeca Namaḥ*.

Lalitā – 53 & 998 – *Shivā* – शिवा & – *Śrīśivā* – श्रीशिवा – *Śiva*'s consort and hence *Śiva* – inseparable from *Śiva*. Embodiment of auspiciousness, bestower of auspiciousness – The *Icchāśakti* of the Supreme Being – Liberation personified. Everything ultimately rests with *Śrī Devī*. Hence *Śiva.*

Lord *Parameśvarā* has eight forms, viz. Earth, Water, Fire, Wind, Space, Sun, Moon and Jīva. *Śiva* in the form wind is called *Īśāna*. **His** consort is *Śiva.*

One who is the blessed *Śrī Śiva.*

She is *Śivai* with *Śrī* (wealth). Since **She** is the sacred consort of *Śiva* and since **She** is an integral part of *Śiva*, **She** got the name as *Śiva.* Hence whatever meaning applicable to *Śiva* is applicable to **Her** also.

Viṣṇu – 27 & 600 – *Śivaḥ* – शिवः – One who is eternally pure. In Him can never be any contamination of the imperfection of *Rajas* and *Tamas*. "Non-apprehension of Reality" is *Tamas* and "misapprehensions of Reality" constitute *Rajas*. In the Reality itself there can be neither of them "He is *Brahmam*; He is *Śiva*", hence the *Upaniṣat* declares of the Absolute Oneness, which is *Viṣṇu*.

Śrī Ādi Śaṇkara in his commentary mentions; since he is pure and not influenced by the three qualities, he is called as *Śiva. Nārāyaŋopaniṣat* advises the integrated form, *Viṣŋu* only is being worshipped as *Śivā*;

Nistraiguŋyatayā Śuddhatvāt Śiva: I *"Sa Brahma Sa Śivaḥ"*
Ityabhedopadeśāt Śivādināmabhiḥ Harireva Stūyate II

Lord *Nārāyaṇa* is adored here as *Śivaḥ* and, at the same time, everyone whether Śaivites or Vaiṣṇavites repeat *Viṣṇu Sahasranāma*. Human prejudices have no logic or reason. *Śrī Nārāyaṇa* is *Śiva* (auspiciousness) and there is no difference between the two. "I am the dweller of Vaikuṇṭa, *Viṣṇu*. Between us there is no difference", so says Lord *Śiva* Himself. *Viṣṇu* is the 'Purifier' (*Śiva*), as his names, when chant and his form-divine, when meditated upon, become a means of quietening the mind and sharpening our perceptions of the subtler and the transcendental.

Colloquially *Śivaḥ* indicates Lord *Śiva* only. But here we see that it indicates *Viṣṇu* also. Even in *Śiva Sahasranāma* the name occurs once only, but in *Viṣṇu Sahasranāma* it occurs twice, indicating no difference between them.

95. ***Śiva*** – 621 – *Viṣṇuḥ* – विष्णुः – One who is in the form of *Viṣṇu*. One who is omnipresent.

In the previous paragraphs, both the Lords *Viṣṇu* and *Śiva* were called as *Śiva*. In this name it is otherwise – both are called as *Viṣṇu*. Everywhere the oneness is elaborated and evidenced.

Lalitā – 339, 892 & 893 – *Viṣŋumāyā* – विष्णुमाया, *Vaiṣŋavee* – वैष्णवी & *Viṣŋurūpiŋee* – विष्णुरूपिणी – One who is *Viṣŋu Māyā Śakti. Vişhŋu* is all-pervading, unlimited by place and time, *Brahmam,* in the form of inner self in all souls, etc. In *Saptaśatī* also we read as;

Yā Devī Sarvabhūteśu Viṣŋu Mayeti Samstitā I
Namastasyai Namastasyai Namastasyai Namo Namaḥ II

The *Kālikā Purāŋā* also says *Viṣŋumāyā* is that which differentiates, everything, into manifested and un-manifested according to the *tamas, rajas* and *satva* qualities. One who is the power/ form of *Viṣŋu.*

She depends on *Viṣŋu.* The *Devī Purāŋa* says, "**She** is sung as *Vaiṣŋavī* because **She** bears the conch, disc and club, the mother of *Viṣŋu* and the destroyer of foes";

Śankha Cakra Gadā Dhatte Viṣŋumātā Tathārihā I
Viṣŋurūpāthā Devī Vaiṣŋavī Tena Gīyate II

Four meanings are provided here. By the word *Arihā,* it is said like *Viṣhŋu,* **She** destroys the demons. The other two are self-clear. For the last one *Viṣŋurūpā* let us consider the following;

(i) In the *Brahmāṇḍa Purāŋa,* in the *Lalitopākhyāna, Śrī Devī* says – my male form bewildering the milk-maids; *Mamaiva pouruśam Rūpam Gopikā Janamohanam* II In the same place *Viṣŋu* says to *Vīrabhadra,* "The ancient *Śakti* of the Lord is divided into four forms, that *Śakti* becomes *Bhavāni* in its ordinary form, in battle **She** takes the form of *Durgā*; in anger that of *Kālī*; and **She** is also my female form";

Ādyā Śaktir Maheśasya Caturdhā Bhinna Vigrahā I
Bhoge Bhavānīrūpā Sā Durgārūpā Ca Samgare II
Kope Ca Kālikārūpā Pumrūpāca Madātmikā II

In the *Kūrma Purāŋa* when *Himavān* praises *Śrī Devī* says, "I salute thy form called *Nārāyaŋa,* Oh! *Lalitā,* which has a thousand heads, which is of infinite energy, having a thousand arms, the ancient person, reclining on the waters";

Sahasra Mūrdhānamananda Śaktim Sahasrabāhūm Puruṣam Purāŋam I
Śayānamabdhou Lalite Tavaiva Nārāyaŋākhyam Praṇatosmirūpam II

Again in the *Kūrma Purāŋa* itself, when *Śiva* showed his universal form to *Mankanaka,* the latter said – "What is the terrible form of thy, facing every side; who is **She** shining by your side?" Thus questioned, *Śiva*, after explaining the glory of his own nature, says, "**She** is my supreme *Māyā* (illusion) and *Prakṛti* (nature) of triple qualities. **She** is said by sages to be the ancient womb of the universe. He bewilders the universe by the illusion, he is the knower of the universe, *Nārāyaṇa*, supreme, unmanifested, in the form of illusion - thus says the *Vedas*";

Mama Sā Paramā Māyā prakṛtis Triguṇātmikā I
Procyate Munibhiḥ Śaktir Jagadyoniḥ Sanātanī II
Sa Eva Māyayā Viśvam Vyāmohayati Viśvavit I
Nārāyaṇaḥ Parovyakto Māyārūpa Iti Srutiḥ II

In the *Sanatkumāra Samhitā*, describing to king *Prabhākara*, the devotion to *Viṣṇu* and describing to his wife *Padminī*, the devotion to *Pārvatī*, it is said – "*Janārdana* is thus in the form of *Devī* as well as in his own form, for the husband and wife being one production, the only one is worshipped as two";

Evam Devyātmanā Svena Rūpeṇa Ca Janārdanaḥ
Dampatyoreka Gāyatvādeka Eva Dvidhārcitaḥ II

The *Bṛhat Parāsara Smṛti* also says, "He who with delighted mind worships *Durgā, Kātyāyanī* and *Vāgdevatā* obtains the world of *Viṣṇu*";

Durgām Kātyāyanīm Caiva Yajan Vāgdevatāmapi I
Cetasā Suprasannene Viṣṇulokamavāpnuyāt II

In the *Padma Purāṇa* also it is mentioned as "One who bathes the image of *Chaṇḍikā* with the juice of the sugarcane and places her on a golden vehicle, enjoys the presence of *Viṣṇu* after death";

Caṇḍikām Snapayedyastu Ikşavena Rasena Ca I
Soupariṇena Ca Yānena Viṣṇunā Saha Modate II

The *Āditya* and *Śiva Purāṇas* say – "**She** who dwells by his side is the young *Pārvati* and *Hari* also is a part of him";

Yā Tasya Pārśvagā Bālā Sā Pārvatyamśajo Hariḥ II

The *Vāmana Purāṇa* also says, "One who, on the full moon day of the month *Māgha,* worships *Śrī Devī* as prescribed, he obtains the benefits of the *Aśvameta* sacrifices and after death he shines in the world of *Viṣṇu*";

Pourŋamāsyām Tu Yo Māghe Pūjayedvidhivacchivām I
Sūśvamedhamavāpnoti Viṣŋuloke Mahīyate II

In *Saptaśatī* (XI-42) it is mentioned that *Śrīdevī* incarnated during *Vaivasvata Manvantara*, in the house of *Nandagopa* to destroy the demons *Śumba* and *Niśumba*;

Nandagopagruhe jātā yaśodā garbha sambhavā I
Tatasthou Nāśayiśyāmi Vindhyācala Nivāsinī II

Then I would be born in the house of Nandagopa to *Yaśodha* and shall live in Vindhya mountains and kill them.

Śree Ādi Śaṇkara comments (for the 2nd name of *Viṣṇu sahasranāma*) as, **He** is the *Māyā* of Universal Absolute. The *Śakti*, which limits this Absolute is illusion.

Gīta (VII–14) also says, this is my divine illusion, consisting of *Guŋas* is hard to surmount – *Daivīhyeśā Guŋamayī Mama Māyā Duratyayā*.

In Tamil, *Thirumazhisai Alwar* (65th verse) says; *Mātāya Mālavanai... Mādhavanai*.

Because of all the common qualities and characters normally *Śrīdevī* is said to be a sister of Lord *Viṣṇu*.

Viṣṇu – 2, 258 & 657 – *Viṣŋuḥ* – विष्णुः – The term *Viṣhŋu* is dissolved as *Veveṣṭi Vyāpnoti iti Viṣṇuḥ*, that pervades everywhere is *Viṣhŋu*. That has the nature of pervasiveness is *Viṣhŋu*. He is the one who pervades all and nothing ever pervades Him. "*Ēsāvāsyam Idam Sarvam*" – all this is indwelt, pervaded by the Lord. This very same idea is described in the typical style of the *Purāṇas*, in the incarnation of the Lord as *Vāmana*, who, with His three feet, measured the entire universe. Because of this act, the Lord got the name *Viṣŋu*, says *Mahābhārata*. *Viṣŋu* Purāṇa (3-1) says: The root *Vis* means "to enter". The entire world of things and beings is pervaded by Him and the *Upaniṣat* emphatically insists in its mantra "whatever that is there is the world of change". Hence it means that He is not limited by space (*desa*), time (*Kāla*) or substance (*vastu*). All-Pervading: Long-Strident. In Mahābhārata (12-

350-43) we also read the Lord Himself explaining to Arjuna, "Because I stand striding across the Universe (*Kramanāt*), Oh! Pārthā, I am known as *Viṣṇu*". One who pervades the entire *Viśvam* is called all-pervading. In His *Viśvarūpa* form in *Gīta* (XI) we have from Arjuna a description of the dazzling wonderment of Him as "All-pervading".

96. ***Śiva*** – 625 – *Dharaḥ* – धर: – He is in the form of *Dhara*, one of the Vasus.

Lalitā – 955 – *Dharā* – धरा – One who is in the form of Earth. It can be taken that cryptically this has cryptically indicated all the other four primary elements also.

She is in the form of *La*, which is the *bhīja* letter of earth. Since **She** supports the entire universe, **She** got this name.

97. ***Śiva*** – 629 – *Savitraḥ* – सवित्र: – One who creates everything.

Lalitā – 699 – *Sāvitrī* – सावित्री – One who is in the form of *Savithrī*, the creator of the world. The creator of this universe is called *Savitā*, a form of *Paramaśiva*. His consort is *Sāvitrī*.

The world is seen because of Sun – i.e. it is known to all through the light of Sun. Hence he is also called as *Savitā* or *Savithrī*. Since **She** is worshipped through all *Vedas* and since by nature **She** is of pure form, **She** is called as *Savithrī*. **She Herself** originates in the form of light and smoothly and continuously flows. Hence **She** is *Savithrī*.

According to *Padma Purāŋa*, the presiding deity at *Puşkara Kşetra* is called *Savitrī*; *Sāvitrī Puşkare Nāmnātīrttānām Pravareśubhe*.

Viṣṇu – 884 & 969 – *Savitā* – सविता – One who brings forth, from Himself, the me-Self functioning through the Sun is called Savitā. He who is the father of All – Who is the eternal father of the entire Universe.

98. ***Śiva*** – 632 – *Vidhātāḥ* – विधाता: – One who orders everyone. Or one who supports all in different ways and means – *vividaprakāreṇa bhośakaḥ*.

Lalitā – 337 – *Vidhātree* – विधात्री – One who supports this universe. Since **She** supports and nourishes the universe, **She** is *Vidhātrī*. **She** is also called *Jagatdhātrī*. *Vidhātā* means *Brahma*. His consort is *Vidhātrī*.

Vi - much, *Dhātri* - myrobalan, because **She** is fond of myrobalans, **She** is *Vidhātrī*. *Dhātrī* – mother, who bears the baby in her womb and releases at the appropriate time. A great mother is *Vidhātrī*.

Viṣṇu – 44 & 484 – *Vidhātāḥ* – विधाता: – One who is the Dispenser of all 'fruits-of-actions'. In the *Karma-kānda* portion of the *Vedas, Ēśvara* is described as the dispenser of fruit (*Karmaphaladātā Ēśvaraḥ*). He is the Lord who is behind this universe of scientific truths and rhythm. He is the One who has not only ordered the laws of the nature, but he is the one afraid of whom, the phenomena dare not disobey his laws anywhere at any time. The light of the sun, the heart is the fire, the sweetness in the sugar, the pains in the sin and the joy s in goodness, are all their 'nature' and none dare ever disobey these laws. The one who is thus the unquestionable law behind the entire universe of laws is *Vidhātā*. All-supporter. As the final sub-stratum for everything, the Lord supports the entire universe of living creatures and nobody supports Him, He alone is His own support. The Lord is at once the material, instrumental and the efficient causes for the universe of forms.

99. ***Śiva*** – 636 – *Varṇavibhāvī* – वर्णविभावी – One who created the four *Varṇas*. Or he shines in different colours. The glowing objects like ice dews, smoke, Sun, wind, fire, glow-worm, lightning, prism, thunder, etc., disclose the *Brahmam* in *yoga*.

Nīhāra tūmārkānilānalānām katyoda vidyud spatikā śanīnīm |
Etāni rūpāni puraḥ sarāni brahmanyapiviyakti karāniyoge ||

Lalitā – 850 – *Varŋarūpiŋī* – वर्णरूपिणी – One who is of the form of letters. *Varŋa* means letters. **She** is of that form. The *Pāŋinisikşā* says, "According to the *Sāmbhava* School there are sixty-four letters, these are promulgated by *Svayambhu* (self-originated) in the *Prākṛt* or Samskrutam language"; **She** is of that form.

Varŋam means caste – **She** is in the form of *Varŋam* in *Varŋāśrama*. Crossing of castes will result in great danger. In *Gīta* (I-41) also *Arjuna* explains the same. The real meaning of this name is *Śrī Devī* is in the form of controls like *varŋas*.

Vişņu – 768 – *Caturgatiḥ* – चतुर्गतिः – The ultimate goal of all the four. Though their means and purposes appear divergent, Śrī Nārāyana alone is the inevitable goal of all activities of the four types (*Varṇas*) of human beings; Thinkers (*Brāhmaṇas*), Rulers and Leaders (*Kśatriyas*), Men of Commerce (*Vaiśyas*) and Workers (*Sūdras*). The Lord, also, is the consummate goal to be achieved by the four stages (*āśramas*) of life; the Age of Study (*Brahmacarya*), the Householder (*Gṛhasta*), the Retirement (*Vānaprasta*) and the Stage of Renunciation (*Sanyāsa*).

100. ***Śiva*** – 638 – *Padmanābhāḥ* – पद्मनाभाः – One who has the lotus, the cause of this world, in his navel – *Vişņusvarūpi*.

Lalitā – 280 – *Padmanābhasahodarī* – पद्मनाभसहोदरी – One who is a sister of *Vişŋu* (*Padmanābhā*). *Vişŋu* created Lotus from his naval and hence *Padmanābhan*.

As per *Mārkaŋḑeya Purāŋā, Śrī Devī* created three pairs of twins as per **Her** desire. The three pairs of brother-sisters are *Brahma* & *Lakshmī* in gold colour, *Vişŋu* & *Śrī Devī* in blue colour and *Śiva* & *Saraswatī* in white colour. Their colours respectively indicate the three qualities (*Guŋas*). As per this *Vişŋu* and *Śrī Devī* are siblings.

Similarly *Brahma Purāŋā*, the *Puruśottamakśetra Mahātmīya* says, *Pārvatī*, who was born from the womb of *Menakā*, wife of *Himavān* in the former birth, in the next birth is born as *Śubhadrā*, sister of *Śrī Kŗşŋa* in the womb of *Yaśoda*.

Again we read *Kātyāyanīti Yā Jātā Kamsa Śatros Sahodarī*.

In another place, *Śrī Devī* alongwith **Her** brother *Śrī Vişŋu* appeared to *Brahma*, the grandsire of all the worlds, who once performed a severe penance in the sacred *Kānchi*. A special interpretation – *Śrī Bhāskararāya* has explained in many a place that each letter of this *Sahasranāmā* is a root letter of one or other *mantra*. Accordingly the name *Padmanābhasahodarī* explain the five letters of the *Vāgbhava* (first) division of *Pancadaśī mantra*. This is the inherent meaning.

Viṣṇu – 48, 196 & 346 – *Padmanābhaḥ* – पद्मनाभ: – One from whose navel (*nābhi*) springs the Lotus (*padma*), which is the seat of the four-faced Creator, Brahma. Lotus represents Truth or any of its manifested powers. The creative faculties in human flow from the navel area (*nābhi*) and manifests as the 'four-faced' inner equipment (*Antaḥkaraṇa*) constituted of the mind, intellect, *chit* and ego.

In the *Yoga-śāstras*, we find a lot of details regarding this concept. According to them every 'idea' springs from Him (Parā) and then at the navel area, each of them comes to be 'perceived' (*Paśyantī*).

Thereafter they play in the bosom as thoughts (*Madhyamā*) and at last they are expressed (*Vaikharī*) in the outer fields-of–activity.

One who supports at His navel the very seat of all creative power. According to *Ādi Śaṅkara*, here the term may mean one who has a navel region, which in its rounded beauty, is as charming as the lotus flower.

One who has the lotus in his navel, is not to be taken literally. Navel (*Nābhi*) is the psychic centre where all un-manifest thoughts first spring forth into our recognition (*Paśyantī*). The seedless state of all thoughts is called in the *Yoga Śastra*, as *Parā*. It therefore means "one in whose bosom lies, in potential, all the possibilities of the universe of expression". It can also mean "One who manifests Himself in the lotus of the heart of his devotee. In some schools the meaning of this name is given as "He who is seated in the pericarp of the lotus".

101. ***Śiva*** – 668 – *Vṛkṣaḥ* – वृक्ष: – One who is in the form of a tree. *Vṛkşebhyo harikeśebhyaḥ paśūnāmpataye namaḥ* - He is in the form of trees which have herbs as long hair. He is also in the form of all animals. We bow such a lord.

Svetāsvātara Upaniṣat (III-9) says – like a tree in ether;

Vṛkṣa Iva Stabdho Divi Tiśtatyekaḥ II

We even worship *Aśvatta* tree along with Neem tree as *Śiva*-Śakti.

In *Śrī Rudra Triśatī Nāmāvalī* also we have 245th name as *Namo Vṛkṣebhyo Namaḥ*.

Viṣṇu – 555 – *Vṛkṣaḥ* – वृक्ष: – In the *Upaniṣats* the world emerging out of the Supreme *Brahmam* is described metaphorically as a 'Tree'; *Samsāra Vṛkṣa* – the Tree of Life has been exhaustively described in the *Kaṭopaniṣat* and in the *Gīta*. In the Purāṇas, again we find, in multiple places, exhaustive descriptions of the world manifested from the Lord as a 'Tree'.

Karpaga tree – all bestowing one, originated from the Milky Ocean, when it was churned for Amṛta. We all bow this tree and he is in that for.

102. ***Śiva*** – 702 – *Prāṇadhāraṇaḥ* – प्राणधारण: – One who protects the lives.

Lalitā – 783 – *Prāŋadā* – प्राणदा – One who gives life to all. The word *Prāŋan* (life) indicates the five breaths viz., *Prāŋa, Apāna, Samāna, Udāna & Vyāna* and again the 11 organs (5 organs of action, 5 organs of knowledge and mind). The verb *Da* means to give. Hence it has to be construed that **She** gives the above said life.

It can also be split as – *Prānān* + *Dyati* – *Gandayati* – to obliterate. That is, it means that **She** wipes out the above said *Prāŋan*.

Viṣṇu – 65, 321, 408 & 956 – *Prāṇadaḥ* – प्राणद: – One who gives (*Dadāti*) the *Prānas* to all. The term *Prānas* used in philosophy indicated "all manifestations of Life in a living body". The Source of Life from which all dynamic activities in the living organisms of the world flow out, meaning, that from which all activities emerge out is *Prānadaḥ*.

Taittrīya Upaniṣat (2-7) exclaims – "Who could then live? Who could breath"? if **He** be not everywhere.

One who gives strength (*Prāna*) to everything, everywhere. The root *'da'* has a meaning of destruction and hence, the term comprehends also the power of destruction everywhere. According to the *Purāṇas*, therefore, He is the One who gives the strength and glory for *Devas* and again, He is the One who supplies special strength to them to win over the brutal forces of the diabolically wicked, the demons subjectively, it is the Self that supplies the mental strength for cultivating the higher values of life and it is the same Source Divine that floods the seekers heart with the courage to annihilate the lower impulses that come to destroy his peace and tranquillity within.

This can also mean "One who gives *'Prāna'* or as one who takes away *'Prāna'*, because, the root *'da'* has both the meanings, 'to give' and 'to break'. Therefore, *Viṣṇu* is the supreme who gives *Prāna* to all creatures in the beginning of the creation and He alone is again the one who destroys all the *Prānās* (movements) at the time of the dissolution.

The term *'Prāna'* in our *Śāatras* means the physiological functions, the manifestations of life in man. Therefore, *Nārāyaṇa*, the self, is the vital Source from which all sense organs, mind and intellect borrow their power of perception, capacities of feeling and their faculties of thinking and understanding.

103. ***Śiva*** – 705 – *Dakṣaḥ* – दक्षः – One who all the skills of this world. One who accomplish**e**s everything so quickly.

Lalitā – 598 – *Dākshāyaŋī* – दाक्षायणी – One who is daughter of *Dakşa.* According to the *Viśva* dictionary, *Dākşyāyaṇī* means, the consort of *Śiva*, alongwith *Rohiṇī* and other constellations (daughters of *Dakşāprajāpati*); It is evidenced through – *Dākşāyanī Tvaparnāyām Rohiṇyām Tārakāsuca.*

Dākshyāna means a certain sacrifice repeating the performance of the *darśa* and *pūrŋamāsa* sacrifices. **She** is in that form.

Vişṇu – 423 – *Dakṣaḥ* – दक्षः – The Smart. One who undertakes the creation, sustenance and destruction of the Whole Cosmos with ease and efficiency, diligence and promptitude. One who augments in the form of the world.

104. ***Śiva*** – 706 – *Satkṛtaḥ* – सत्कृत: – Who is properly worshipped by all.

Lalitā – 627 – *Trijagadvandyā* – त्रिजगद्वन्द्या – One who is worshipped by all the three worlds. One who is worshipped in all the three worlds. In the meditation verse of *Śrī Lalitā Sahasranāma* itself we read as *Sakalasuranutām* – worshipped by all *Devas*.

Viṣṇu – 241 & 242 – *Satkartā* – सत्कर्ता & *Satkṛtā* – सत्कृता – One who revels and adores those who are good and wise. His palace is ever lit up with His hospitality and He Himself presides over the loving reception of the righteous.

One who is adored by all good people, not only is He adored and worshipped by great men of wisdom and devotion – as the *Sanatkumāras*, Nārada and others – but He is invoked and worshipped consciously by all living creatures.

The *Upaniṣat* describes every experience of all living creatures as a *Yajna* in which the stimuli received are the 'Oblations' poured at which the inner Consciousness flares up into brilliancy.

105. ***Śiva*** – 709 – *Gopatiḥ* – गोपति: – One who rules the earth. Or one who is in the form of Sun, who is the head of rays – *raṣmīnām patiḥ sūryādhiḥ*.

Viṣṇu – 495 & 592 – *Gopatiḥ* – गोपति: – The **She**pherd. As one who played the part of a cowherd in His Krishna-incarnation. The term 'Go' in Samskrutam has got four meanings: the cattle, the earth, the speech and the Vedas. In all these meanings He is the Lord (*Patiḥ*) – Lord of the cattle; Lord of Earth; Lord of speech; the Lord about whom all the *Vedas* speak of as the very Goal.

The husband of the Earth. Or, one who is the Lord protecting all those who are weary of their *sansāric* life of passions and desires. Such ones, exhausted by grassing in the pastures of dissipation and enervated from the world of happenings, are comparable to cows. 'Go' also may be interpreted as 'sense-organs'. In this way the term suggests "Lord of the Sense Organs," Śrī *Narāyaṇa*, the Self.

106. ***Śiva*** – 722 – *Ratiḥ* – रतिः – One who is in the form of delight.

Lalitā – 315 & 316 – *Ratirūpā* – रतिरूपा & *Ratipriyā* – रतिप्रिया – One who is in the form of *Rati* (Cupid's consort). One who is beloved of *Rati*.

Rati is the external interest and involvement on anything. Unless it is achieved people do not get peace. *Rati* is the consort of Cupid. Cupid's goal is the person who has wish. *Rati* helps Cupid by creating love and interest on things. *Śrī Devī*'s power only comes out in the form *Rati* and hence *Ratirūpa.*

Rati means copulation and erotic art. For instance, in *Rāmāyana, Dasaratha*, after fixing up the crowning of *Rāmā* as prince, went to the palace of *Kaikeyī*. This has been mentioned as *Ratyārtam*.

Soundaryalaharī (9th verse), says that the *Kuṇḍalinī* energy has united happily with the consort at *Sahasrāram;*

Sahasrāra Padme Saha Rahasi Patyā Viharase.

Viṣṇu – 297 – *Kāmaḥ* – कामः – One who is the beloved. Not only He is the beloved of the devotees, but every activity of all living creatures is an attempt at courting and winning bliss and happiness. The Blissful Self is the goal of all creatures in life. Even insignificant unicellular organisms revolt against pain and they too seek happiness. Human is no exception. The Infinite Bliss which is experienced only on transcending the body, mind and intellect, is that which is constantly demanded by every organism that breathes in this universe. In the ignorance of this All Satisfying Goal, the world suffers. That Lord is the beloved of all devotees and in fact, He is also the beloved of even those who deny Him and run after the sense- objects. The theist seeks Him through devotion or meditation. The atheist too seeks Him only in and through all his diligent pursuits of the sense-stimuli.

107. ***Śiva*** – 723 & 873 – *Naraḥ* – नरः – One who is in the form of human being. One who conducts everything. *Nayati prāpayati brahmāṇḍamiti naro virāt* – the *Virātpuruş*, who conducts this *Brahmāṇḍa*.

One who does not ask for anything – does not have wish on anything. *Na rāti ādatte iti naraḥ*.

Viṣṇu – 246 – *Naraḥ* – नर: – The Guide. One who guides all creatures strictly according to their actions is none other than the Ancient (*Sanātana*) Self.

108. ***Śiva*** – 730 – *Calaḥ* – चल: – One who cannot apprehended or seized by anyone. In that fashion he continuously moves on.

Viṣṇu – 746 – *Calaḥ* – चल: – Moving. One who moves in the form of air. By the juxtaposition of these two opposite qualities like *Calaḥ* and *Acalaḥ*, we are reminded that the apparent world of plurality that constitutes the realm of change is also nothing other than the immovable Ātman interpreted through our personal equipment of experiences. Unconditioned by the body, mind and intellect, the Lord in His Infinitude is motionless, but as conditioned by the vehicles He apparently seems to move. It is something like a traveller, though himself sleeping, is able to travel all the night since he is conditioned by the vehicle which carries him.

109. ***Śiva*** – 742 – *Guṇādhikaḥ* – गुणाधिक: – He is above all by his *Guṇas* (characters).

Lalitā – 604 – *Guṇanidhiḥ* – गुणनिधि: – One who is the treasure house of qualities. Though the qualities are of specifically three viz. *satva*, *rajas* and *tamas*, they have endless modifications. **She** is the treasure house of all such qualities.

Guṇa means aggregate (*Vyūhas*). Like nine *nidhies*, these *vyūhas* also are nine in number. *Parameśvara* is of the form of these nine aggregates of qualities. They are; *Kālavyūha* (time), *Kulavyūha* (family race), *Nāmavyūha* (name), *Gnānavyūha* (knowledge), *Cittavyūha* (mind), *Nādavyūha* (*Nāda*), *Binduvyūha* (*Bindu*), *Kalpavyūha* (*Kalpa*) and *Jīvavyūha* (soul). Since **She** is of all these forms **She** is called as *Guṇanidhi*. These are also described in the 36th verse of *Soundaryalaharī* starting as *Tavāgnā Cakrastham*.

The word *Guṇa* also means rope. The rope called *Valrikā*, which tied the ship during the *pralaya*; *Nidhi*, the deity to whom it was tied. The following story occurs in the *Matsya* and *Kālika Purāṇas* thus; at the time of dissolution all seeds and sages entered the boat at the command of *Manu*, who was directed by the Lord *Vişŋu* and the boat was tied to the horn of the fish-incarnation. That rope became firm when *Śrī Devī* held it. "Make a great rope of hides to be called *Vatrikā*, nine *Yojanas* long and three cubits broad. *Śrī Devī* who is the protector of the universe, the great *Māyā*, the mother of the world, the world itself, will make that rope firm so that it will not give away".

Vişṇu – 839 & 840 – *Guṇabhṛt* – गुणभृत् & *Nirguṇaḥ* – निर्गुण: – One Who supports – maintains and expresses through the three Guṇas. Through *rajas* He creates; through *Sattva* He preserves and through *tamas* He annihilates. He, as Consciousness, expresses Himself through these three textures of *vāsanās*.

840th name *Nirguṇaḥ* – निर्गुण is also worth noting here – Without any qualities. That which has property is matter-perishable, changeable and finite. The Imperishable, the Changeless, the Infinite is property-less; it is the Consciousness that illumines all properties (Gunas). With the matter equipments, in His Incarnations He manifests as having 'form' (*Guṇabhṛt*) and in His Absolute Nature He is 'form-less' the Non-dual Self.

110. ***Śiva*** – 767 – *Jīvanaḥ* – जीवन: – He is the life in all human beings.

Vişṇu – 930 – *Jīvanaḥ* – जीवन: – The Life-Spark in all living creatures. The Flame-of-Existence that warns an organism to life is the presiding Consciousness Supreme, the Self. This Self is *Nārāyaṇa*. Permeating the earth, I support all beings by (My) energy; and having become the juicy Moon I nourish all herbs – is the declaration of *Bhagavān*.

111. ***Śiva*** – 774 – *Mūlaḥ* – मूल: – One who is the root of this entire world. *Gīta* (XV-1) compares this world to *Aśvatta* tree, which has roots above and branches beneath –

Ūrdva mūlamataḥ cākamśvattam prāhuravyayam.

Lalitā – 840 – *Mūlavigraharūpiŋee* – मूलविग्रहरूपिणी – One who is the root from where all other powers (*Śaktis*) originate. *Bala, Bagalā* and all other *Śaktis* originate from the three forms *Śāmbavee, Vidyā* and *Śyāma*. Those three forms originate from *Śrī Devī*.

Viṣṇu – 99 – *Sarvādiḥ* – सर्वादिः – One who is the very beginning (*ādi*) of all and is naturally the Primary Cause (*Mūla-Kāraṇa*). One who was in existence earlier than everything else. Even before effects arise, the Cause. The Infinite which was before creation and from which the created beings had emerged out, as an effect.

112. ***Śiva*** – 776 – *Amṛtaḥ* – अमृतः – One who was never conquered by anyone. One who cannot be conquered by anybody. One who cannot be conquered by the three *guṇas* – *Guṇātītaḥ*. He is like the nectar.

Lalitā – 296 – *Anādinidhanā* - अनादिनिधना – One who exists without a beginning or an end. The Supreme Being has neither a beginning nor an end – neither a birth nor a death. On the other hand, the human being begins in the middle and ends in the middle.

Viṣṇu – 119 – *Amṛtaḥ* – अमृतः – One who is deathless. One who is immortal and immutable. *Mṛta* = death. It can also mean as one who is of the nature of Nectar (*Amṛtam*) – a sure cure for those who are suffering from malady of ignorance. *Amṛtaḥ* also means *mokṣa*; and thus it is indicated, **He** is ever-liberated – the Pure State of Being. *Brihadāraṇyaka Upaniḥad* (4.4-25) says *ajaromaraḥ* – un-aging and deathless.

113. ***Śiva*** – 798 – *Śaśiḥ* – शशिः – One who is in the form of Moon.

Lalitā – 746 – *Bhāgyābdhicandrikā* – भाग्याब्धिचन्द्रिका – One who is the Moon beam illuminating the ocean of good fortune. Welfare happens only by the virtues done in the previous births. Welfare can be enjoyed in peace only by the self. But, when others recognise the welfare of one person, then his happiness multiplies – the total dimension of the welfare does not increase (since it is the result of virtues of previous births, it has been already fixed).

The ocean boils because of the beams of Moon. The tide waves heavily – but there is no change in the quantity of water in the ocean. Similarly, **She** makes the sea of good fortune swell for **Her** devotees, just as the Moon makes the ocean swell into high tide. **She** is in the form of Moon. With **Her** compassion, **She** makes the others recognise the welfare enjoyed by **Her** devotees.

Viṣṇu – 285 – *Śaśibinduḥ* – शशिबिन्दुः – The patch in the moon looks like the silhouette of a rabbit for the naked eye; that which has a "beauty-spot" (*Bindu*) in the shape of a rabbit (*Śaśa*) is called *Śaśibindu* – the Moon. Since the Lord is the nourisher of all and He Himself is the entire world of matter, He Himself is the Moon "that nourishes with essence all plant kingdom".

114. ***Śiva*** – 808 – *Sumukhaḥ* – सुमुखः – One who has a beautiful face. Or since he initiates all *vidyās* to the devotees he is *sumukha* –
yo brahmāṇam vidadāti pūrvam yovai vedāmccha brahiṇoti tasmai.

Lalitā – 459 – *Sumukhī* – सुमुखी – One who has a lovely face. **She** has a beautiful and splendid face. It is told that with wisdom, the luster of the face is enhanced. In many a place the *Veda* says, "One who knows this (*Brahmam*), his face shines"; *Chāndokya Upaniṣat* (IV-14-2) – *Śobhate'sya Mukhamya Evam Veda* – "Oh dear child, your face shines like that of a sage (*brahmavit*)"; *Brahmavidiva Te Soumya Mukhamābhāti*.

The first in the sixteen great names of Lord *Gaŋesha* is *Sumukhaḥ*. This appears in *Gaŋesh Sahasranāmā* also. The *śakti* of *Sumukhaḥ* is *Sumukhī*.

Sumukhī is a type of meter in music. As per *Vṛddha Ratnāvali* of *Venkatesar*, its character is – *Na Ja Ja La Ga*. But, as per *Vṛddha Maŋimālā* of *Baingānādu Gacchapī Gaŋapati Sastrigal*, its character is of 10 letters – *Sa Sa Ja*.
Viṣṇu – 456 – *Sumukhaḥ* – सुमुखः – One who has an enchanting face. Truth is beauty and Beauty is truth. In all conditions the Lord is ever cheerful and brings to His face the dignified beauty of calm repose. When the devotees come and surrender at His sacred feet *Nārāyaṇa* is the one of infinite mercy who beams with joy at the devotion of the surrender.

Śrī Ādi Śaṇkara in his commentary mentions as;

- One who has a handsome face. The verse from *Viṣŋu Purāŋa* has been quoted – *Prasanna Vadanam Cāru Padmapadrāyadekṣaṇam*.
- He teaches all the knowledge (*vidyās*) and hence *Sumukhaḥ*. The *Svetavastara Upaniṣat* (6-18) verse starting from *Yo Brahmāṇam* has been quoted.

115. ***Śiva*** – 815 – *Mahādhanuḥ* – महाधनुः – One who has a great bow, called *Pināka* and hence he is called as *Pinākapāṇī*. *Rudram* says – *Namaste astu dhanvane* – the bow of *Rudra* is in the form of *Vedas*. *Vālmīki Rāmāyaṇa* (6-75.36) says;

Bhagavāniva sankṛto bhavo vedamayam dhanuḥ.

Lalitā – 594 – *Indradhanuḥprabhā* – इन्द्रधनुःप्रभा – One who has brightness like that of a rainbow. *Indradhanuś* (bow of *Indra*) indicates rainbow.

Viṣṇu – 434 – *Mahādhanuḥ* – महाधनुः – One who is supremely rich with the wealth of bliss, which he can give to His devotees. *Viṣṇu* is one from whom His devotees gain great wealth.

The Samskrutam word *dhanu* is interpreted as a bow and as wealth in different places.

116. ***Śiva*** – 832 – *Daṇḍiḥ* – दण्डिः – He punishes the criminals. He stands as a *brahmachāri* holding the *Daṇḍa* in his hands.

Lalitā – 608 – *Daŋḍanītisthā* – दण्डनीतिस्था – One who administers justice by punishing the culprits. *Daŋḍanīti* is the *śāstra,* which describes the crimes and the corresponding punishments for the criminals. The *Devī Purāŋa* says, because **She** leads to certainty men who wander into good and bad ways by restraining and by soothing them, **She** is called *Daŋḍanītisthā*;

Nayānayagatān Lokān Avikalpe Niyojanāt I
Daŋḍanāt Damanād Vāpi Daŋḍanītiriti Smṛtā II

Viṣṇu – 859 – *Daṇḍaḥ* – दण्डः – One who punishes the wicked. In *Gīta*, *Bhagavān* declares Himself to be the policeman of the Universe. The term can also mean the 'Sceptre' the insignia of kingship. Śrī Narāyaṇa, the King of kings in the entire, limitless universe, holds the Sceptre of total royalty.

117. ***Śiva*** – 837 & 972 – *Vajriḥ* – वज्रिः – One who is in the form of *Devendra* holding *Vajrāyuta* in his hands.

Lalitā – 468 & 944 – *Vajriṇī* – वज्रिणी & *Vajreshvaree* – वज्रेश्वरी – One who is the in the form of *Indrāṇī*, consort of *Indra*, the possessor of the weapon *Vajra*. Or one who has the thunderbolt in hand. Or adorned with jewels like diamond and other gems.

Kaṭopaniṣat (VI-2) says, "The great terrible *Vajra*". *Vajra* means *Brahmam*. *Śrī Devī* is called *Vajriṇī* as **She** is related with *Brahmam* as its limitator;

Mahadbhayam Vajramudyatam.

One who is in the form of the deity called *Vajreśvarī*. *Pāvanopaniṣat* says that three *Devīs* viz., *Kāmeśvarī, Vajreśvarī* and *Bagamālinī*.

The *Śrī Cakra* has twelve walls, all built of diamonds; in the centre of the eleventh, there is a river called *Vajramayī* and **She** is its deity. Sage *Durvāsa* in his *Lalitāstavarathan*, (44 and 45) says, "There let the ever flowing river called *Vajra*, be everlasting, filled with the sound of the sweet notes of the swans gliding on the beautiful waves; on the pleasant bank of that river *Vajreshī* flourishes decked with diamond ornaments praised by *Devas* headed by *Indra*, the hurler of the thunder-bold";

Tatra Sadā Pravahanti Tatinī Vajrāpbhidhā Ciram Jīyāt I
Catolormi Jāta Nṛtyat Kalahamsī Kula Kalakvanita Puṣṭā II
Rodhasi Tasyā Rucire Vajreśī Jayati Vajra Bhūśādyā I
Vajra Pradāna Tośita Vajrimukha Tridaśa Vinutacāritrā II

The *Brahmāṇḍa Purāṇa* says, when *Indra* performed penance in the water, "From that water *Śrī Devī* arose and gave *Indra* the weapon called *Vajra*.

Viṣṇu – 62 – *Pavitram* – पवित्रं – The term *Pavi* means – the weapon *vajra* (thunderbolt). One who saves (*tram*) his devotees from the thunderbolt of *Indra* is *Pavitram*. This can also be interpreted as the *giridhara* episode where the lord saves his devotees from *Indra's* wrath.

Earlier the name *Pavitram* was interpreted differently as pure. Now another perspective is given. It may be noted that we use a kind of ring by *darba* grass for all religious rites and it is also called as *Pavitram*. Such a ring is a must for all *para* or *apara* rites.

118. ***Śiva*** – 839 – *Sahasrapāt* – सहस्रपात् – One who has thousand feet. Here thousand should not be considered as literally meaning 1000. It means thousands of feet.

Lalitā – 284 – *Sahasrapāt* – सहस्रपात – One who has countless feet.

Viṣṇu – 227 – *Sahasrapāt* – सहस्रपात् – Thousand-footed Lord. In *Puruṣasūkta* of Ṛg-Veda also, the similar terms like thousand-headed, thousand-eyed, thousand-footed, etc., are used in describing the Infinite form of the Mighty Truth - *Sahasra Śīrśāḥ Puruṣaḥ Sahasrākṣa Sahasrapāt.*

The "many heads" (224th name), "many eyes" (226th name) and "many legs" (227th name), together indicate that, through all these equipments of thinking (head), of action (leg) and of perception (eyes), the Thinker, the Doer and the Seer, the One Infinite Consciousness expresses everywhere, in all forms, at all times and He is the Lord *Viṣṇu*.

119. ***Śiva*** – 840 – *Sahasramūrdhāḥ* – सहस्रमूर्धा: – One who has many heads. The heads every other person is his only.

Sarvadaḥpāṇi pātam sarvatokṣi śiromukham.

Lalitā – 532 – *Sarvatomukhī* – सर्वतोमुखी – One who has faces in all round directions.

Viṣṇu – 224 – *Sahasramūrdhāḥ* – सहस्रमूर्धा: – One who has endless number of heads. All living creatures are His manifestations and He Himself is the One who has become the many. Therefore all heads are His, just as in a factory the proprietor considers all the employees as his own 'hands'. As indicated earlier, here the term *Sahasra* means innumerable. The *Viśvarūpa* shown to *Arjuna* while advising *Gīta* (XIII-13) can be imagined here;

Sarvato'kṣiśiromukham – Everywhere eyes, heads and mouths.

120. ***Śiva*** – 842 – *Guruḥ* – गुरु: – One who is in the form of a *guru* (teacher). We bow to him, who is the teacher of the entire world and the doctor for the patients suffering from the disease of birth –

Gurave sarvalokānām bhiśaje bhavaroginạm
nitaye sarva vidyānām Dakşiṇāmūrthaye namaḥ

When we talk about *Guru* the definition given by *Kānchi Paramācārya* is worth mentioning. *Guru* means huge or more weight – i.e. a person with fame and superiority. *Gu* = darkness and *ru* = to remove – i.e. *Guru* means remover of darkness. Once a person finds an appropriate *Guru* and becomes his disciple, then he provides him the knowledge by removing the darkness of ignorance.

Another interesting fact about *Guru* mentioned by *Paramācārya*: Normally a *guru* is supposed to be on the higher plane in all respects like age, status, seating, etc., than the disciple(s) or students and also he would be talking and the students would be silently hearing. But there are three special types of *gurus* ironical in nature like:

i. A young *guru* teaching without uttering even a single word to four elderly students – *Dakşiṇāmūrthy*.
ii. Young boy teaching his father – *Swāmināthа Swāmy*.
iii. As a charioteer sitting in a lower plane teaches (advises *Śrīmad Bhagavad Gīta*) to Arjuna, who is sitting on the higher plane, being a king – Lord Kṛşṇa

Lalitā – 209 – *Gurumūrtiḥ* – गुरुमूर्तिः – One who assumes the form of a teacher.

The confirmed opinion of the *mantra śāstras* is – the teacher, the *mantra* and the deity are all one and the same and should not be distinguished. *Śrī Devī* **Herself** reaches the devotee in the form of a teacher and gives him invocation of *mantras Aruŋagirinadar* also sings about Lord Muruga in Tamil as "*Guruvāi Varuvāi Arulvāi Guhane*".

The letter *Gu* is a existence (*Sat* letter) and *Ru* is knowledge (of *Brahmam*) and because one is with the knowledge of *Brahmam*, he is called *guru*.

Vişṇu – 209 – *Guruḥ* – गुरुः – The teacher, who initiates the seekers into the secrets of the sacred scriptures is called the *Guru*. Since the Lord, the infinite alone, is the very author and knower of the Vedas, He is the Teacher in all spiritual study. *Ātman* being the Light, that illumines the knowledge in the teacher, his very capacity to speak and the very ability in the student to hear, understand and apprehend this great Truth, He alone is the Teacher wherever there is any transference of knowledge.

Śrī Ādi Śaṇkara in his commentary of mentions – **He** is called *Guru* since **he**; (invocates/ advises all *Vidyās* or gave birth to all living beings (as a father).

120. ***Śiva*** – 853 – *Padmagarbhaḥ* – पद्मगर्भः – One who is in the form of *Brahma*, who originated from Lotus flower.

Lalitā – 638 – *Svarŋagarbhā* – स्वर्णगर्भा – One who is in the form of *Hiraŋyagarbha*. *Hiraŋyagarbhā* is interested in the group of subtle bodies. This group shines like gold. Hence he was called as *Hiraŋyagarbha.* The same is called as *Svarŋagarbhā* also.

She gives holiness to the *Mātrukās* (*bījaksharas*). I.e. since **She** has them in **Her** *mantras* they become *Su Arnas* (holy or excellent) and contained in **Her** womb.

Viṣṇu – 348 – *Padmagarbhaḥ* – पद्मगर्भः – One who is being meditated upon in the centre of the lotus-of-the-heart.

121. ***Śiva*** – 857 – *Gabhastiḥ* – गभस्तिः – One who has the rays of light – *raśmimān – vareṇyam bhargo devasya dhīmahi.*

Lalitā – 6 – *Udyadbhānusahasrābhā* – उध्यद्बानुसहस्राभा – Her luster is equal to thousands of rising suns. The word *Sahasram* also means infinite. **Her** luster is equal to infinite (thousands) rays of rising suns. The word *Sahasram* can be attributed to 'Sun' or its 'rays'. In that case **Her** splendor can be equated to countless (thousands) number of rising Suns or countless number of rays of a rising Sun.

Viṣṇu – 486 – *Gabhastinemiḥ* – गभस्तिनेमिः – The Centre of the Supreme planetary system. The Samskrutam word '*Gabhasti*' means 'rays' and the *'nemiḥ'* means the 'spokes'. Therefore, the term indicates "One who is the hub of the wheel of light in which the spokes are His own rays of brilliancy". Astronomically, we can consider this as the Sun, the centre of the Solar system. Subjectively, He is the *Ātman*, the Self – the Effulgent Consciousness beaming out Himself to the whirls of matter (the five *koşas* – Sheaths).

122. ***Śiva*** – 858 – *Brahmakṛt* – ब्रह्मकृत् – One who created the Vedas.

Lalitā – 287 – *Nijāgyārāpanigamā* – निजाज्ञारूपनिगमा – One who has the *Vedas* as the expressions of **Her** commands. *Veda* statements command human beings with the do's and don'ts in this life what set forth the object to be attained, the means and the practical directions. These commands limit the social divisions and castes. These *Vedas* originated from *Śrī Devī* . The same meaning is said in *Kūrma Purāŋā* as; the ancient and supreme energy called *Vedas*, which are my commandments, are manifested at the beginning of creation in the form of *Rig Yajus* and *Sāman*;

Mamaivākgyā Parāśakti: *Veda Samgyā Purādanee* I
Rigyajussāma Rūpena Sargadou Sampravarttate II

Vişņu – 662 – *Brahmakṛt* – ब्रह्मकृत् – One who performs *Brahma* or tapas/ penance (austerity).

123. ***Śiva*** – 859 – *Brahmī* – ब्रह्मी – One who chants the vedas.

Lalitā – 675 – *Brāhmee* – ब्राह्मी – One who is in the form of *Sarasvatī*, the consort of *Brahma*. **She** is in the form of speech and hence can be taken as *Vāgīśvarī*. The senior most among the eight mothers. **She** shines alongwith the vehicle swan, the chanting garland (*japamālā*) and *kamaŋḍalu* (a vessel with water used by sages) in hand. **She** killed the enemies just by sprinkling the water from *kamaŋḍalu* through *darpa* grass (a sacrificial grass).

There are 8 *Prakatayoginīs* as *Matrukā Devī s*, in the middle layer of *Catusrā* (*Nūpurā*) of *Śrī Cakra*. *Brahmī* is the first among them. Each of these has 8 *yoginīs* as allied *Devī s*. Each of these 8 yoginīs has one crore as retinue. Hence the total becomes 8 x 8 = 64 crores *yoginīs*. Hence *Śrī Devī* is called as being served by these *yoginees*. *Mahācatuşśaşţikoţiyoginīgaŋasevita.*

Viṣṇu – 668 – *Brahmī* – ब्रह्मी – One Who is with Brahma. The term Brahma meaning – Austerities, *Vedas*, Truth and Knowledge-divine. One in whom is established the entities such as *tapas*, *Vedas*, mind, *prāṇa*, etc., which are parts of *Brahma* and hence called as *Brahma*.

124. ***Śiva*** – 860 – *Brahmavit* – ब्रह्मिवत् – One who understands the inner meanings of *Vedas*. *Gīta* (XV-15) says *Vedāntakṛt vedavideva cāham*.

Lalitā – The very meaning of *Veda* is to explain that the *Brahmam* has no characters like form, etc. There is no single name conveying the same meaning. But, *Śrī Devī* has been mentioned as formless, attributeless (*Guṇādītā*), etc., in many a place in *Lalitā Sahasranāma*.

Viṣṇu – 666 – *Brahmavit* – ब्रह्मिवत् – One who knows the Vedas and their real meaning.

125. ***Śiva*** – 861 – *Brāhmaṇaḥ* – ब्राह्मण: – He, in the form of a Brāhmin, imparts *Vedas* to the world.

Among the three gods *Shiva* is considered as *Brāhmin* and *Viṣŋu* as *Kṣatriya.* The Chānkokya *Upaniṣat* (VIII-14-I) says – Thou art *brāhmaṇa* among the *Devas*, I am the *brāhmaṇa* among men, (he who thinks thus) attains *Brahmam*. In the same way, the *Parāsara*, *Aditya*, *Koorma*, *Vāshishţa* and *Linga Purāŋas* also confirm this – The divine *Śambhu* the consort of *Śrī Devī* , is *Brāhmaṇa* and is the deity of *Brāhmaṇas*. A *Brāhmaṇa* especially should take refuge in *Rudra*, the Lord";

Brahmaŋo Bhagavān Śambo Brāhmanānām Hi Daivatam I
Viseśāt Brāhmano Rudram Īśānam Śaranam Vraja II

Lalitā – 661 – *Brāhmaŋī* – ब्राह्मणी – A brahmin lady. According to the *Viśva* dictionary the word *Brāhmaŋī* has many a meaning viz., harlot, a brahmin lady, a certain herbal plant, wisdom, etc. **She** is of all these forms. The *Samayācāra Smruti* says – *Brāhmaŋi* means divine wisdom crowned with the white flower (*satva*);

Brāhmanee Sveta Pushpādyā Samvitsā Devatātmika

Being consort of *Shiva*, **She** is *Brāhmanee*, because *Śiva* belongs to the *brāhmin* caste.

Viṣṇu – 667 – *Brāhmaṇaḥ* – ब्राह्मण: – One who is in the form of Brahmin instructs the whole world, saying, it is demanded so and so in the *Vedas*.

126. ***Śiva*** – 865 – *Svayaṁbhuvastigmatejasaḥ* – स्वयंभुवस्तिग्मतेजस: – One who originated himself. One who does not have source neither end – *ādianta*.

Lalitā – 850 – *Varŋaroopiŋī* – वर्णरूपिणी – The *Pāŋinīsikṣā* says, "According to the *Sāmbhava* School there are sixty-four letters, these are promulgated by *Svayambhu* (self-originated) in the *Prākṛt* or Samskrutam language"; **She** is of that form. *Varŋa* means letters. **She** is of that form.

Viṣṇu – 37 – *Svayaṁbhuḥ* – स्वयंभू: – The one who manifests Himself from Himself is considered as self-made. Everything born or produced must have a cause. The Supreme is the cause from which all effects arise and itself has no cause. This un-caused Cause-of-all, this Ultimate Cause, with reference to which everything else is considered as 'effects' is in itself the Absolute Cause. This idea is indicated by the term Self-made (*Svayambhūḥ*).

127. ***Śiva*** – 886 – *Damanaḥ* – दमन: – One who controls of evil people. Or one who smells like *davana*. Or who is worshipped with *damana*.

P.S. *Damana* or *davana* is a kind of stems of a plant green colour with a good fragrance. This is used in pujas and also stitched in garlands for colour and smell as well.

Lalitā – 743 – *Pāpāraŋyadavānalā* – पापारण्यदवानला – One who is the forest fire that burns and destroys all the sins. The forest fire consuming the forest of sin.

Viṣṇu – 190 – *Damanaḥ* – दमन: – One who restrains and controls every demonic impulse within the bosom. In the forms of the ten incarnations, He had controlled the irresistible tyrannies of the vicious against the good. In the form of pain and agitation, sorrow and death, it is He, who is the Controller, *Damanaḥ*, of all negative tendencies in everyone's Heart.

128. **Śiva** – 890 – *Paramātmāḥ* – परमात्मा: – One who is above all. *Annamaya prāṇamaya vijānamaya, ānandamayabhyaḥ pancabhyo paramebhya ātmabhyonyaḥ śaṣṭṭa ānandamātrsvarūpaḥ.*

Lalitā – 618 – *Paramā* – परमा – One who is the great in all things and all ways. **She** who limits and shows us the immeasurable *Brahmam*. The word *Parama* means "at a distance". I.e. **She** is at a distance for those who do not have devotion. If *ātma* (617th name) is considered as *Jīvātma* as a meaning, this name is *Paramātma*.

According to *Viṣŋu Purāŋa*, the Supreme Being has four forms viz., Male, Twice Born (Brahmin), Time and *Param*. **She** is of the fourth form *Param*.

Viṣṇu – 11 – *Paramātmāḥ* – परमात्मा: – The Supreme. That which transcends all limitations and imperfections of matter: in short, the Transcendental Reality. The Spirit is other than matter and that in its presence, the vestures of matter, borrowing their dynamism from Him, play their parts rhythmically at all times. This has been the ascertained unanimously in all the *Upaniṣat*s and in almost all the *Vedāntic* literatures. Śrī Ādi Śaṅkara in his *Ātmabodha* points out that the Self is other than the three bodies and that He functions in the microcosm as a king in the nation. It was also said therein that matter borrows its energy from the Spirit and continues its activity "as the world from the Sun".

Kaṭopaniṣat and the *Gīta* guide us from the outer levels of our personality, stage by stage, into the inner-most sanctum and there, the teachers declare, is He the Infinite, transcending all, reigning in His own glory. "In short, that which remains other than the cause and effect – *Māyā* and matter – is **He**, the *Paramātman*. In *Viṣṇu Purāṇa* (6.4.10.) this Supreme is glorified as *Mahā Viṣṇu* (*Paramātmā*)". In other *Purāṇas* this *Paramātmā* is mentioned as that concerned Lord(s).

129. ***Śiva*** – 920 & 921 – *Sat* – सत् & *Asat* – असत् – The *Brahmam* which is of the form only truth. Or the one which is the cause of everything.

In *Śrī Rudra Triśatī Nāmāvalī* also we have 38th name as *Satvanām Pataye Namaḥ*.

Lalitā – 661 – *Sadasadrūpadhāriṇī* – सदसद्रूपधारिणी – One who is the form of being and non-being.

Sat is eternal and *asat* is impermanent. Both are the forms of *Śrī Devī* only. *Sat* is *Brahmam*, which is eternal and the *asat* is the universe which originated from *sat* and is destructible. **She** is in the form of this universe and hence impermanent. It does not mean that it is not available from the root. All activities are till the beginning of the universe only. The form of *Brahmam* is also herself. Hence this combined name.

When seen from the angle of the soul **She** is split into two both *sat* and *asat*. But seen from **Her** both are same – *sat* only. *Skanda Purāṇa* says;

Yatyatasti Tayā Bhātiyannāsti Tayabhi Cha I
Tat Tat Sarvam Mahādeva Māyayā Parikalpitam II

Māṇickavācakar says in Tamil; *Unmaiyumāi Inmaiyumai* – Both as truth and untruth.

Aruṇagirinadar also says in Tamil; *Ulatāi Ilatāi* – Both existent and not existent.

Ṛg Veda (VII-104-12) says, "Out of *Sat* and *Asat*, *Śiva* with *Umā* protects the *Sat* and destroys *Asat*";

Sacchāsaccha Vacasī Pasprghāte I
Tayoryassatyam Yataradṛ Jīyastaditsomovati Hantyāsat II

Viṣṇu – 478 & 479 – *Sat* – सत् & *Asat* – असत् – The Existence in all things and beings is the same ever and it is all-pervading. The Sun exists; the space between the sun and the earth exists; the ocean and the creatures therein exist; the physiological organs and their functions, mind and its activities, the intellect and its agitations -all exist. This ever-present principle of existence is *Śrī Nārāyaṇa*. That which remains the same without any change in and through all changes, unaffected ever, same in the past, present and the future is called in *Vedānta* as *'Satya'*. One who has all these natures is called *Sat-Puruṣa*. In the *Upaniṣats*, the Supreme *Brahmam* is indicated as *'Satya'* – "This, indeed was *Sat*". In *Gīta* while describing the changeless factor behind the eternally changing matter, Bhagavān says; "That which is the all-pervading in this world, that alone is indestructible and no one can destroy it".

Asat is the Conditioned; Limited; the One who appears at this moment as the limited, conditioned and therefore confined only to the world of plurality. That which actually is not, but apparently seems to be there, is called a delusion and this is indicated by the word *'Asat'*. In the *Vedāntic* terminology, higher-Self (*Param*) is ever Immutable and Eternal, while the lower-Self (*Aparam*) constituted of all the universe of manifested things and beings, is mutable and ephemeral. *Śrī Nārāyaṇa* Himself is, in His *Apara* nature, expressing as the world of the many that we today recognise around us. *Bhagavān* confesses to Arjuna in *Gīta*; Arjuna! I am at once immortality and mortality. I am both existence and non-existence".

As the *Aparabrahmam* has manifested as the world He is called *asat* (not having reality). *Cāndokya Upaniṣat* (6.1.4) says – the manifest exists only in name as a mere play of words; *Vacārambhāṇam vikāro nāmadheyam*

130. ***Śiva*** – 925 & 1006 – *Mātāḥ* – माता: & *Śrīmān* – श्रीमान् – One who is in the form of a mother to all. When compared to father mother will have more affection to the children. Also children will be freer with mother than with father. Hence Lord takes mother form to bestow his full compassion.

One who has *yoga aiśwarya* and who bestows *aiśwarya* to devotees.

Lalitā – 1, 457 & 934 – *Śrīmātā* – श्रीमाता, *Mātā* – माता & *Viśvamātā* – विश्वमाता – One who is the form of a mother. The supreme mother. Since *Śree Devee* is the mother of this entire universe, **She** is *Māta.* When we are in deep trouble, the first word uttered by us involuntarily is *Ma.* Human beings are afflicted by three kinds of *Tapas* (difficulties), which cannot be solved by the mother in her human form. The possession of the power to resolve these difficulties makes **Her** the "Superior Mother". Worshipping **Her**, who has given birth to the whole world, will prevent birth again in this world from the mother's womb. The best of love is mother's affection. Hence to contemplate and worship **Her** as the mother will give us proximity to Her.

Śrī means *Lakşmī* (goddess of wealth). Hence *Śrīmātā* means *Lakşmī's* mother. *Śrī* also means *Saraswathī* (goddess of learning). **She** is mother of both *Lakşmī* and *Saraswathī.*

Mā means 'to measure'. *Śrīmātā* therefore means that **She** is capable of measuring wealth. One that measures is superior to the one that is measured. *Ma* also be interpreted to mean one who 'distributes' or 'classifies'. **She** is the one who classified the *Vedas*. From this angle, *Śrī Devī* can also be indicated as *Brahma* and/ or *Vyasa. "Rico Yajumśi Sāmāni Sāhi Śrīḥ Amŗtā Sadām"* – when interpreted in the manner this name is masculine. The prefix *Śrī* is used to refer respectable men or objects – for instance *Śrī Cakra, Śrī Vidyā, Śrī Sailam*, etc. Thus **She** is aptly called as *Śrīmātā*, as **She** is the mother of the whole world. Moreover, the word *Śrī* is itself auspicious. Is it not, hence, appropriate to commence this series of thousand names with *Śrī*?

Mother here also indicates that **She** has given birth to the entire universe. It indicates one of the three main functions of the Supreme Being viz. creation. *Vedās* also reflect the same sense in *Yato Vā Imanī Bhūtānī Jāyantī.*

In *Saptashatee* also we read

Yā Devī Sarvabhūteśu Mātru Rūpeṇa Samstitā I
Namastasyai Namastasyai Namastasyai Namo Namaḥ II (V-71)

One who is the mother of the universe. This has been accepted by all right from *Mūlaprakŗti* till the creation of this universe.

Vişņu – 22 – *Śrīmān* – श्रीमान् – One who is always with *Śrī* (*mān*). *Śrī* is Mother *Lakşmī.* In the *Purānic* terminologies *Lakşmī* stands for all powers, all faculties. The total manifested power potential in the Omnipotent is *Lakşmī*. These powers are ever in Him and therefore, He is the *Śrīmān*.

Viśva means *Vişŋu*. The very first name of *Vişŋu Sahasranāma* is *Viśva*.

131. ***Śiva*** – 923 – *Avyaktaḥ* – अव्यक्त: – One who cannot be identified as this or that with any character or parameter. One who can be accessed with focused devotion;

Na vividena rūpeṇa eti prāpnotyenam sātaka iti avyaya: ekāgracitta prāpyaḥ

Lalitā – 398 – *Avyaktā* – अव्यक्ता – One who is not visibly seen – is in an un-manifested state. When the Brahmam (*Vicikīrşā*) feels to create, the form taken by it on account of *māyā* (illusion) is called *Avyaktam*. It is said in the *Samkhyasaptami* that is the *avyakta* which is subtle, without characteristics, inanimate, without beginning or end, capable of production, without parts, one and universal;

Sūkşmam Alingam Acetanam Anāḍinidanam Tathā Prasavadharmi
Niravayavam Ekameva Hi Sādhāranam Etat Avyaktam II

Virūpākşa Pancaśikhā also says, *Pradhāna*, say the wise, is the *avyakta*, which is without beginning or middle, beyond *mahat* and permanent. It is the collective form of the three qualities;

Anāḍimadhyam Mahata: *Param Dhṛvam* I
Pradhānam Avyaktam Uşanti Śūrāya: II

The *Samkhya Sūtra* (VI-39) says, *Satva* and the rest are not qualities of that *Brahmam*, because they are the qualities of that *avyakta*;

Sattvādeenāmetaddharmatvam Tadrūpatvāt

By the word *Avyakta* the *Brahmam* is indicated. In *Brahma Sūtra* (III-2-23) it is said, that *Brahmam* is *avyakta* for the scriptures say so; *Tadavyaktamāha Hi. Śrī Ādi Śaṇkara* explains this with the following *Veda* statements – *Muŋḍaka Upanişat* (III-1-8), He is not to be felt by the eyes, nor by the speech, nor by the other senses, nor by penance, nor by actions;

Nachakshushā Gruhyate Nāpi Vāchā Nanyaidevais Tapasā Karmanā Va.

Further this has been evidenced through *Brahāraŋya Upanişat* (III-9-26), *Muŋḍaka Upanişat* (II-1-6) and *Taitreeya Upansihad* (II-7-1).

The *Linga Purāŋa* says that *avyakta* means *Vişŋu*. The names of *Vişŋu*, who is ever capable of creation, are *Pradhāna, Avyaya, Yoni* (origin), *Avyakta, Prakruti* and *Tamas*. This name stresses that *Śrī Devī* is in the form of *Vişŋu*.

Pradhānamavyayam Yoni: *Avyaktam Prakrutis Tama*: I
Vishnoretāni Nāmāni Nityam Prabhava Dharmina: II

Vişņu – 305 & 722 – *Vyaktarūpaḥ* – व्यक्तरूप & *Avyaktaḥ* – अव्यक्त: – One who cannot be clearly described as 'this' even though he has many forms.

His gross form as universe can be clearly perceived. It need not be mentioned that this is opposite to the meaning of *Avyakta*.

Gīta (II-25) also – this *ātman* is said to be unmanifested, unthinkable and immutable. Therefore, knowing it as such you should not grieve;

Avyakto'yamachintyo'yam Avikāryo'yamuchyate I
Tasmādevam Viditvainam Nanushochitumarhasi II

132. ***Śiva*** – 931 – *Nirvāṇaḥ* – निर्वाण: – One who is in the form of liberation (*Mokşa*). Actually he is the path to reach liberation and he himself is *Mokşa*. He is both *Upāya* and *Upeya*.

Lalitā – 390 – *Nirvāŋasukhadāyinī* – निर्वाणसुखदायिनी – One who confers the bliss of *nirvāna*.

Vāna (or *bāna*) means body; *Prasna Upanişat* (II-2) says; *Etad Bānamavaśţambhya* - Holding this bow (body) and in the word *Gīrvāṇa* by *Mimāmsakas* this word has been used in the same sense as body. Also in *Amarakośa*, for the word *Bāna* two meanings, body and bow, are given. Hence *nirvāna* means without body. That is the meaning of this name is – **She** offers bliss indescribable by words to **Her** devotees.

In *Kūrma Purāŋa* – *Śrī Devī* says to *Himavān*; if you neglect me, Oh King of mountains! you cannot attain the pure rest of the supreme *nirvāna*, hence seek refuge in me;

Mām Anādrutya Paramam Nirvāṇam Amalam Padam I
Prapyate Nahi Śailendra Tato Mām Śaraṇam Vraja II

Viṣṇu – 577 – *Nirvāṇam* – निर्वाणम् – The Lord is of the very nature of "ever-liberated and ever-free". There is no trace of imperfection and sorrow in Him whose nature is, All-Bliss.

The *Gīta* (V-24 & 25) says; He whose happiness is within, whose delight is within, whose illumination is within only, that yogi becomes *Brahmam* and gains the beatitude of *Brahmam*. With sins destroyed, doubts removed, minds disciplined, being delighted in the welfare of all beings, the sages attain the beatitude of *Brahmam*.

Yo'ntaḥ Sukho'ntarārāmastathāntajyortireva Yaḥ I
Sa Yogi Brahmaŋirvānam Brahmabhūto'dhigacchati II
Labhante Brahmaŋirvānamṛdhayaḥ Kṣīṇakalmaśāḥ I
Cinnadvaidhā Yatātmānaḥ Sarvabhūtahite Ratā: II

133. ***Śiva*** – 951 & 997 – *Acintyaḥ* – अचिन्त्य: & *Acintyayaḥ* – अचिन्त्यय: – Who is beyond *upāsana* or meditation or worship. *Kenopaniṣat* says; *"Tadeve Brahmatvam vitthi netam tatitamupāsate"*.

Lalitā – 554 – *Achintyarūpā* – अचिन्त्यरूपा – One who is of unthinkable form or inaccessible to mind. Because **She** is free from connection with the qualities, **Her** nature is unthinkable. 139th name *Nirguŋā* and 415th name *Manovāchāmagocharā* may also be referred.

Viṣṇu – 832 – *Acintyaḥ* – अचिन्त्य: – One who is not determinable by any criteria or parameter of knowledge, being himself the witnessing Self certifying all knowledge. Or one who, being transcendent, cannot be subject to though.

134. ***Śiva*** – 955 – *Trivikramaḥ* – त्रिविक्रम: – One who pervades all the three worlds. Or who is in the form of *Vāmana* incarnation of *Viṣṇu*.

Lalitā – 626 & 627 – *Tripurā* – त्रिपुरा & *Trijagadvandyā* – त्रिजगद्वन्द्या – One who is elder to the three Gods viz., *Brahma, Viṣṇu* and *Rudra*. **She** takes three forms as *Brahma, Viṣṇu* and *Rudra* to do the three tasks viz., creation, protection and destruction. Hence **She** is elder or senior to these three gods;

Mūrtitrāyasyāpi Purātanatvāt Tatambikāyās Tripuretināma.

One who is worshipped by all the three worlds. Or one who is worshipped in all the three worlds.

Viṣṇu – 530 – *Trivikramaḥ* – त्रिविक्रमः – One who has taken the three steps. One who has, in three steps, conquered the three worlds in his *Vāmana* incarnation. The spiritual seeker has only to take three steps to reach the Centre of the Self in him-self. Once he has stepped across the fields-of-experiences in the waking, dream and deep-sleep conditions, he has reached the Infinite Consciousness, the Atman. The very term *'Tri'* in Samskrutam means 'the three-worlds'. *Harivamsa* says – The greatest men of reflection have declared the three fields-of-experiences (*Loka*) by the simple term 'Tri'.

135. ***Śiva*** – 957 – *Virajaḥ* – विरजः – One who is blemish-less.

Lalitā – 779 – *Virajā* – विरजा – One who is without any stain or sin originated by the *Rajo* character. When such meaning is said, the prefix *'Vi'* has to be taken in the opposite sense – i.e. without the character called *Rajo*.

The verses of *Mahānārāyaṇopaniṣat* (20th chapter) may be compared here;

Virajā Vipāpma...

The word *Rajas* means splendour, water and world. While accepting these meanings the prefix *'Vi'* has to be specifically considered.

Viṣṇu – 396 – *Virajaḥ* – विरजः – Passionless. One who is not associated with the agitations (*Rajas*) of the mind. The mind gets agitated when it identifies with the sense-objects of the world outside. The Atman, the Self, in its Pure Nature, has no such identifications and, therefore, He is recognised as 'passionless'.

136. ***Śiva*** – 967 – *Sūkşmaḥ* – सूक्ष्मः – One who is in subtle form. One who has minute knowledge. One who is difficult to understand. *Māndukya Upansişad* says – *Adṛśṭa mavyavahārya magrāhya malakşaṇa macintya mavyapadeśya megātma pratyayasāram śāntam śiva madvaitam*.

Lalitā – 467 – *Sūkşmarūpiṇī* – सूक्ष्मरूपिणी – One who has a very subtle, not to be easily be recognised, form. *Kaivalyopanişat* (16) says – it is subtler than the subtle and eternal; *Sūkşmāt Sūkşmataram Nityam*. *Kaţopanishad* (II-20) says – it is subtler than an atom; *Anoranīyān*.

The sacrificial fire done in the fire at *Kunḍalinī*, in the midst of *Mūladāram*, is subtle. It is called *Rahoyāgam*. This indicates, in the *Navāvarṇa Pūja*, after establishing the vessels through *mantras*, offering special *argyās*, offering prayers to teacher, the following are offered as oblations in the fire of *Kunḍalinī*; virtues, sins, decisions, indecisions, justice, injustice, actions and inactions. This *homa* (sacrificial fire) is explained in *Tantra Rāja Tantra* in verses starting from *Nityā Nityodite* ending with *Evam Dvādaśadhā Homamakşaraiḥ Syādudhīritaiḥ*. **She** is in the form of that *homa*.

Vişṇu – 457 – *Sūkṣmaḥ* – सूक्ष्मः – One who is subtler than the subtlest. In Vedanta terminology subtlety indicates pervasiveness. Therefore, the term means All-Pervasive. *Muṇḍakopanişat* (I-1-6) says that the Lord is all-pervading, subtler than the subtlest – *Sarvagatam susūkşmam*.

Śrī Ādi Śaṇkara in his commentary mentions as; the ether and all are material causes. Since there is no material cause like sound, etc., he is subtle.

137. ***Śiva*** – 976 – *Kāntaḥ* – कान्तः – One who is the border or limit of the supreme bliss – *kasya sukhasya antaḥ sīmā ānantasya parākāşṭedyarttaḥ*

Lalitā – 329 – *Kāntā* – कान्ता – One who is beautiful. Since **She** is effulgent, **She** is looks like the Ultimate beauty. The luster is the beauty and brightness of the body. *Kam* – *Brahmam. Anta* – final. Unconditioned *Brahmam* is her final form.

The presiding deity of the eleventh night of the dark fortnight of the lunar month is called *Kānta.* **She** is in that form. **She** is in the form of all the presiding deities of all the days and nights and hence this is very apt.

Viṣṇu – 296 & 654 – *Kāntaḥ* – कान्तः – One who is of enchanting form. Infinite Beauty is the very nature of the Self and the *Upaniṣats* define the Self as *Śāntam Śivam Sundaram*.

The aestheticism in man craves for harmony and where we experience the greatest of harmony, there we detect the presence of beauty. In front of beauty, the entire personality of an intelligent man becomes calm and peaceful, hushed in silence, transported to ecstasy. These are moments when the meditator has transcended his Sheaths and is in union with the Pure Self. Naturally therefore, the pure personality of an intelligent man becomes calm and peaceful. Self is indicated here as *Kāntaḥ* - Divine Auspicious form of Absolute Beauty. Of Enchanting-Form; 'Supremely-Handsome'; the "Beauty of Beauty itself". In all His Incarnations we find Him described as extremely charming with His Grace and Beauty. In Samskrutam the term *Kaḥ* means the Creator, *Brahma*. In this sense, therefore, *Kāntaḥ* can suggest "One Who destroys even the Creator during the dissolution".

138. ***Śiva*** – 984 – *Nirāmayaḥ* – निरामयः – One who does not do any mistake or error. He has nothing wrong in him. *Nirdośaḥ*

Lalitā – 876 – *Nirāmayā* – निरामया – One who is free from all ailments. Sickness affects both body and mind. **She** is without any disease. Since **She** is the medicine for all the diseases, how can any disease affect **Her**?

Viṣṇu – 689 – *Anāmayaḥ* – अनामयः – One who has neither the mental or physical diseases. Of pure unstained divine essence is his nature. He is not involved in karmas, thus the resultant of the karmas which visit us in terms of mental restlessness or physical pangs, never touch Him.

139. ***Śiva*** – 998 – *Satyavrataḥ* – सत्यव्रतः – One who has *satya* as vow. *Satyam* is *brahmam*. The penance or vow to reach *Brahmam* is *Śiva*. *Satyam brahma tatarttānyeva vratāni tapāmsi yasya*.

Śiva Sūtra (III-27) says developing the body is a *vrata* (vow). This indicates that maintaining the body without any disease and nourishing it is a *vrata*. A commentator of this says; protecting the body which is filled with the nectar in the form of devotion to *Shiva* is a vow. This has to be definitely followed. There cannot be carelessness on this;

Śivabhaktisudhāpūrṇe Śarīre Vruttirasya Yā I
Vratametatanuśteyam Na Tuccham Taccha Dhāranam II

Lalitā – 817 – *Satyavratā* – सत्यव्रता – One who is vowed to truth. A *vrata* (vow) is a self-imposed control to reach a goal. That is to bring the thought, speech and action under control. **She** has the truth itself as **Her** vow.

She is attainable by following the vow to speak and follow the truth.

The truth indicates *Brahmam*. *Vrata* (vow) is, some places, used on edible things. For instance, in *Sruti* statement; *Payovratam Brāhmanasya* – the word *vrata* indicates eatables. Hence, like eatables, **She** has liking on *Brahmam*. *Satyam* (truth) also indicates low hanging fruits (which gives faster results). That is, the vows on **Her** give quick results. For instance, *Śrīmad Viṣṇu Bhāgavatam* (X-22) says, the vow followed by *Gopika* ladies to marry *Śrī Kriṣṇa*, followed the *Kātyāyanee Vrata*.

Śrī Bhagavān, in his incarnation as *Śrī Rāma – Śreemad Rāmāyanam* (VI-18-33, 34) says; *Sakrudeva Prapannāya Tavvsmīti Ca Yācate* I
Abhayam Sarvadā Tasmai Dadāmyetadvratam Mama II

Like this **She** has very great and interpretable vows. (There are some variations in this verse in South India). For the sake of devotion on *Śree Devee*, such a vow is a must and truth. Hence **She** is *Satyavrata.*

Paṭṭotpalar also preys in this regard, "let this body, nourished by the devotion called nectar, be there for a long time for your adoration sake";

Antarullasita Svacchaśakti Pīyūśa Pośitam I
Bhavatpūjopabhoghāya Śarīramidamastu Me II

In *Devī Bhāgavatam* (book 3), *Satyavrata* was earlier an idiot that he shouted loudly '*I*', '*I*' when he was scared of the forest pig. This shouting was treated as *'Im'* without the *bīja* sound *'M'*. He later became a very big poet by the compassion of *Śrī Devī*. This is described in *Lagustuti* also. It can also be said that **She** is no different from that *Satyavrata*.

Viṣṇu – 106 – *Satyaḥ* – सत्य: – He is the Real. The term *Satyam* used in philosophy has a special connotation. That which remains the same in all the three periods of time is called *Satyam*. That which seemingly exists, but which never was nor shall ever be, is considered as a false delusion, *Asatya*. He who remains the same, before the creation, during the existence and even after the dissolution, is the Infinite Truth, *Satyaḥ*. The *Taitrīya Upaniṣat* (2-1) thunders that the Eternal Truth is "Truth, Knowledge, Bliss": *"Satyam, Jnānam, Anantam Brahma"*.

Commonalities between *Lalitā* and *Viṣṇu Sahasranāmas* only

140. ***Lalitā*** – 121 – *Bhayāpahā* – भयापहा – One who dispels all fears. **She** drives away all the fears from water and earth. Hence *Bhayāpaha. Veda* says – One who has reached eternal bliss knows no fear.

Ānandam Brahmaṇo Vidwan Na Bhibheti Kutascana

In the *Vāyu Purāṇa* also it is mentioned that when frightened the very thought of *Śrī Devī* alleviates all fears.

Viṣṇu – 834 & 935 – *Bhayanāshana*: – भयनाशन: & *Bhayāpaha*: – भयापह: – Destroyer of all fear, is the Supreme Lord. The *Upaniṣats* repeatedly – declare the State of Self-Knowledge to be the only state of absolute fearlessness. From a sense of otherness or plurality alone can fear spring forth. In the One Reality, where there is no other, how can there be fear? *Śrī Nārāyaṇa* alone is the only harbour from all fears.

One who removes all fear in the *samsāric* life. Naturally, Lord *Nārāyaṇa* is the one sure harbour wherein the boats of life, tossed mercilessly on the high seas of passions, can find their calm of peace and total security.

Śrī Ādi Śaṇkara says – One who relieves the fear of cycle of birth and death. **He** destroys the fear for those who do follow the convention of caste and *ashramas*.

141. **Lalitā** – 122 – *Shāmbhavī* – शाम्भवी – Consort of *Shambu*. Mother of devotees of Lord *Shiva*.

Vişņu – 38 – *Śambhuḥ* – शंभुः – He who brings Auspiciousness – both inner goodness and outer prosperity to His devotees. *Śambhuḥ* is one of the famous names of Lord Siva. By using this term in invoking *Viśṇu*, by its suggestion, it declares that *Viśṇu* and *Śiva* are not two Divine Entities, but they are both manifestations of the One Essential Reality.

Śrī Ādi Śaṇkara says – One who gives comfort to the devotees is *Śambhu*.

142. **Lalitā** – 124 – *Śarvāŋī* – शर्वाणी – Consort of Lord *Paramaśiva*. One of the eight forms of Lord *Paramaśiva* is earth. His consort is *Sukesī*. Their son is *Angārakā* (Mars).

Vişņu – 26 – *Śarvaḥ* – शर्वः – The Auspicious One – meaning, the One who gives auspiciousness to those who hear of Him, to those who have a vision of Him and to those who meditate upon Him.

Śrī Ādi Śaṇkara in writes that he destroys all the living beings during the great dissolution of the universe (*Pralaya* period).

143. **Lalitā** – 127 – *Śrīkarī* – श्रीकरी – One who gives prosperity. For the word *Śrī* many a meaning has been provided like; prosperity, wealth, goddess *Lakşmī*, auspiciousness, splendour, , beauty, luster, etc.

Vişņu – 611 – *Śrīkaraḥ* – विष्णुः – One who confers Śrī upon His devotees who remember Him continuously, reflect upon His nature and meditate upon His Glories. *Śrī Ādi Śaṇkara* interprets this as – one who gives affluence to the devotees.

144. **Lalitā** – 139 – *Nirguŋā* – निर्गुणा – One who is beyond the three characters – *Guŋas*. In *Svetāsvatara Upanişat* (VI-11) we read *Sākşī Cetā Kevalo Nirguŋasca* – Witness, the philosopher, one who is uncontaminated and who is free from attributes. This has been explained in *Matsya* and *Padma purānās*. The traits of *Devas* are their identities;

characters are related to bodies. Since *Śrī Devī* is in the form of *Chit*, **She** has no attributes neither identity.

Viṣṇu – 840 – *Nirguṇā* – निर्गुणा – Without any attributes. That which has property/ attribute is matter perishable, changeable and finite. The Imperishable, the Changeless and the Infinite is property-less; it is the Consciousness that illuminates all properties (*Guṇas*). With the matter equipments, in His Incarnations He manifests as having 'form' (*Guṇabhṛt*) and in His Absolute Nature He is 'form-less'-the Non-dual Self. *Śrī Ādi Śaṇkara* quotes the same verse from *Vedas* and gives the same meaning.

145. ***Lalitā*** – 167 – *Pāpanāśinī* – पापनाशिनी – One who destroys the sins of devotees. By the repetition of Her *mantra*, etc., **She** destroys the sins of devotees.

In *Cāndokya Upaniṣat* (IV–24–3) says; *Yateśikā Tūlamagnou Pradūyataiva Mevāsya Papmanaḥ Pradūyante* – Like the point of reed in the fire, so all the sins are burnt up.

Viṣṇu – 924 & 992 – *Duśkṛtihā* & *Pāpanāśanaḥ* says – He destroys the bad act of sin or one who does sinful acts. *Kṛti* means actions; *Duśkṛti* means bad actions. When actions are undertaken, prompted by sensuous desires, they leave impressions (*vāsanās*) and these always have a tendency to make us repeat similar actions. When one turns the mind towards Nārāyaṇa, the Self, he is emptied of his existing *vāsanās*, so Lord is indicated as the destroyer (*Hā*) of the sins.

Meditating upon whom, all *vāsanās* (sins) are liquidated. When the individuals, surrendering in love to Him, acts and fulfils his duties, all his existing *vāsanās* are destroyed and no new ones are created –this is the very root in the theory of *Karma Yoga* in the *Vedas*. Through meditation upon the self, all sins are dissolved and totally removed.

Śrī Ādi Śaṇkara in his commentary says that **he** destroys the sins in bunches, of those people, who sings hymns in praise of him, or worship him or meditate upon him or just remember him.

146. ***Lalitā*** – 200 – *Sarvamangalā* – सर्वमंगला – One who is the source of all that is auspicious. **She** is the root of all those. Or, *Sarvamangala* is a *Thiti Nityā Devī*. Hence it can be inferred that this name indicates the *Praṇavā* (in the *mantra* of *Sarva mangalā*) sound (*Om*).

Viṣṇu – 63 – *Maṇgalamparam* – मङ्गलंपरं – *Mangalam* is that which not only removes the dark pains of evil, but brings the bright joys of merit. *Param Mangalam* is Supreme *Mangalam* and it can be none other than He, by whose mere remembrance all inauspiciousness gets lifted up and all Auspiciousness comes to flood our hearts. The *Upaniṣat* declares - "May That *Brahmam* who removes all inauspiciousness in man and gives man all auspiciousness, by a mere remembrance of Him, give us all auspiciousness.

While chanting *Viṣŋu Sahasranāma* in the initial parts, we recite *Mangalānām Mangalam* – he is the most auspicious among auspicious things.

147. ***Lalitā*** – 201 – *Sadgatipradā* – सद्गतिप्रदा – One who leads along the path of salvation. The word *sadgati* means all stages from heaven to *mokṣa* as per our wish. **She** who gives various stages of liberation as per eligibility. *Gati* – goal. Heaven and *moksa* are attainable goals by two ways. *Śrī Devī* guides to reach the goals easily.

Gati – wisdom; *Śrī Devī* gives good knowledge. *Gati* – way to reach; *Śrī Devī* enlightens good path. *Sat* – eternal absolute. *Śrī Devī* provides the path to reach it (path to knowledge). *Satgati* means the path followed by good people. *Śrī Devī* enables us to reach the good place.

Sat – **She** is the *Sat*. *Gati* – the goal to reach is also Herself. I.e. **She** is the path and the goal.

Viṣṇu – 699 – *Sadgatiḥ* – सद्गतिः – The goal of good and noble seekers. Lord *Nārāyaṇa* is the Spiritual Goal to be reached. "The Good" here means those who know the existence of Brahmam, for the *Upaniṣat* says: "If a person knows that *Brahmam* exists, then the wise call him good. Śrī Ādi Śaṇkara, says;

(i) He who can be reached by those who understands that the *Brahmam* is the truth.
(ii) He has elegant, best *Gati* – knowledge.

148. ***Lalitā*** – 267 – *Govindarūpiṇī* – गोविन्दरूपिणी – One who is in the form of *Govinda* that is, *Viṣṇu.* The protector of the universe *Viṣṇu*, who predominantly has *Satva* character, is also in the form of *Śrī Devī* only.

Go – speech. *Govinda* – who can be understood by it (speech). The Supreme Being is beyond reach by speech. Since *Govinda* has taken the protection task, once he hears the crying of the soul, he immediately appears to him.

Go – earth. Once the creation of the universe is complete the earth, on account of overweight it became unstable and started to sub–merge in the water. *Viṣṇu* bore it. Also when *Hiranyākṣa*, the demon, seized the earth *Viṣṇu* only protected it from him. Hence among all the names of *Viṣṇu*, the name *Govinda* stresses the task of protection. *Śrī Devī* herself is in the form of *Govinda*.

Viṣṇu – 187 & 539 – *Govindaḥ* – गोविन्दः – The word *Go* in Samskrutam has four meanings: 'Earth', 'Cow', 'Speech' and *'Vedas'*. As the earth is the supporter of everything that is existing, He, who is the supporter of everything within the individual, is called *Govinda*; He, who is the Protector of the Cow's and played the part of *Gopāla* in Gokula, is the very controller of the animal instincts and passions in the bosom of man.

Kenopaniṣat says – One, without whom, no speech can ever emerge out of any throat-He being the very Life in all Creatures and the Highest Speech is the declaration of Truth in the *Vedas*. The Lord Himself is the very Theme and the Author of the Vedas. This great Self is *Mahāviṣṇu*. *Śrī Ādi Śaṇkara* mentions;

1. Since he bore and takes out the earth that is being destructed, he is *Govinda*.
2. Head of cows.
3. One who makes speech to him.
4. One who can be reached through languages (*Gobhiḥ*)

5. One who understands the souls through the statements of *Vedānta*.

149. ***Lalitā*** – 271 – *Ĕśvarī* – ईश्वरी – One who is in the form of *Ĕśvar*. One who does the fourth task called *Tirodhāna* is *Ĕśvar*, completely in the form *satva* quality. *Śrī Devī* is in this form.

The quality of *Esvara* is Lordship, activity, independence, conscious ness, etc. Since *Śrī Devī* is with all these qualities, **She** is called *Ĕśvari*.

Viṣṇu – 36 – *Ĕśvaraḥ* – ईश्वर: – One who has the ability to do anything without the help of other beings or things is called *Ĕśvara*. *Śrī Ādi Śaṇkara* mentions; one who has all the wealth without being affected by any type of sorrows (natural rule).

150. ***Lalitā*** – 279 – *Bhagavatī* – भगवती – One who is with prosperity. As **She** knows the origin and dissolution, the going and coming of beings, knowledge and ignorance, **She** is called *Bhagavatī*.

Viṣṇu – 558 – *Bhagavān* – भगवान् – The word *Bhaga*, according to the *Viṣṇu Purāṇa* means, "One who has all the Six Great Glories – Wealth, Power, *Dharma*, Fame, Character, Knowledge and Dispassion –is called *Bhagavān*". Again, *Viṣṇu Purāṇa* says "He is named *Bhagavān* who knows (a) the beginning and the end, (b) the arrival and departure of beings and also (c) *Vidyā* and *Avidyā*". One who has all the six glorious in himself alone in *Bhagavān* and these great mighty power atomically come to Him, because his equipment is the Total-mind. *Śrī Ādi Śaṇkara,* quotes the verse with the meaning below and says that one who has all these is called *Bhagavān*. *Bhaga* means complete wealth, charity, glory, richness, relinquishment and liberation from all the bondage. He has all these and hence *Bhagavān*; or he knows everything about the living beings like birth, death, destruction, movement, knowledge, ignorance, etc., hence *Bhagavān*.

151. ***Lalitā*** – 283 – *Sahasrākṣī* – सहस्राक्षी – One who has countless eyes.

Viṣṇu – 226 – *Sahasrākṣaḥ* – सहस्राक्ष: – One who has many (thousands of) eyes. In describing the macro-cosmic form of the Lord we have an endorsement of this declaration in *Gīta*.

152. ***Lalitā*** – 374 – *Kṛtagyā* – कृतज्ञा – One who knows all that is done. **She** knows all the actions done by those who live in this world. The Sun, the Moon, the god of death (*yama*), time and the five elements, these nine are the witnesses of good and bad actions. Only *Śrī Devī* is in all these nine forms.

Kṛta – done (good) actions, *Gnā* – knowledge (gives as a reward). **She** does this with gratitude.

Kṛta (*vat*) – **She** possess already available (self–acquired) knowledge.This expression is that **She** always conquers when **She** casts the dice with *Śiva*.

Viṣṇu – 82 – *Kṛtagnaḥ* – कृतज्ञ: – He who knows all that is done by all: the One Knower who knows all physical activities, all emotional feelings and all intellectual thoughts and motives. He illumines them all, in all, at all times. Hence He is called *Kṛtagna*. *Viṣṇu* is the One who knows clearly the exact depth of sincerity, the true ardency of devotion, the real amount of purity in the bosom of all his devotees, and, accordingly, brings joy and bliss to their hearts.

Śrī Ādi Śaṇkara says – he who knows the sins and virtues of the living beings.

153. ***Lalitā*** – 377 – *Jayā* – जया – One who is with the name *Jaya*. According to the *Padma Purāṇa, Jayā* is the deity worshipped in the *Varāha* Mountain.

Jayā – victory. **She** is in that form. In the *Śilpaśāstra* (science of sculpture), mention is made about a house by name *Jaya.* **She** is in that form.

According to *Kaṭapayādhi* numbering system *Jaya* is equated to the number Eighteen. Some schools mention this comparing with that of 18 days *Kuruśetra* battle, *Gīta* having 18 chapters and so on.

Viṣṇu – 509 – *Jayaḥ* – जयः – The Victorious. One who has conquered all the matter. It connotes that in order to experience the 'Self' we have to conquer all the lower matter-realms and their by-products. Realizing the Self, the seeker himself becomes the Self. At that time he has conquered all.

Śrī Ādi Śaṇkara comments – one who is victorious of all the living beings.

154. ***Lalitā*** – 383 – *Sadyaḥ Prasādinī* – सद्यः प्रसादिनी – One who immediately bestows Her grace. Made pleased by the secret method and *Rahaḥtarpaŋam*. *Śrī Devī* right away bestows Her blessings to the devotees.

In the same fashion, *Paramaśiva* also gets pleased early – *Āśutośi.* This has been mentioned in the 88th chapter, *Uttarārttam,* 10th *Kāndam* of *Śrīmad Bhāgavatam*.

Viṣṇu – 905 – *Svastidakṣiṇa* – स्वस्तिदक्षिणः – Lord is ever engaged in smartly distributing Auspiciousness. The word *Dakşiṇā* has, apart from the meaning of 'gift', also has another meaning: "One who is efficient and quick". Therefore, the term indicates that *Śrī Nārāyaṇa* quickly and efficiently will reach His sincere seekers to give them the experience of auspiciousness which is the Lord's very nature.

Śrī Ādi Śaṇkara says – *Swasti Dakşiŋaḥ* has three meanings; one among them is "He has the capability to bestow fortunes early".

155. ***Lalitā*** – 396 – *Parameśvarī* – परमेश्वरी – One who is the Sovereign Supreme. **She** is the *Ĕśvari,* the *śakti* of the universal absolute.

Viṣṇu – 377 – *Parameśvaraḥ* – परमेश्वरः – The Supreme (*Parama*) Lord (*Ēśvara*). The fanatics generally interpret the word to mean as "the only Lord", in the sense that all other concepts of God are wrong. The large-hearted, tolerant Rishis of old, could have never meant such a meaning. It could only mean "that He is the Supreme Consciousness whose expressions are all the deities". The term *Ēśvara* indicates both might and glory. Therefore, Parameśvara means "One who is Omnipotent and All-glorious".

Śrī Ādi Śaṇkara in his commentary of *Viṣŋu Sahasranāma* for the 377th name – *Parameśvaraḥ* – he is *Parameśvaraḥ* since he has great wealth and supreme ruling power.

156. ***Lalitā*** – 807 – *Parandhāma* – परंधाम – One who is in the form of Supreme abode above all. Here the word *Dhāma* has many a meaning viz., lustre, dwelling place, state (state of mind, etc.). All these meanings fit Her.

Viṣṇu – 719 – *Dīptamūrtiḥ* – दीप्तमूर्तिः – Of the Resplendent Form. As Consciousness, He is never bright and fully effulgent illuming all experiences at all times. *Sanjaya* reports in Mahābhārata – If the splendour of a thousand Suns were to blaze out at once in the sky that would be like the splendour of that Mighty Being.

Śrī Ādi Śaṇkara mentions; He who has the bright form of knowledge. He is self–illuminating, bright and lustrous and hence *Dīptamūrtiḥ*

157. ***Lalitā*** – 814 – *Amūrtā* – अमूर्ता – One who is without form or shape. That which has form is called *mūrtā* – Earth, water, fire, etc.; *Amūrtā* means air, ether, etc., which are formless.

Mūrtā – the five gross elements mingled with each other; *Amūrtā*– the subtle elements which are not mingled with each other. *Brahadāraŋya Upaniṣat* (II–3–1) says, "*Brahmam* has two forms, *Mūrtā* and *Amūrtā*" – *Dve Vāva Brahmaŋo Rūpe Mūrtam Cāmūrtam Ca* I

Mūrtā – universe, *Amūrtā* – *Brahmam*. The *Viṣŋu Purāŋa* says, that *Brahmam* has two forms, *Mūrtā* and *Amūrtā*, these two are respectively perishable and imperishable and both are in all beings. The imperishable is the ever remaining *Brahmam*, the perishable is the whole universe. The Logicians explain the word *Mūrtā*s that which has motion, but we should not adopt their theory as it has no foundation.

Viṣṇu – 720 – *Amūrtimān* – अमूर्तिमान् – Having no Form. Though He was described earlier as *Dīptamūrtiḥ* "of the resplendent form"; *Mahāmūrtiḥ* "of great form"; *Viśvamūrtiḥ* "of the universal-Form" – He has, in reality, "No-Form"; *Amūrtimān*. He pervades all, but nothing limits Him. The limited alone has a form-the unlimited, like 'Space', has no form. The Infinite Brahman being so subtle. "Subtler than the subtlest". *Śrī Nārāyaṇa* as the Self-in-all, allows everything to remain in Him, but He is not conditioned by anyone of them.

Śrī Ādi Śaṇkara comments that he is formless because he does not have the bondage and actions (*karmās*).

158. ***Lalitā*** – 827 – *Pracaṇḍā* – प्रचण्डा – One who is wrathful. Anger is a symbol of *Brahmam*. The *Taitirīya Upaniṣat* (III–8–1) says "For fear of Him the wind, fire and Sun do their respective duties".

Viṣṇu – 315, 776 & 833 – *Krodhakṛtkartā* – क्रोधकृत्कर्ता, *Duratikramaḥ* – दुरतिक्रमः & *Bhayakṛt* – भयकृत् – One who generates in a sincere and serious seeker anger against the lower tendencies when they manifest – *Krodhakrit*. Also He is the very creative impulse *Kartā* behind the lower tendencies; because all things come out from Him alone. Some commentators consider this term as two different words, but the majority consider them as an integrated one.

One who is difficult to be disobeyed; This term declares a truth which is proven upon observation of this scientifically precise world where no object or being dares to disobey the Lord, the Cosmos The Rishi in *Kaṭopaniṣat* says "through fear of Him the Fire burns, through fear of Him shines the Sun, through fear of Him functions Indra, Vāyu and *Yama* itself is the fifth" – as though He is behind each one with uplifted thunderbolt. The term '*Atikromaḥ*' means 'going beyond', therefore the term, as it stands, indicates "a state beyond which no one can go" – meaning *Śrī Nārāyaṇa* is the final and the absolute destination of all evolution He is the transcendental Reality and other than He there is no more a beyond to he achieved.

Lord is the "Giver of fear". He is a terror to the evil-minded. In all His Incarnations, He gives fear to the evil-hearted, that they may ultimately be swayed to the path of *Dharma*.

Śrī Ādi Śaṇkara in his commentary says that all these three names convey the same message.

159. **Lalitā** – 838 – *Mukundā* – मुकुन्दा – One who bestows salvation. *Mukuḥ* means salvation. **She** bestows it.

Viṣṇu – 515 – *Mukundaḥ* – मुकुन्दः – One who gives liberation. To those who are trying to free themselves from the imperfections of the matter-conditionings and who are struggling hard to end their delusions, Śrī *Nārāyaṇa*, being the very Goal, ultimately gives complete liberation for all devotees who reach Him in the true spirit of total surrender.

160. **Lalitā** – 887 – *Viprapriyā* – विप्रप्रिया – One who is fond of those who know *Vedas* and *Śāstras*. The *Brahma Vaivarta Purāṇa* says – "A Brahmin should be known by his birth. He is called *Dvijā*, (twice born) on account of his purification ceremonies. He becomes a *vipra* by knowledge. One who possesses all these is called *srotriya*";

Viṣṇu – 670 – *Brāhmaṇapriyaḥ* – ब्रामणप्रियः – One who is the beloved or and One Who is the lover of true men of full realisation, the Brahmins. Not the caste, but the men of supreme experience-divine. The Lord is dear to them and they too are dear to Him.

Śrī Ādi Śaṇkara mentions as; He is fond of Brahmins – those who have the knowledge of *Brahmam*. He is liked by Brahmins.

161. **Lalitā** – 889 – *Viśvabhramaṇakāriṇī* – विश्वभ्रमणकारिणी – One who is causing the revolution of the earth. *Viśva* – all the *Brāhmic* eggs, *Bhramana* – their creation, preservation,and destruction. The *Svesvatara Upaniṣat* (VI–1) says, "Some wise call it nature, some confused call it time, that by which the wheel of *Brahmam* is revolving, is the glory of the Lord";

Viṣṇu – 1 – *Viśwam* – विश्वं – He whose manifestation is the whole universe of forms: the *Virāṭ Puruṣa*. The cause is always present in the effects and as such that form from which the whole universe has emerged out can only be its own manifestation. The whole cosmos of gross forms is His own expression and hence, He is called as *Virāṭpuruṣa. Sa eva sarva bhūtātmā Viśvarūpo Yatovyayaḥ*. The Samskrutam word *Viśvam* comes from the root *Viś* means to enter. Thus it means He who has created_and entered into the entire universe, as the all-pervading reality. It can also mean that into which the entire universe has entered to remain therein established. In the *Upaniśads* also we have assertions of similar ideas. It is only when intellectually, we view the Lord that we come to recognise Him as the cause for the universe. When viewed through contemplation, since the effect is nothing other than the cause, there can be no world other than Him. In fact, there is nothing other than the Supreme. In the *Māṇḍukya Upaniṣat* we read *Omkāra Evedam Sarvam*. In *Gīta* we have *Om Ityekākṣaram Brahma*.

Viśvam means *Viṣŋu*, for the word *Viśva* is explained thus "causing confusion to him". This story occurs in the *Kālika Purāŋa* – "*Viṣŋu* once travelling through the sky, mounted on his vehicle *Garuḍa* (the bird Eagle), passed by the *Devī* named *Kāmakyā,* residing in the *Nilācala* mountain in the *Kāmarūpa* country, without saluting her; then by the force of her anger he fell into the ocean and there he remained confused; after a long time *Lakṣmī* (his consort) began to look for him and hearing of this event from *Nārada*, **She** appeased *Śrī Devī*, by penance and freed *Viṣŋu* from his confusion. Afterwards he worshipped *Śrī Devī* and reached *Vaikuŋṭa*.

162. ***Lalitā*** – 899 – *Vīrā* – वीरा – One who is valourous. **She** herself is a warrior in battles, has valour and has killed lots of demons. A *vīrā* is a lady living with her husband and sons.

Viṣṇu – 658 – *Vīraḥ* – वीरः – The Valiant – The Courageous – the One of heroic exploits. The root *Vi* often means creation, radiance existence, involution or motion. One who has all these powers is called *Vīraḥ*.

Śrī Ādi Śaṇkara mentions as ; to go, to spread, to create, to enlighten, to throw, to eat, etc. The meaning of the verb *Vī* is a person who does all these actions.

163. ***Lalitā*** – 927 – *Stotrapriyā* – स्तोत्रप्रिया – One who is fond of praises

(*stotras*). The praises are of two types – *Vaidhīka* (based on *Vedas*) and *loukīka* (not based on *Vedas*). The attributes of *loukīka stotras* have been divided into six types by learned. They are, "Salutation (*namaskāra*), blessing (*Āśirvāda*), praising the attainments (telling about the *siddhāntās*), praising exploits (*parākrama*), rehearsing glory (*vibhūti*) and prayer for prosperity (*prārtanā*). The *Lalitā Sahasranam*, covers all these six types. The 1000 names entirely fit in any one of these 6 types.

Viṣṇu – 679 & 680 – *Stavyaḥ* – स्तव्य: & *Sthavapriyaḥ* – स्तवप्रिय: – One Who is the object of all praise – meaning, one who deserves all our praise but one who has none top praise, he is praised by all and he praises none. The *jīva* invokes him; the self, the atman, never invokes the ignorant *jīva*.

One who is invoked through the loving chants of the devoted hearts. When a devoted seeker melts away in singing the praise of the lord, his physical, mental and intellectual preoccupations with objects, emotions and thoughts silently roll away from him. In such quiet moments they rise above their present nature and explode into the realms of experiences of the higher state of divine consciousness – Śrī *Nārāyaṇa*.

Śrī Ādi Śaṇkara says – He is praised by all, but he does not praise anybody and hence *Stavyaḥ*. Because of this he is interested in praising – *Stotrapriyāḥ*

164. ***Lalitā*** – 953 – *Śarmadā* – शर्मदा – One who is the bestower of happiness. *Śarma* means the eternal bliss. After this there is no question of sorrow. *Śrī Ādi Śaṇkara* in his commentary of *Viṣṇu Sahasranāma* for the 459th name – *Sukhadāḥ* mentions – Since he bestows happiness to those who have good habits and destroys the happiness of those who have bad habits, He is *Sukhadāḥ*. The 889th name *Sukhadāḥ* – He gives the happiness of salvation to the devotees.

Viṣṇu – 459 & 889 – *Sukhadaḥ* – सुखद: – One who confers happiness. It can also mean in Samskrutam one who is the destroyer of joy (*Da* = to destroy). Here, of course, it means that one who gives joy to His devotees and takes away joy from those who are un-divine. One who gives the experience of eternal Bliss to the devotees at their final spiritual destination (*Mokṣa*). As the term stands in the verse, some would read it – *Asukhada* in which case the nominative would mean; One who removes all the discomforts and pains of the devotees. *Śree Ādi Śaṇkara* mentions – Since he bestows happiness to those who have good habits and destroys the happiness of those who have bad habits. **He** gives the happiness of salvation to the devotees.

*****

Only One God

The above discussions is only a sample – a drop from an ocean to establish that there exists only one God – be it *Śaṇmata* (Hinduism), Christianity, Muslim, Jainism, Buddhism or any other religion.

Concept of God in Hinduism: some Hindus believe in the existence of three gods, some believe in thousands of gods and some others in thirty three crore i.e. 330 million Gods. However, learned, who are well versed in the scriptures, insist that a Hindu should believe in and worship only one God. We can gain a better understanding of the concept of God in Hinduism by analysing Hindu scriptures.

Gīta (VII-20) says – Those whose intelligence has been stolen by material desires surrender unto demigods and follow the particular rules and regulations of worship according to their own natures. That people who are materialistic worship demigods i.e. Gods besides the True God.

The *Upanişats* are considered sacred scriptures by the Hindus. The following verses from the *Upanişats* refer to the Concept of God:

Cāndokya Upanişat (6:2:1) says – *Ekam evadvitiyam* – He is One only without a second.

Svetāsvāstara Upanişat (6:9) says – *Na casya kascijjanita na cadipaḥ* – Of Him there are neither parents nor lord.

Svetāsvāstara Upanişat (4:19) says – *Na tasya pratima asti* – There is no likeness of Him.

Svetāsvāstara Upanişat (4:20) says – *Na samdrse tişṭati rūpam asya na cakşuśa paśyati kaścanainam* – His form is not to be seen; no one sees Him with the eye.

The following verses from the *Yajurveda* (32-3) echo a similar concept of God: *na tasya pratima asti* – There is no image of Him.

Yajurveda (32-3) – *Śudhāma pāpvidham* – He is bodiless and pure.

Yajurveda (40-8 & 9) – *Andatama praviśanti ye asambhūti mupaste* – They enter darkness, those who worship the natural elements (Air, Water, Fire, etc.). They sink deeper in darkness, those who worship *sambhūti*. *Sambhūti* means created things, for example table, chair, idol, etc. The *Yajurveda* (40-16) contains the following prayer: Lead us to the good path and remove the sin that makes us stray and wander.

The *Atarvaveda* (20-58-3) praises God – *Devmahosi* – God is verily great

Ṛgveda (1-164-46) states – Sages (learned Priests) call one God by many names.

The *Ṛgveda* gives several different attributes to Almighty God. Many of these are mentioned in *Ṛgveda* (2-1). Among the various attributes of God, one of the beautiful attributes is *Brahma*. *Brahma* means "The Creator". Describing Almighty God in anthropomorphic terms also goes against the following verse of *Yajurveda* (32-3) – *Na tasya Pratima asti* – There is no image of Him. It has been mentioned in many a place as God is *Nirguṇa* – i.e. without any attributes.

Another beautiful attribute of God mentioned in the *Ṛgveda* (II-1-3) is *Viṣṇu*. *Viṣṇu* means "The Sustainer".

The following verse from the *Ṛgveda* (8-1-1) refer to the Unity and Glory of the Supreme Being – *Ma cid anyad vi sansata sakhayo ma riśanyata* – Oh! Friends, do not worship anybody but Him, the Divine One. Praise Him alone."

Again *Ṛgveda* (5-1-81) says – *Devasya samituk pariṣṭutiḥ* – Verily, great is the glory of the Divine Creator.

The *Brahma Sūtra* says – *Ekam Brahma, dvitīya naste neḥ na naste kincan* – There is only one God, not the second; not at all, not at all, not an iota.

Thus only a dispassionate study of the Hindu scriptures can help one understand the concept of single God in Hinduism.

The worship of multiple gods – probably multiple forms of God – is really not polytheism. Rather, it represents the many different paths that people take to reach the same *Brahmam* (the infinite oneness of existence). The above samples are speaking against worshipping these gods simply for limited or material ends rather than for union with the ultimate *Brahmam*.

In Tamil *Thirumoolar* also in his *Thirumantiram* says

Onre Kulam Oruvane Devan - ஒன்றே குலம் ஒருவனே தேவன்

which means there is only one religion and only one God.

Puttabarthi Sai Baba has categoricaly advised:

- There is only one religion, the religion of Love;
- There is only one language, the language of the Heart;
- There is only one caste, the caste of Humanity;
- There is only one law, the law of *Karma*;
- There is only one God, He is Omnipresent.

True devotion must not get dispirited; nor elated or satisfied with lesser gains; it must fight against failure, loss, calumny, calamity, ridicule and against egoism and pride, impatience and cowardice.

Let the different faiths exist, let them flourish, let the glory of God be sung in all languages in a variety of tunes. That should be the ideal. Respect the differences between the faiths and recognize them as valid so far as they do not extinguish the flame of unity.

Should each person live the ideals propounded by the founders of his religion, unaffected by greed or hate, then the world will be a happy and peaceful habitation for man.

In spiritual terms all of mankind belongs to one and the same class, race, and religion.

The followers of each religion call upon One God who is omnipresent and listens to their prayers, be they from any race or whatever language they speak; but it is the same God who confers happiness on all of mankind. No religion has a separate God showering grace only on those who profess to abide by that faith.

There is only one God, one Goal, one Law, one Truth, one Religion and one Reason.

Be like the lions in the spiritual field, rule over the forest of the senses and roam fearlessly with full faith in victory.

Reach the point where churches, temples, mosques do not matter, where all roads end, from where all roads run.

Honor all religions. Each is a pathway to God. That is the right way of life. Devotion has to be non-intermittent, uninterrupted, like the flow of oil from one vessel to another.

- Nations are many, but Earth is one;
- Beings are many, but Breath is one;
- Stars are many, but Sky is one;
- Oceans are many, but Water is one;
- Religions are many, but God is one;
- Jewels are many, but Gold is one;
- Appearances are many, but Reality is One.

God will not ask you when and where you did service. He will ask, with what motive did you do it? What was the intention that prompted you? You may weigh the service and boast of its quantity. But God seeks quality - the quality of heart, the purity of mind, the holiness of motive.

Spend a few minutes every morning and evening in the Silence of your own shrine or home; spend them with the highest of all the Powers that you know of. Be in His elevating and Inspiring company; worship Him mentally; offer unto Him all the work you do; you will come out of the silence nobler and more heroic than when you went in.

The mind carries the divine principle (the light of love) and conveys it to all who contact it.

God is the mother and father of the world. Our parents are the mother and father of this body. God is one; there are not many Gods, one for each tribe among men.

Human being can realise the mission on the earth only when he knows himself as Divine and when he reveres all others as Divine.

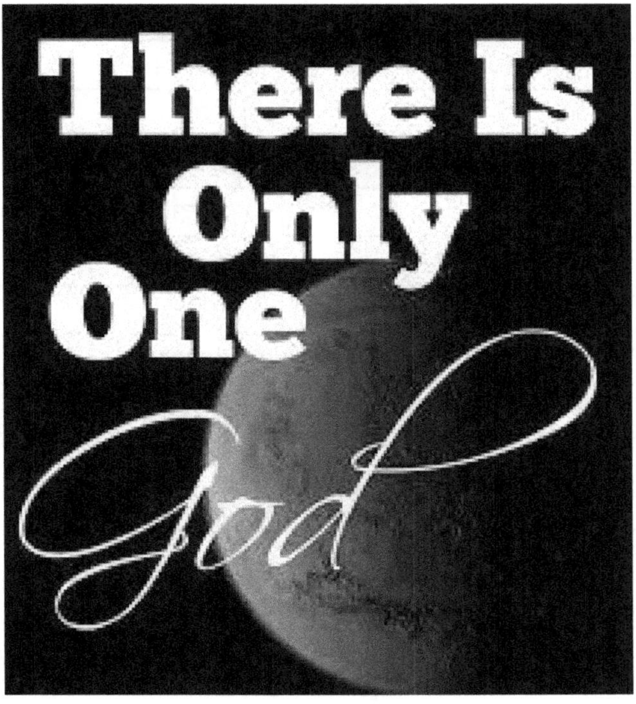

*****

Śrī Śiva Sahasranāmāvali

Om Namaḥ Śivāya

#	Name in English	Name in Samskrutam
1.	*Sthiraḥ*	स्थिर:
2.	*Sthāṇuḥ*	स्थाणु:
3.	*Prabhuḥ*	प्रभु:
4.	*Bhīmaḥ*	भीम:
5.	*Pravaraḥ*	प्रवर:
6.	*Varadaḥ*	वरद:
7.	*Varaḥ*	वर:
8.	*Sarvātmaḥ*	सर्वात्म:
9.	*Sarvavikhyātaḥ*	सर्वविख्यात:
10.	*Sarvaḥ*	सर्व:
11.	*Sarvakaraḥ*	सर्वकर:
12.	*Bhavāḥ*	भव:
13.	*Jatiḥ*	जटि:
14.	*Carmiṇaḥ*	चर्मिण:
15.	*Śikhaṇḍi:*	शिखण्डि:
16.	*Sarvāṁgaḥ*	सर्वांग:
17.	*Sarvabhāvanaḥ*	सर्वभावन:
18.	*Haraḥ*	हर:
19.	*Hariṇākşaḥ*	हरिणाक्ष:
20.	*Sarvabhūtaharaḥ*	सर्वभूतहर:
21.	*Prabhuḥ*	प्रभु:

#	Name in English	Name in Samskrutam
22.	*Pravṛttaḥ*	प्रवृत्त:
23.	*Nivṛttaḥ*	निवृत्त:
24.	*Niyataḥ*	नियत:
25.	*Śāśvataḥ*	शाश्वत:
26.	*Dhravaḥ*	ध्रव:
27.	*Śmaśānavāsaḥ*	श्मशानवास:
28.	*Bhagavān*	भगवान्
29.	*Khacaraḥ*	खचर:
30.	*Gocaraḥ*	गोचर:
31.	*Ardanaḥ*	अर्दन:
32.	*Abhivādayaḥ*	अभिवाद्य:
33.	*Mahākarmā*	महाकर्मा
34.	*Tapasvīḥ*	तपस्वी:
35.	*Bhūtabhāvanaḥ*	भूतभावन:
36.	*Unmattaveṣa Pracchannaḥ*	उन्मत्तवेष प्रच्छन्न:
37.	*Sarvaloka Prajāpatiḥ*	सर्वलोक: प्रजापति:
38.	*Mahārūpaḥ*	महारूप:
39.	*Mahakāyaḥ*	महाकाय:
40.	*Vṛṣarūpaḥ*	वृषरूप:
41.	*Mahāyaśāḥ*	महायशा:
42.	*Mahātman*	महात्मन्
43.	*Sarvabhūtātman*	सर्वभूतात्मन्
44.	*Viśvarūpaḥ*	विश्वरूप:

#	Name in English	Name in Samskrutam
45.	*Mahāhanuḥ*	महाहनुः
46.	*Lokapālaḥ*	लोकपालः
47.	*Antarhitātman*	अन्तर्हितात्मन्
48.	*Prasādaḥ*	प्रसादः
49.	*Hayagardabhiḥ*	हयगर्दभिः
50.	*Pavitram*	पवित्रम्
51.	*Mahat*	महत्
52.	*Niyamaḥ*	नियमः
53.	*Niyamāśritaḥ*	नियमाश्रितः
54.	*Sarvakarmā*	सर्वकर्मा
55.	*Svayaṁbhūtaḥ*	स्वयंभूतः
56.	*Ādayaḥ*	आदयः
57.	*Ādikaraḥ*	आदिकरः
58.	*Nidhiḥ*	निधिः
59.	*Sahasrākṣaḥ*	सहस्राक्षः
60.	*Viśālākṣaḥ*	विशालाक्षः
61.	*Somaḥ*	सोमः
62.	*Nakṣatrasādhakaḥ*	नक्षत्रसाधकः
63.	*Candraḥ*	चन्द्रः
64.	*Sūryaḥ*	सूर्यः
65.	*Śaniḥ*	शनिः
66.	*Ketuḥ*	केतुः
67.	*Grahaḥ*	ग्रहः

#	Name in English	Name in Samskrutam
68.	*Grahapatiḥ*	ग्रहपतिः
69.	*Varaḥ*	वरः
70.	*Atrayaḥ*	अत्रयः
71.	*Atrayānamaskartaḥ*	अत्रयानमस्कर्तः
72.	*Mṛgabaṇārpaṇaḥ*	मृगबणार्पणः
73.	*Anaghaḥ*	अनघः
74.	*Mahātapaḥ*	महातपः
75.	*Goratapaḥ*	घोरतपः
76.	*Adeenaḥ*	अदीनः
77.	*Deenasādhakaḥ*	दीनसाधकः
78.	*Saṁvatsarakāraḥ*	संवत्सरकारः
79.	*Mantraḥ*	मन्त्रः
80.	*Pramāṇaḥ*	प्रमाणः
81.	*Paramāyatapaḥ*	परमायतपः
82.	*Yogiḥ*	योगिः
83.	*Yojyaḥ*	योज्यः
84.	*Mahābeejaḥ*	महाबीजः
85.	*Mahāretaḥ*	महारेतः
86.	*Mahābalaḥ*	महाबलः
87.	*Svarṇaretaḥ*	सुवर्णरेतः
88.	*Sarvagnaḥ*	सर्वज्ञः
89.	*Subeejaḥ*	सुबीजः
90.	*Bhījavāhanaḥ*	बीजवाहनः

#	Name in English	Name in Samskrutam
91.	*Daśabāhuḥ*	दशबाहु:
92.	*Animiṣaḥ*	अनिमिष:
93.	*Nīlakaṇṭhaḥ*	नीलकण्ठ:
94.	*Umāpatiḥ*	उमापति:
95.	*Viśvarūpaḥ*	विश्वरूप:
96.	*Svayaṁśreṣṭhaḥ*	स्वयंश्रेष्ठ:
97.	*Balaveeraḥ*	बलवीर:
98.	*Abalogaṇaḥ*	अबलोगण:
99.	*Gaṇakartā*	गणकर्ता
100.	*Gaṇapatiḥ*	गणपति:
101.	*Digvāsaḥ*	दिग्वास:
102.	*Kāmaḥ*	काम:
103.	*Mantravit*	मन्त्रवित्
104.	*Paramamantraḥ*	परममन्त्र:
105.	*Sarvabhāvakaraḥ*	सर्वभावकर:
106.	*Haraḥ*	हर:
107.	*Kamaṇḍaludharaḥ*	कमण्डलुधर:
108.	*Dhanvaḥ*	धन्व:
109.	*Bāṇahastaḥ*	बाणहस्त:
110.	*Kapālavān*	कपालवान्
111.	*Aśanaḥ*	अशन:
112.	*Śataghnaḥ*	शतघ्न:
113.	*Khadgaḥ*	खड्ग:

#	Name in English	Name in Samskrutam
114.	*Paṭṭiśaḥ*	पट्टिश:
115.	*Āyudhaḥ*	आयुध:
116.	*Mahān*	महान्
117.	*Struvahastaḥ*	स्त्रुवहस्त:
118.	*Surūpaḥ*	सुरूप:
119.	*Tejasaḥ*	तेजस:
120.	*Tejaskaranidhaḥ*	तेजस्करनिध:
121.	*Uṣnīṣiṇaḥ*	उष्णीषिण:
122.	*Suvaktraḥ*	सुवक्त्र:
123.	*Udagraḥ*	उदग्र:
124.	*Vinataḥ*	विनत:
125.	*Dīrghaḥ*	दीर्घ:
126.	*Harikeśaḥ*	हरिकेश:
127.	*Sutīrthaḥ*	सुतीर्थ:
128.	*Kṛṣṇaḥ*	कृष्ण:
129.	*Srugālarūpaḥ*	सृगालरूप:
130.	*Siddhārthaḥ*	सिद्धार्थ:
131.	*Muṇḍaḥ*	मुण्ड:
132.	*Sarvaśubhamkaraḥ*	सर्वशुभंकर:
133.	*Ajaḥ*	अज:
134.	*Bahurūpaḥ*	बहुरूप:
135.	*Gandhadhārī*	गन्धधारी
136.	*Kapardiḥ*	कपर्दि:

#	Name in English	Name in Samskrutam
137.	*Ūrdhvaretaḥ*	ऊर्ध्वरेत:
138.	*Ūrdhvalingaḥ*	ऊर्ध्वलिङ्ग:
139.	*Ūrdhvaśāyaḥ*	ऊर्ध्वशाय:
140.	*Nabhaḥsthalaḥ*	नभ:स्थल:
141.	*Trijaṭaḥ*	त्रिजट:
142.	*Cīravāsāḥ*	चीरवासा:
143.	*Rudraḥ*	रुद्र:
144.	*Senāpatiḥ*	सेनापति:
145.	*Vibhuḥ*	विभु:
146.	*Ahaścaraḥ*	अहश्चर:
147.	*Naktarancaraḥ*	नक्तरंचर:
148.	*Tigmamanyuḥ*	तिग्ममन्यु:
149.	*Suvarcasaḥ*	सुवर्चस:
150.	*Gajagnaḥ*	गजज्ञ:
151.	*Daityagnaḥ*	दैत्यज्ञ:
152.	*Kālaḥ*	काल:
153.	*Lokadhātāḥ*	लोकधाता:
154.	*Guṇākaraḥ*	गुणाकर:
155.	*Simhaśārdūlarūpaḥ*	सिंहशार्दूलरूप:
156.	*Ārdracarmāmbarāvṛtaḥ*	आर्द्रचर्मांबरावृत:
157.	*Kālayogiḥ*	कालयोगि:
158.	*Mahānādaḥ*	महानाद:
159.	*Sarvakāmaḥ*	सर्वकाम:

#	Name in English	Name in Samskrutam
160.	*Catuṣpathaḥ*	चतुष्पथ:
161.	*Niśācaraḥ*	निशाचर:
162.	*Pretacāraḥ*	प्रेतचार:
163.	*Bhūtacāraḥ*	भूतचार:
164.	*Maheśvaraḥ*	महेश्वर:
165.	*Bahubhūtaḥ*	बहुभूत:
166.	*Bahudaraḥ*	बहुधर:
167.	*Svarbhanuḥ*	स्वर्भानु:
168.	*Amitaḥ*	अमित:
169.	*Gatiḥ*	गति:
170.	*Nṛtyapriyaḥ*	नृत्यप्रिय:
171.	*Nityanartaḥ*	नित्यनर्त:
172.	*Nartakaḥ*	नर्तक:
173.	*Sarvalālasaḥ*	सर्वलालस:
174.	*Ghoraḥ*	घोर:
175.	*Mahātapāḥ*	महातपा:
176.	*Pāśaḥ*	पाश:
177.	*Nityaḥ*	नित्य:
178.	*Giriruhaḥ*	गिरिरुह:
179.	*Nabhaḥ*	नभ:
180.	*Sahasrahastaḥ*	सहस्रहस्त:
181.	*Vijayaḥ*	विजय:
182.	*Vyavasāyaḥ*	व्यवसाय:

#	Name in English	Name in Samskrutam
183.	*Atandritaḥ*	अतन्द्रित:
184.	*Aghamarṣaṇaḥ*	अघमर्षण:
185.	*Darṣaṇatmanaḥ*	धर्षणात्मन:
186.	*Yagnaḥ*	यज्ञ:
187.	*Kāmanāśakaḥ*	कामनाशक:
188.	*Dakṣayāgāpahāraḥ*	दक्षयागापहार:
189.	*Susahāyaḥ*	सुसहाय:
190.	*Madhyamaḥ*	मध्यम:
191.	*Tejopahāraḥ*	तेजोपहार:
192.	*Balagnaḥ*	बलज्ञ:
193.	*Muditaḥ*	मुदित:
194.	*Artthaḥ*	अर्त्थ:
195.	*Ajitaḥ*	अजित:
196.	*Avaraḥ*	अवर:
197.	*Gambhīraghoṣaḥ*	गंभीरघोष:
198.	*Gambhīraḥ*	गंभीर:
199.	*Gambhīrabalavahanaḥ*	गंभीरबलवाहन:
200.	*Nyagrodharūpaḥ*	न्यग्रोधरूप:
201.	*Nyagrodhaḥ*	न्यग्रोध:
202.	*Vṛkṣakarṇasthitiḥ*	वृक्षकर्णस्थिति:
203.	*Vibhavaḥ*	विभव:
204.	*Sutīkṣṇadaśanaḥ*	सुतीक्ष्णदशन:
205.	*Mahākāyaḥ*	महाकाय:

#	Name in English	Name in Samskrutam
206.	*Mahānanaḥ*	महानन:
207.	*Viṣvaksenaḥ*	विष्वक्सेन:
208.	*Hariḥ*	हरि:
209.	*Yagnaḥ*	यज्ञ:
210.	*Saṁyugapīḍavāhanaḥ*	संयुगापीडवाहन:
211.	*Dhīkṣṇatāpaḥ*	दीक्ष्णताप:
212.	*Haryaśvaḥ*	हर्यश्व:
213.	*Sahāyaḥ*	सहाय:
214.	*Karmakālavit*	कर्मकालवित्
215.	*Viṣṇuprasāditaḥ*	विष्णुप्रसादित:
216.	*Yagnaḥ*	यज्ञ:
217.	*Samudraḥ*	समुद्र:
218.	*Badavāmukhaḥ*	बडवामुख:
219.	*Hutāśanasahāyaḥ*	हुताशनसहाय:
220.	*Praśāntātmaḥ*	प्रशान्तात्म:
221.	*Hutāśanaḥ*	हुताशन:
222.	*Ugratejaḥ*	उग्रतेज:
223.	*Mahātejaḥ*	महातेज:
224.	*Janyaḥ*	जन्य:
225.	*Vijayakālavit*	विजयकालवित्
226.	*Jyotiṣāmayaḥ*	ज्योतिषामय:
227.	*Siddhiḥ*	सिद्धि:
228.	*Sarvavigrahaḥ*	सर्वविग्रह:

#	Name in English	Name in Samskrutam
229.	Śikhiḥ	शिखि:
230.	Muṇḍīḥ	मुण्डी:
231.	Jaṭīḥ	जटी:
232.	Jvāliḥ	ज्वालि:
233.	Mūrtijāyaḥ	मूर्तिजाय:
234.	Mūrdhagaḥ	मूर्धग:
235.	Balīḥ	बली:
236.	Vaiṣṇavīḥ	वैष्णवी:
237.	Paṇavīḥ	पणवी:
238.	Talīḥ	ताली:
239.	Khalīḥ	खली:
240.	Kālakaṭamkaṭaḥ	कालकटंकट:
241.	Nakṣatravigrahamataḥ	नक्षत्रविग्रहमत:
242.	Guṇabuddhiḥ	मुणबुद्धि:
243.	Layaḥ	लय:
244.	Āgamaḥ	आगम:
245.	Prajāpatiḥ	प्रजापति:
246.	Visvabāhuḥ	विश्वबाहु:
247.	Vibhāgaḥ	विभाग:
248.	Sarvagaḥ	सर्वग:
249.	Amukhaḥ	अमुख:
250.	Vimocanaḥ	विमोचन:
251.	Sudaraṇaḥ	सुदरण:

#	Name in English	Name in Samskrutam
252.	*Hiraṇyakavacodbhavaḥ*	हिरण्यकवचोद्भव:
253.	*Medrajaḥ*	मेड्रज:
254.	*Balacārīḥ*	बलचारी:
255.	*Mahīcarīḥ*	महीचरी:
256.	*Stutāyaḥ*	स्तुताय:
257.	*Sarvatūryavinodī*	सर्वतूर्यविनोदी
258.	*Sarvatodyaparigrahaḥ*	सर्वतोद्यपरिग्रह:
259.	*Vyālarūpaḥ*	व्यालरूप:
260.	*Guhāvāsī*	गुहावासी
261.	*Guhaḥ*	गुह:
262.	*Malī*	मली
263.	*Tarangavit*	तरंगवित्
264.	*Tridaśaḥ*	त्रिदश:
265.	*Trikāladṛtaḥ*	त्रिकालधृत:
266.	*Karmaḥsarvabandhavimocanaḥ*	कर्म:सर्वबन्धविमोचन:
267.	*Asurendraṇāmbandhanaḥ*	असुरेन्द्रणांबन्धन:
268.	*Yudhiśatruvināśanaḥ*	युधिशत्रुविनाशन:
269.	*Sānkhyaprasādaḥ*	सांख्यप्रसाद:
270.	*Durvāsaḥ*	दुर्वास:
271.	*Sarvasādhuniṣevitaḥ*	सर्वसाधुनिषेवित:
272.	*Praskandanaḥ*	प्रस्कन्दन:
273.	*Vibhāgagnaḥ*	विभागग्न:
274.	*Atulyaḥ*	अतुल्य:

#	Name in English	Name in Samskrutam
275.	*Yagnabhāgavit*	यज्ञभागवित्
276.	*Sarvavāsaḥ*	सर्ववास:
277.	*Sarvacarīḥ*	सर्वचारी:
278.	*Durvāsaḥ*	दुर्वास:
279.	*Vāsavaḥ*	वासव:
280.	*Amaraḥ*	अमर:
281.	*Haimaḥ*	हैम:
282.	*Hemakaraḥ*	हेमकर:
283.	*Yagnaḥ*	यज्ञ:
284.	*Sarvadhārī*	सर्वधारी
285.	*Darotamaḥ*	धरोत्तम:
286.	*Lohitākṣaḥ*	लोहिताक्ष:
287.	*Mahākṣaḥ*	महाक्ष:
288.	*Vijayākṣaḥ*	विययाक्ष:
289.	*Viṣāradaḥ*	विशारद:
290.	*Saṁgrahaḥ*	संग्रह:
291.	*Nigrahaḥ*	निग्रह:
292.	*Kartā*	कर्ता
293.	*Sarpaceeranivāsanaḥ*	सर्पचीरनिवासन:
294.	*Mukhyaḥ*	मुख्य:
295.	*Amukhyaḥ*	अमुख्य:
296.	*Dehaḥ*	देह:
297.	*Kāhaliḥ*	काहलि:

#	Name in English	Name in Samskrutam
298.	*Sarvakāmadaḥ*	सर्वकामद:
299.	*Sarvakālaprasādaḥ*	सर्वकालप्रसाद:
300.	*Subalaḥ*	सुबल:
301.	*Balarūpadhṛt*	बलरूपधृत्
302.	*Sarvakāmavaraḥ*	सर्वकामवर:
303.	*Sarvadaḥ*	सर्वद:
304.	*Sarvatomukhaḥ*	सर्वतोमुख:
305.	*Ākāśanirvirūpaḥ*	आकाशनिर्विरूप:
306.	*Nipātīḥ*	निपाती:
307.	*Avaśaḥ*	अवश:
308.	*Khagaḥ*	खग:
309.	*Roudrarūpaḥ*	रौद्ररूप:
310.	*Amśava:*	अंशव:
311.	*Ādityaḥ*	आदित्य:
312.	*Bahuraśmiḥ*	बहुरश्मि:
313.	*Suvarcasī*	सुवर्चसी
314.	*Vasuvegaḥ*	वसुवेग:
315.	*Mahāvegaḥ*	महावेग:
316.	*Manovegaḥ*	मनोवेग:
317.	*Niśācaraḥ*	निशाचर:
318.	*Sarvavāsī*	सर्ववासी
319.	*Śriyāvāsī*	श्रियावासी
320.	*Upadeśakaraḥ*	उपदेशकर:

#	Name in English	Name in Samskrutam
321.	*Akara:*	अकर:
322.	*Muniḥ*	मुनि:
323.	*Ātmannirālokaḥ*	आत्मनिरालोक:
324.	*Saṁbhagnaḥ*	संभग्न:
325.	*Sahasradaḥ*	सहस्रद:
326.	*Pakṣiḥ*	पक्षि:
327.	*Pakṣarūpaḥ*	पक्षरूप:
328.	*Atidīptaḥ*	अतिदीप्त:
329.	*Viśāmpatiḥ*	विशाम्पति:
330.	*Unmādaḥ*	उन्माद:
331.	*Madanaḥ*	मदन:
332.	*Kāmaḥ*	काम:
333.	*Aśvatthaḥ*	अश्वत्त्थ:
334.	*Arthakaraḥ*	अर्थकर:
335.	*Yaśaḥ*	यश:
336.	*Vamadevaḥ*	वामदेव:
337.	*Vamāḥ*	वाम:
338.	*Prācaḥ*	प्राच:
339.	*Dakṣiṇaḥ*	दक्षिण:
340.	*Vāmanaḥ*	वामन:
341.	*Siddhayogiḥ*	सिद्धयोगि:
342.	*Maharṣiḥ*	महर्षि:
343.	*Siddhārthaḥ*	सिद्धार्थ:

#	Name in English	Name in Samskrutam
344.	*Siddhasādhakaḥ*	सिद्धसाधकः
345.	*Bikṣuḥ*	भिक्षुः
346.	*Bikṣurūpaḥ*	भिक्षुरूपः
347.	*Vipaṇaḥ*	विपणः
348.	*Mrudhuḥ*	मृदुः
349.	*Avyayaḥ*	अव्ययः
350.	*Mahāsenaḥ*	महासेनः
351.	*Viṣākhaḥ*	विशाखः
352.	*Ṣaṣṭibāgaḥ*	षष्टिभागः
353.	*Gavāmpatiḥ*	गवांपतिः
354.	*Vajrahastaḥ*	वज्रहस्तः
355.	*Viṣkambhīḥ*	विष्कम्भीः
356.	*Camūstambhanaḥ*	चमूस्तम्भनः
357.	*Vṛttāvṛtakaraḥ*	वृत्तावृत्तकरः
358.	*Tālāḥ*	तालाः
359.	*Madhuḥ*	मधुः
360.	*Madhukalocanaḥ*	मधुकलोचनः
361.	*Vācaspatiḥ*	वाचस्पतिः
362.	*Vājasanaḥ*	वाजसनः
363.	*Nityamāśritapūjitaḥ*	नित्यमाश्रितपूजितः
364.	*Brahmacārīḥ*	ब्रह्मचारीः
365.	*Lokacārīḥ*	लोकचारीः
366.	*Sarvacārīḥ*	सर्वचारीः

#	Name in English	Name in Samskrutam
367.	*Vicāravit*	विचारवित्
368.	*Īśānaḥ*	ईशानः
369.	*Īśvaraḥ*	ईश्वरः
370.	*Kālaḥ*	कालः
371.	*Niśācārīḥ*	निशाचारीः
372.	*Pinākavān*	पिनाकवान्
373.	*Nimittastaḥ*	निमित्तस्थः
374.	*Nimittaḥ*	निमित्तः
375.	*Nandaḥ*	नन्दः
376.	*Nandakaraḥ*	नन्दकरः
377.	*Hariḥ*	हरिः
378.	*Nandeeśvaraḥ*	नन्दीश्वरः
379.	*Nandīḥ*	नन्दीः
380.	*Nandanaḥ*	नन्दनः
381.	*Nandivardhanaḥ*	नन्दिवर्धनः
382.	*Bhagahārīḥ*	भगहारीः
383.	*Nihantaḥ*	निहन्तः
384.	*Kālaḥ*	कालः
385.	*Brahmāḥ*	ब्रह्माः
386.	*Pitāmahaḥ*	पितामहः
387.	*Caturmukhaḥ*	चतुर्मुखः
388.	*Mahālingaḥ*	महालिङ्गः
389.	*Cārulingaḥ*	चारुलिङ्गः

#	Name in English	Name in Samskrutam
390.	*Lingādhyakṣaḥ*	लिङ्गाध्यक्ष:
391.	*Surādhyakṣaḥ*	सुराध्यक्ष:
392.	*Yogādhyakṣaḥ*	योगाध्यक्ष:
393.	*Yugāvahaḥ*	युगावह:
394.	*Bhījādhyakṣaḥ*	बीजाध्यक्ष:
395.	*Bhījakartāḥ*	बीजकर्ता
396.	*Adyātmānugataḥ*	अद्यात्मानुगत:
397.	*Balaḥ*	बल:
398.	*Itihāsaḥ*	इतिहास:
399.	*Kalpaḥ*	कल्प:
400.	*Goutamaḥ*	गौतम:
401.	*Niśākaraḥ*	निशाकर:
402.	*Dambhaḥ*	दम्भ:
403.	*Hyadambhaḥ*	ह्यदम्भ:
404.	*Vaidambhaḥ*	वैदम्भ:
405.	*Vasyaḥ*	वस्य:
406.	*Vaśakaraḥ*	वशकर:
407.	*Kaliḥ*	कलि:
408.	*Lokakartā*	लोककर्ता
409.	*Paśupatiḥ*	पशुपति:
410.	*Mahākartā*	महाकर्ता
411.	*Anouṣadhaḥ*	अनौषध:
412.	*Akṣaraḥ*	अक्षर:

#	Name in English	Name in Samskrutam
413.	*Parabrahmaḥ*	परब्रह्म:
414.	*Balavaḥ*	बलव:
415.	*Śakraḥ*	शक्र:
416.	*Nītiḥ*	नीति:
417.	*Anītiḥ*	अनीति:
418.	*Śuddhātmaḥ*	शुद्धात्म:
419.	*Śuddhaḥ*	शुद्ध:
420.	*Mānyaḥ*	मान्य:
421.	*Gatāgataḥ*	गतागत:
422.	*Bahuprasādaḥ*	बहुप्रसाद:
423.	*Susvapnaḥ*	सुस्वप्न:
424.	*Darpaṇaḥ*	दर्पण:
425.	*Amitrajit*	अमित्रजित्
426.	*Vedakāraḥ*	वेदकार:
427.	*Mantrakāraḥ*	मन्त्रकार:
428.	*Vidvān*	विद्वान्
429.	*Samaramardanaḥ*	समरमर्दन:
430.	*Mahāmeghanivāsī*	महामेघनिवासी
431.	*Mahāgoraḥ*	महाघोर:
432.	*Vaśīḥ*	वशी:
433.	*Karaḥ*	कर:
434.	*Agnijvālaḥ*	अग्निज्वाल:
435.	*Mahājvālaḥ*	महाज्वाल:

#	Name in English	Name in Samskrutam
436.	*Atidhūmraḥ*	अतिधूम्रः
437.	*Hutaḥ*	हुतः
438.	*Haviḥ*	हविः
439.	*Vṛṣaṇaḥ*	वृषणः
440.	*Śaṅkaraḥ*	शंकरः
441.	*Nityavarcasvīḥ*	नित्यवर्चस्वीः
442.	*Dhūmaketanaḥ*	धूमकेतनः
443.	*Nīlaḥ*	नीलः
444.	*Angalubdhaḥ*	अङ्गलुब्धः
445.	*Śobhanaḥ*	शोभनः
446.	*Niravagrahaḥ*	निरवग्रहः
447.	*Svastidaḥ*	स्वस्तिदः
448.	*Svastibhāvaḥ*	स्वस्तिभावः
449.	*Bhāgaḥ*	भागः
450.	*Bhāgakāraḥ*	भागकरः
451.	*Laghuḥ*	लघुः
452.	*Utsangaḥ*	उत्सङ्गः
453.	*Mahāngaḥ*	महाङ्गः
454.	*Mahāgarbhaparāyaṇaḥ*	महागर्भपरायणः
455.	*Kṛṣṇavarṇaḥ*	कृष्णवर्णः
456.	*Suvarṇaḥ*	सुवर्णः
457.	*Sarvadehināmindriyāyaḥ*	सर्वदेहिनांइन्द्रियायः
458.	*Mahāpādaḥ*	महापादः

#	Name in English	Name in Samskrutam
459.	*Mahāhastaḥ*	महाहस्तः
460.	*Mahākāyaḥ*	महाकायः
461.	*Mahāyaśaḥ*	महायशः
462.	*Mahāmūrdhāḥ*	महामूर्धा
463.	*Mahāmātraḥ*	महामात्रः
464.	*Mahānetraḥ*	महानेत्रः
465.	*Niśālayaḥ*	निशालयः
466.	*Mahāntakaḥ*	महान्तकः
467.	*Mahākarṇaḥ*	महाकर्णः
468.	*Mahoṣṭaḥ*	महोष्टः
469.	*Mahāhanuḥ*	महाहनुः
470.	*Mahānāśaḥ*	महानाशः
471.	*Mahākambuḥ*	महाकम्बुः
472.	*Mahāgreevaḥ*	महाग्रीवः
473.	*Śmaśānabhājaḥ*	श्मशानभाजः
474.	*Mahāvakṣaḥ*	महावक्षः
475.	*Mahoraskaḥ*	महोरस्कः
476.	*Antarātmaḥ*	अन्तरात्मः
477.	*Mṛgālayaḥ*	मृगालयः
478.	*Lambanaḥ*	लम्बनः
479.	*Labhitoṣṭaḥ*	लम्बितोष्ट
480.	*Mahāmāyaḥ*	महामायः
481.	*Payonidhiḥ*	पयोनिधिः

#	Name in English	Name in Samskrutam
482.	*Mahādantaḥ*	महादन्तः
483.	*Mahādamṣṭraḥ*	महादंष्ट्रः
484.	*Mahājihvaḥ*	महाजिह्वः
485.	*Mahāmukhaḥ*	महामुखः
486.	*Mahānakhaḥ*	महानखः
487.	*Mahāromaḥ*	महारोमः
488.	*Mahākeśaḥ*	महाकेशः
489.	*Mahājaṭaḥ*	महाजटः
490.	*Prasannaḥ*	प्रसन्नः
491.	*Prasādaḥ*	प्रसादः
492.	*Pratyayaḥ*	प्रत्ययः
493.	*Girisādhanaḥ*	हिरिसाधनः
494.	*Snehanaḥ*	स्नेहनः
495.	*Asnehanaḥ*	अस्नेहनः
496.	*Ajitaḥ*	अजितः
497.	*Mahāmuniḥ*	महामुनिः
498.	*Vṛkṣākaraḥ*	वृक्षाकरः
499.	*Vṛkṣaketuḥ*	वृक्षकेतुः
500.	*Analaḥ*	अनलः
501.	*Vāyuvāhanaḥ*	वायुवाहनः
502.	*Gaṇḍalīḥ*	गण्डलीः
503.	*Merudhāmaḥ*	मेरुधामः
504.	*Devādhipatiḥ*	देवाधिपतिः

#	Name in English	Name in Samskrutam
505.	*Atharvaśeerṣaḥ*	अथर्वशीर्ष:
506.	*Sāmāsyaḥ*	सामास्य:
507.	*Ṛksahasrāmitakṣaṇaḥ*	ऋक्सहस्रामितक्षण:
508.	*Yajuḥpādabhujaḥ*	यजु:पादभुज:
509.	*Guhyaḥ*	गुह्य:
510.	*Prakhāśaḥ*	प्रकाश:
511.	*Jangamaḥ*	जंगम:
512.	*Amoghārthaḥ*	अमोघार्थ:
513.	*Prasādaḥ*	प्रसाद:
514.	*Abhigamyaḥ*	अभिगम्य:
515.	*Sudarśanaḥ*	सुदर्शन:
516.	*Upakāraḥ*	उपकार:
517.	*Priyaḥ*	प्रिय:
518.	*Sarvaḥ*	सर्व:
519.	*Kanakaḥ*	कनक:
520.	*Kāncanacchaviḥ*	काञ्चनच्छवि:
521.	*Nābhiḥ*	नाभि:
522.	*Nandikaraḥ*	नन्दिकर:
523.	*Bhāvaḥ*	भाव:
524.	*Puṣkaraḥ*	पुषकर:
525.	*Sthapatiḥ*	स्थपति:
526.	*Sthiraḥ*	स्थिर:
527.	*Dvādaśasāstrāsanaḥ*	द्वादशसास्त्रासन:

#	Name in English	Name in Samskrutam
528.	*Ādyaḥ*	आद्य:
529.	*Yagnaḥ*	यज्ञ:
530.	*Yagnasamāhitaḥ*	यज्ञसमाहित:
531.	*Naktaḥ*	नक्त:
532.	*Kaliḥ*	कलि:
533.	*Kālaḥ*	काल:
534.	*Makaraḥ*	मकर:
535.	*Kālapūjitaḥ*	कालपूजित:
536.	*Sagaṇaḥ*	सगण:
537.	*Gaṇakāraḥ*	गणकार:
538.	*Bhūtavāhanasārathiḥ*	भूतवाहनसारथि:
539.	*Bhasmāśayaḥ*	मस्माशय:
540.	*Basmagoptāḥ*	भस्मगोप्ता:
541.	*Basmabhūtaḥ*	भस्मभूत:
542.	*Tharuḥ*	तरु:
543.	*Gaṇaḥ*	गण:
544.	*Lokapālaḥ*	लोकपाल:
545.	*Alokāḥ*	अलोका:
546.	*Mahātmāḥ*	महात्मा:
547.	*Sarvapūjitaḥ*	सर्वपूजित:
548.	*Śuklaḥ*	शुक्ल:
549.	*Triśuklaḥ*	त्रिशुक्ल:
550.	*Saṁpannaḥ*	संपन्न:

#	Name in English	Name in Samskrutam
551.	*Śucaḥ*	शुचः
552.	*Bhūtaniṣevitaḥ*	भूतनिषेवितः
553.	*Āśramasthaḥ*	आश्रमस्थः
554.	*Kriyāvasthaḥ*	क्रियावस्थः
555.	*Viśvakarmamataḥ*	विश्वकर्ममतः
556.	*Varaḥ*	वरः
557.	*Viśālaśākhaḥ*	विशालशाखः
558.	*Tamroṣṭhaḥ*	ताम्रोष्ठः
559.	*Ambujālaḥ*	अम्बुजालः
560.	*Suniścalaḥ*	सुनिश्चलः
561.	*Kapilaḥ*	कपिलः
562.	*Kapiśaḥ*	कपिशः
563.	*Śuklaḥ*	शुक्लः
564.	*Āyuḥ*	आयुः
565.	*Paraḥ*	परः
566.	*Aparaḥ*	अपरः
567.	*Gandharvaḥ*	गन्धर्वः
568.	*Aditiḥ*	अदितिः
569.	*Ārkṣyaḥ*	आर्क्ष्यः
570.	*Suvigneyaḥ*	सुविज्ञेयः
571.	*Suśāradaḥ*	सुशारदः
572.	*Paraśvadhāyudhaḥ*	परश्वधायुधः
573.	*Devaḥ*	देवः

#	Name in English	Name in Samskrutam
574.	*Anukārīḥ*	अनुकारी:
575.	*Subāndhavaḥ*	सुबान्धव:
576.	*Tumbaveeṇaḥ*	तुम्बवीण:
577.	*Mahākrodhaḥ*	महाक्रोध:
578.	*Ūrdhvaretaḥ*	ऊर्ध्वरेत:
579.	*Jaleśayaḥ*	जलेशय:
580.	*Ugraḥ*	उग्र:
581.	*Vaśaṅkaraḥ*	वशंकर:
582.	*Vamśaḥ*	वंश:
583.	*Vamśanādaḥ*	वंशनाद:
584.	*Aninditaḥ*	अनिन्दित:
585.	*Sarvāngarūpaḥ*	सर्वाङ्गरूप:
586.	*Māyāvīḥ*	मायावी:
587.	*Suhṛdaḥ*	सुहृद:
588.	*Anilaḥ*	अनिल:
589.	*Analaḥ*	अनल:
590.	*Bandhanaḥ*	बन्धन:
591.	*Bandhakartāḥ*	बन्धकर्ता:
592.	*Subandhanavimocanaḥ*	सुबन्धनविमोचन:
593.	*Sayagnāriḥ*	सयज्ञारि:
594.	*Sakāmāriḥ*	सकामारि:
595.	*Mahādamṣṭraḥ*	महादंष्ट्र:
596.	*Mahāyudhaḥ*	महायुध:

#	Name in English	Name in Samskrutam
597.	*Bahudhāninditaḥ*	बहुधानिन्दित:
598.	*Sarvaḥ*	शर्व:
599.	*Śaṅkaraḥ*	शंकर:
600.	*Śaṅkaraḥ*	शंकर:
601.	*Aghanaḥ*	अघन:
602.	*Amareśaḥ*	अमरेश:
603.	*Mahādevaḥ*	महादेव:
604.	*Visvadevaḥ*	विश्वदेव:
605.	*Surārighnaḥ*	सुरारिघ्न:
606.	*Ahirbudhnyaḥ*	अहिर्बुध्न्य:
607.	*Anilābhaḥ*	अनिलाभ:
608.	*Cekitānaḥ*	चेकितान:
609.	*Haviḥ*	हवि:
610.	*Ajaikapāḥ*	अजैकपा:
611.	*Kāpālīḥ*	कापाली:
612.	*Triśankuraḥ*	त्रिशङ्कुर:
613.	*Ajitaḥ*	अजित:
614.	*Śivaḥ*	शिव:
615.	*Dhanvantariḥ*	धन्वन्तरि:
616.	*Dhūmaketuḥ*	धूमकेतु:
617.	*Skandaḥ*	स्कन्द:
618.	*Vaiśravaṇaḥ*	वैश्रवण:
619.	*Dhātraḥ*	धात्र:

#	Name in English	Name in Samskrutam
620.	*Śakraḥ*	शक्र:
621.	*Viṣṇuḥ*	विष्णु:
622.	*Mitraḥ*	मित्र:
623.	*Tvaṣṭā*	त्वष्टा:
624.	*Druvaḥ*	ध्रुव:
625.	*Dharaḥ*	धर:
626.	*Prabhāvaḥ*	प्रभाव:
627.	*Sarvagayavāyuḥ*	सर्वगायवायु:
628.	*Aryamaḥ*	अर्यम:
629.	*Savitraḥ*	सवित्र:
630.	*Raviḥ*	रवि:
631.	*Uṣangaḥ*	उषङ्ग:
632.	*Vidhātāḥ*	विधाता:
633.	*Māndhātāḥ*	मान्धाता:
634.	*Bhūtabhāvanaḥ*	भूतभावन:
635.	*Vibhuḥ*	विभु:
636.	*Varṇavibhāvī*	वर्णविभावी
637.	*Sarvakāmaguṇāvahaḥ*	सर्वकामगुणावह:
638.	*Padmanābhāḥ*	पद्मनाभा:
639.	*Mahāgarbhaḥ*	महागर्भ:
640.	*Candravaktraḥ*	चन्द्रवक्त्र:
641.	*Anilaḥ*	अनिल:
642.	*Analaḥ*	अनल:

#	Name in English	Name in Samskrutam
643.	*Balavān*	बलवान्
644.	*Upaśāntaḥ*	उपशान्तः
645.	*Purāṇaḥ*	पुराणः
646.	*Puṇyacanca:*	पुण्यचङ्चः
647.	*Ī*	ई
648.	*Kurukartāḥ*	कुरुकर्ताः
649.	*Kuruvāsī*	कुरुवासी
650.	*Kurubhūtaḥ*	कुरुभूतः
651.	*Guṇouṣadhaḥ*	गुणौषधः
652.	*Sarvāśayaḥ*	सर्वाशयः
653.	*Darbhacārī*	दर्भचारी
654.	*Sarveṣāmprāṇināmpatiḥ*	सर्वेषांप्राणिनांपतिः
655.	*Devadevaḥ*	देवदेवः
656.	*Sukhāsaktaḥ*	सुखासक्तः
657.	*Sat*	सत्
658.	*Asat*	असत्
659.	*Sarvaratnavit*	सर्वरत्नवित्
660.	*Kailāsagirivāsī*	कलासगिरिवासी
661.	*Himavadgirisaṁśrayaḥ*	हिमवद्गिरिसंश्रयः
662.	*Kūlahārī*	कूलहारी
663.	*Kūlakartā*	कूलकर्ता
664.	*Bahuvidyāḥ*	बहुविद्याः
665.	*Bahupradaḥ*	बहुप्रदः

#	Name in English	Name in Samskrutam
666.	*Vaṇijaḥ*	वणिज:
667.	*Vardhakīḥ*	वर्धकी:
668.	*Vṛkṣaḥ*	चृक्ष:
669.	*Vakulaḥ*	वकुल:
670.	*Candanaḥ*	चन्दन:
671.	*Chadaḥ*	छद:
672.	*Sāragrīvaḥ*	सारह्रीव:
673.	*Mahājatruḥ*	महाजत्रु:
674.	*Alolaḥ*	अलोल:
675.	*Mahouṣadhaḥ*	महौषध:
676.	*Siddhārthakārī*	सिद्धार्थकारी
677.	*Siddhārthachandovyākara-ṇottaraḥ*	सिद्धार्थछन्दोव्याकरणोत्तर:
678.	*Simhanādaḥ*	सिंहनाद:
679.	*Simhadamṣṭraḥ*	सिंहदंष्ट्र:
680.	*Simhagaḥ*	सिंहग:
681.	*Simhavāhanaḥ*	सिंहवाहन:
682.	*Prabhāvātmā*	प्रभावात्मा
683.	*Jagatkālaḥ*	जगत्काल:
684.	*Lokahitaḥ*	लोकहित:
685.	*Taraḥ*	तर:
686.	*Sārangaḥ*	सारङ्ग:
687.	*Navacakrāngaḥ*	नवचक्राङ्ग:
688.	*Ketumālī*	केतुमाली

#	Name in English	Name in Samskrutam
689.	*Sabhāvanaḥ*	सभावन:
690.	*Bhūtālayaḥ*	भूतालय:
691.	*Bhūtapatiḥ*	भूतपति:
692.	*Ahorātraḥ*	अहोरात्र:
693.	*Aninditaḥ*	अनिन्दित:
694.	*Vāhitāḥ*	वाहिता:
695.	*Sarvabhūtānām Vāhitraḥ*	सर्वभूतानां वाहित्र:
696.	*Nilayaḥ*	निलय:
697.	*Vibhurbhavaḥ*	विभुर्भव:
698.	*Amoghaḥ*	अमोघ:
699.	*Saṁyataḥ*	संयत:
700.	*Aśvaḥ*	अश्व:
701.	*Bhojanaḥ*	भोजन:
702.	*Prāṇadhāraṇaḥ*	प्राणधारण:
703.	*Dṛtimān*	धृतिमान्
704.	*Matimān*	मतिमान्
705.	*Dakṣaḥ*	दक्ष:
706.	*Satkṛtaḥ*	सत्कृत:
707.	*Yugādhipaḥ*	युगाधिप:
708.	*Gopālaḥ*	गोपाल:
709.	*Gopatiḥ*	गोपति:
710.	*Grāmaḥ*	ग्राम:
711.	*Gocarmacasanaḥ*	गोचर्मचसन:

#	Name in English	Name in Samskrutam
712.	*Hariḥ*	हरिः
713.	*Hiranyabāhuḥ*	हिरण्यबाहुः
714.	*Guhāpālaḥpraveśikaḥ*	गुहापालःप्रवेशिकः
715.	*Prakṛṣṭāriraḥ*	प्रकृष्टारिरः
716.	*Mahāharṣaḥ*	महाहर्षः
717.	*Jitakāmaḥ*	जितकामः
718.	*Jitendriyaḥ*	जितेन्द्रियः
719.	*Gāndhāraḥ*	गान्धारः
720.	*Suvāsaḥ*	सुवासः
721.	*Tapaḥsaktaḥ*	तपःसक्तः
722.	*Ratiḥ*	रतिः
723.	*Naraḥ*	नरः
724.	*Mahāgītaḥ*	महागीतः
725.	*Mahānṛtyaḥ*	महानृत्यः
726.	*Apsarogaṇasevitaḥ*	अप्सरोगणसेवितः
727.	*Mahāketuḥ*	महाकेतुः
728.	*Mahādhātuḥ*	महाधातुः
729.	*Naikasānucaraḥ*	नैकसानुचरः
730.	*Calaḥ*	चलः
731.	*Āvedaneyaḥ*	आवेदनेयः
732.	*Adeśaḥ*	आदेशः
733.	*Sarvagandhasukhāvahaḥ*	सर्वगन्धसुखावहः
734.	*Toranaḥ*	तोरनः

#	Name in English	Name in Samskrutam
735.	*Tāranaḥ*	तारन:
736.	*Vātaḥ*	वात:
737.	*Paridhīḥ*	परिधी:
738.	*Patikhecaraḥ*	पतिखेचर:
739.	*Saṁyogāyavardhanaḥ*	संयोगायवर्धन:
740.	*Vṛddhaḥ*	वृद्ध:
741.	*Ativṛddhaḥ*	अतिवृद्ध:
742.	*Guṇādhikaḥ*	गुणाधिक:
743.	*Nityamātmasahāyaḥ*	नित्यमात्मसहाय:
744.	*Devāsurapatiḥ*	देवासुरपति:
745.	*Patiḥ*	पति:
746.	*Yuktaḥ*	युक्त:
747.	*Yuktabāhuḥ*	युक्तबाहु:
748.	*Divisuparvarga Devaḥ*	दिविसुपवर्ग देव:
749.	*Āṣāḍhaḥ*	आषाढ:
750.	*Suṣāḍhaḥ*	सुषाढ:
751.	*Druvoḥ*	ध्रुवो:
752.	*Hariṇaḥ*	हरिण:
753.	*Haraḥ*	हर:
754.	*Āvartamānebhyovapuṣa:*	आवर्तमानेभ्योवपुष:
755.	*Vasuśreṣṭaḥ*	वसुश्रेष्ट:
756.	*Mahāpathaḥ*	महापथ:
757.	*Śirohāri Vimarśaḥ*	शिरोहारि विमर्श:

#	Name in English	Name in Samskrutam
758.	*Sarvalakṣaṇalakṣitaḥ*	सर्वलक्षणलक्षित:
759.	*Akṣaya Rathayogīḥ*	अक्षय रथयोगी:
760.	*Sarvayogīḥ*	सर्वयोगी:
761.	*Mahābalaḥ*	महाबल:
762.	*Samāmnāyaḥ*	समाम्नाय:
763.	*Asamāmnāyaḥ*	असमाम्नाय:
764.	*Tīrthadevaḥ*	तीर्थदेव:
765.	*Mahārathaḥ*	महारथ:
766.	*Nirjīvaḥ*	निर्जीव:
767.	*Jīvanaḥ*	जीवन:
768.	*Mantraḥ*	मन्त्र:
769.	*Śubhākṣaḥ*	शुभाक्ष:
770.	*Bahukarkaśaḥ*	बहुकर्कश:
771.	*Ratnaprabhuḥ*	रत्नप्रभु:
772.	*Raktāngaḥ*	रक्ताङ्ग:
773.	*Mahārṇavanipānavit*	महार्णवनिपानवित्
774.	*Mūlaḥ*	मूल:
775.	*Viśālaḥ*	विशाल:
776.	*Amṛtaḥ*	अमृत:
777.	*Vyaktāvyaktaḥ*	व्यक्ताव्यक्त:
778.	*Taponidhiḥ*	तपोनिधि:
779.	*Ārohaṇaḥ*	आरोहण:
780.	*Adhirohaḥ*	अधिरोह:

#	Name in English	Name in Samskrutam
781.	*Śīladhārī*	शीलधारी
782.	*Mahāyaśāḥ*	महायशाः
783.	*Senakalpaḥ*	सेनाकल्पः
784.	*Mahākalpaḥ*	महाकल्पः
785.	*Yogiḥ*	योगिः
786.	*Yugakaraḥ*	युगकरः
787.	*Hariḥ*	हरिः
788.	*Yugarūpaḥ*	युगरूपः
789.	*Mahārūpaḥ*	महारूपः
790.	*Mahānāgahanaḥ*	महानागहनः
791.	*Vadhaḥ*	वधः
792.	*Nyāyanirvapaṇaḥ*	न्यायनिर्वपणः
793.	*Pādaḥ*	पादः
794.	*Paṇḍitaḥ*	पण्डितः
795.	*Acalopamaḥ*	अचलोपमः
796.	*Bahumālaḥ*	बहुमालः
797.	*Mahāmālaḥ*	महामालः
798.	*Śaśiḥ*	शशिः
799.	*Harasulocanaḥ*	हरसुलोचनः
800.	*Vistāra Lavaṇa Kūpastriyugaḥ*	विस्तार लवण कूपस्त्रियुगः
801.	*Saphalodayaḥ*	सफलोदयः
802.	*Trilocanaḥ*	त्रिलोचनः
803.	*Viṣaṇṇāngaḥ*	विषण्णाङ्गः

#	Name in English	Name in Samskrutam
804.	*Maṇividdhaḥ*	मणिविद्धः
805.	*Jaṭādharaḥ*	जटाधरः
806.	*Binduḥ*	बिन्दुः
807.	*Visargaḥ*	विसर्गः
808.	*Sumukhaḥ*	सुमुखः
809.	*Śaraḥ*	शरः
810.	*Sarvāyudhaḥ*	सर्वायुधः
811.	*Sahaḥ*	सहः
812.	*Nivedanaḥ*	निवेदनः
813.	*Sukhājātaḥ*	सुखाजातः
814.	*Sugandhāraḥ*	सुगन्धारः
815.	*Mahādhanuḥ*	महाधनुः
816.	*Gandhapālī Bhagavān*	गन्धपाली भगवान्
817.	*Sarvakarma Utthānaḥ*	सर्वकर्म उत्थानः
818.	*Manthāna Bahula Vāyuḥ*	मन्थान बहुल वायुः
819.	*Sakalaḥ*	सकलः
820.	*Sarvalocanaḥ*	सर्वलोचनः
821.	*Talastālaḥ*	तलस्तालः
822.	*Karasthālīḥ*	करस्थालीः
823.	*Urdhvasaṁhananaḥ*	ऊर्ध्वसंहननः
824.	*Mahān*	महान्
825.	*Chatraḥ*	छत्रः
826.	*Succhatraḥ*	सुच्छत्रः

#	Name in English	Name in Samskrutam
827.	*Vikhyātalokaḥ*	विख्यातलोकः
828.	*Sarvāśrayakramaḥ*	सर्वाश्रयक्रमः
829.	*Muṇḍaḥ*	मुण्डः
830.	*Virūpaḥ*	विरूपः
831.	*Vikṛtaḥ*	विकृतः
832.	*Daṇḍiḥ*	दण्डिः
833.	*Kuṇḍiḥ*	कुण्डिः
834.	*Vikurvaṇaḥ*	विकुर्वणः
835.	*Haryakṣḥ*	हर्यक्षः
836.	*Kakhubhaḥ*	ककुभः
837.	*Vajriḥ*	वज्रिः
838.	*Śatajihvāḥ*	शतजिह्वाः
839.	*Sahasrapāt*	सहस्रपात्
840.	*Sahasramūrdhāḥ*	सहस्रमूर्धाः
841.	*Devendrasarvadevamayaḥ*	देवेन्द्रसर्वदेवमयः
842.	*Guruḥ*	गुरुः
843.	*Sahasrabāhuḥ*	सहस्रबाहुः
844.	*Sarvāngaḥ*	सर्वाङ्गः
845.	*Śaraṇyaḥ*	शरण्यः
846.	*Sarvalokakṛt*	सर्वलोककृत्
847.	*Pavitraḥ*	पवित्रः
848.	*Trikakunmantraḥ*	त्रिककुन्मन्त्रः
849.	*Kaniṣṭaḥ*	कनिष्टः

#	Name in English	Name in Samskrutam
850.	*Kṛṣṇapingalaḥ*	कृष्णपिङ्गल:
851.	*Brahmadaṇḍavinirmātāḥ*	प्रह्मदण्डविनिर्माता:
852.	*Śatagnīpāśaśaktiman*	शतग्नीपाशशक्तिमान्
853.	*Padmagarbhaḥ*	पद्मगर्भ:
854.	*Mahāgarbhaḥ*	महागर्भ:
855.	*Brahmagarbhaḥ*	ब्रह्मगर्भ:
856.	*Jalodbhavaḥ*	जलोद्भव:
857.	*Gabhastiḥ*	गभस्ति:
858.	*Brahmakṛt*	ब्रह्मकृत्
859.	*Brahmī*	ब्रह्मी
860.	*Brahmavit*	ब्रह्मिवत्
861.	*Brāhmaṇaḥ*	ब्राह्मण:
862.	*Gatiḥ*	गति:
863.	*Anantarūpaḥ*	अनन्तरूप:
864.	*Naikātmāḥ*	नैकात्मा:
865.	*Svayaṁbhuvastigmatejasaḥ*	स्वयंभुवस्तिग्मतेजस:
866.	*Ūrdhvagātmāḥ*	ऊर्ध्वगात्मा:
867.	*Paśupatiḥ*	पशुपति:
868.	*Vātaranhāḥ*	वातरंहा:
869.	*Manojavaḥ*	मनोजव:
870.	*Candanīḥ*	चन्दनी:
871.	*Padmanālāgraḥ*	पद्मनालाग्र:
872.	*Surabhyuttaraṇaḥ*	सुरभ्युत्तरण:

#	Name in English	Name in Samskrutam
873.	*Naraḥ*	नर:
874.	*Karṇikāramahāsragvīḥ*	कर्णिकारमहास्रग्वी:
875.	*Nīlamouliḥ*	नीलमौलि:
876.	*Pinākadṛt*	पिनाकधृत्
877.	*Umāpatiḥ*	उमापति:
878.	*Umākāntaḥ*	उमाकान्त:
879.	*Jāhnavīdṛguḥ*	जाह्नवीधृगु:
880.	*Umādhavaḥ*	उमाधव:
881.	*Varavarāhaḥ*	वरवराह:
882.	*Varadaḥ*	वरद:
883.	*Vareṇyaḥ*	वरेण्य:
884.	*Sumahāsvanaḥ*	सुमहास्वन:
885.	*Mahāprasādaḥ*	महाप्रसाद:
886.	*Damanaḥ*	दमन:
887.	*Śatruhāḥ*	शत्रुहा:
888.	*Śvetapiṇgalaḥ*	श्वेतपिङ्गल:
889.	*Prītātmāḥ*	प्रीतात्मा:
890.	*Paramātmāḥ*	परमात्मा:
891.	*Prayatātmāḥ*	प्रयतात्मा:
892.	*Pradhānadṛt*	प्रधानधृत्
893.	*Sarvapārśvamukhaḥ*	सर्वपार्श्वमुख:
894.	*Trayakṣaḥ*	त्रयक्ष:
895.	*Dharmasādhāraṇavaraḥ*	धर्मसाधारणवर:

#	Name in English	Name in Samskrutam
896.	*Carācarātmaḥ*	चराचरात्म:
897.	*Sūkṣmātmaḥ*	सूक्ष्मात्म:
898.	*Amṛtagovṛṣeśvaraḥ*	अमृतगोवृषेश्वर:
899.	*Sādhyarṣaḥ*	साध्यर्ष:
900.	*Vasurādityaḥ*	वसुरादित्य:
901.	*Vivasvat Savitāmṛtaḥ*	विवस् वत् सवितामृत:
902.	*Vyāsaḥ*	व्यास:
903.	*Sargasusaṁkṣepa Vistaraḥ*	सर्गसुसंक्षेप विस्तर:
904.	*Paryayo Naraḥ*	पर्ययो नर:
905.	*Ṛtuḥ*	ऋतु:
906.	*Saṁvatsaraḥ*	संवत्सर:
907.	*Māsaḥ*	मास:
908.	*Pakṣaḥ*	पक्ष:
909.	*Saṁkhyāsamāpanaḥ*	संख्यासमापन:
910.	*Kalāḥ*	कला:
911.	*Kaṣṭāḥ*	काष्टा:
912.	*Lavāḥ*	लवा:
913.	*Mātrāḥ*	मात्रा:
914.	*Muhūrtākṣapāḥ*	मुहूर्ताक्षपा:
915.	*Kṣaṇāḥ*	क्षणा:
916.	*Visvakṣetraḥ*	विश्वक्षेत्र:
917.	*Prajābījaḥ*	प्रजाबीज:
918.	*Lingaḥ*	लिङ्ग:

#	Name in English	Name in Samskrutam
919.	*Ādhyanirgamaḥ*	आध्यनिर्गमः
920.	*Sat*	सत्
921.	*Asat*	असत्
922.	*Avyaktaḥ*	अव्यक्तः
923.	*Pitāḥ*	पिताः
924.	*Mātāḥ*	माताः
925.	*Pitāmahaḥ*	पितामहः
926.	*Svargadvāraḥ*	स्वर्गद्वारः
927.	*Prajādvāraḥ*	प्रजाद्वारः
928.	*Mokṣadvāraḥ*	मोक्षद्वारः
929.	*Triviṣṭapaḥ*	त्रिविष्टपः
930.	*Nirvāṇaḥ*	निर्वाणः
931.	*Hlādanaḥ*	ह्लादनः
932.	*Brahmalokaḥ*	ब्रह्मलोकः
933.	*Parāngatiḥ*	पराङ्गतिः
934.	*Devāsuravinirmātā*	देवासुरविनिर्माता
935.	*Devāsuraparāyaṇaḥ*	देवासुरपरायणः
936.	*Devāsuraguruḥ*	देवासुरगुरुः
937.	*Devaḥ*	देवः
938.	*Devāsuranamaskṛtaḥ*	देवासुरनमस्कृतः
939.	*Devāsuramahāmātraḥ*	देवासुरमहामात्रः
940.	*Devāsuragaṇāsrayaḥ*	देवसुरगणाश्रयः
941.	*Devāsuragaṇadhyakṣaḥ*	देवासुरगणाध्यक्षः

#	Name in English	Name in Samskrutam
942.	*Devāsuragaṇāgraṇīḥ*	देवासुरगणाग्रणी:
943.	*Devātidevaḥ*	देवातिदेव:
944.	*Devarṣiḥ*	देवर्षि:
945.	*Devāsuravarapradaḥ*	देवासुरवरप्रद:
946.	*Devāsureśvaraḥ*	देवासुरेश्वर:
947.	*Viśvaḥ*	विश्व:
948.	*Devāsuramaheśvaraḥ*	देवासुरमहेश्वर:
949.	*Sarvadevamayaḥ*	सर्वदेवमय:
950.	*Acintyayaḥ*	अचिन्त्यय:
951.	*Devatātmaḥ*	देवतात्म:
952.	*Ātmasaṁbhavaḥ*	आत्मसंभव:
953.	*Udbhiḥ*	उद्भि:
954.	*Trivikramaḥ*	त्रिविक्रम:
955.	*Vaidhyaḥ*	वैध्य:
956.	*Virajaḥ*	विरज:
957.	*Nīrajaḥ*	नीरज:
958.	*Amaraḥ*	अमर:
959.	*Īḍyaḥ*	ईड्य:
960.	*Hastīśvaraḥ*	हस्तीश्वर:
961.	*Vyāgraḥ*	व्याघ्र:
962.	*Devasimhaḥ*	देवसिंह:
963.	*Nararṣabhaḥ*	नरर्षभ:
964.	*Vibudhaḥ*	विबुध:

#	Name in English	Name in Samskrutam
965.	*Agravaraḥ*	अग्रवर:
966.	*Sūkṣmaḥ*	सूक्ष्म:
967.	*Sarvadevaḥ*	सर्वदेव:
968.	*Tapomayaḥ*	तपोमय:
969.	*Suyuktaḥ*	सुयुक्त:
970.	*Śobhanaḥ*	शोभन:
971.	*Vajraḥ*	वज्र:
972.	*Prāsānāmprabhavaḥ*	प्रासानांप्रभव:
973.	*Avyayaḥ*	अव्यय:
974.	*Guhaḥ*	गुह:
975.	*Kāntaḥ*	कान्त:
976.	*Nijaḥ*	निज:
977.	*Sargaḥ*	सर्ग:
978.	*Pavitraḥ*	पवित्र:
979.	*Sarvapāvanaḥ*	सर्वपावन:
980.	*Sṛngīḥ*	शृंगी:
981.	*Sṛngapriyaḥ*	शृंगप्रिय:
982.	*Babhrūḥ*	बभ्रू:
983.	*Rājarājaḥ*	राजराज:
984.	*Nirāmayaḥ*	निरामय:
985.	*Abhirāmaḥ*	अभिराम:
986.	*Suragaṇaḥ*	सुरगण:
987.	*Virāmaḥ*	विराम:

#	Name in English	Name in Samskrutam
988.	*Sarvasādhanaḥ*	सर्वसाधन:
989.	*Lalāṭākṣaḥ*	ललाटाक्ष:
990.	*Viśvadevaḥ*	विश्वदेव:
991.	*Hariṇaḥ*	हरिण:
992.	*Brahmavarcasaḥ*	ब्रह्मवर्चस:
993.	*Sthāvarāṇāmpatiḥ*	स्थावराणांपति:
994.	*Niyamendrayavardhanaḥ*	नियमेन्द्रयवर्धन:
995.	*Siddhārthaḥ*	सिद्धार्थ:
996.	*Siddhabhūtārthaḥ*	सिद्धभूतार्थ:
997.	*Acintyaḥ*	अचिन्त्य:
998.	*Satyavrataḥ*	सत्यव्रत:
999.	*Śuciḥ*	शुचि:
1000.	*Vratādhipaḥ*	व्रताधिप:
1001.	*Paraḥ*	पर:
1002.	*Brahmaḥ*	ब्रह्म:
1003.	*Bhaktānāmparamāgatiḥ*	भक्तानांपरमागति:
1004.	*Vimuktaḥ*	विमुक्त:
1005.	*Muktatejasaḥ*	मुक्ततेजस:
1006.	*Śrīmān*	श्रीमान्
1007.	*Śrīvardhanaḥ*	श्रीवर्धन
1008.	*Jagataḥ*	जगत:

*****

Śrī Lalitā Sahasranāmāvali

Om Namaḥ Lalitāmbikāyai

#	Name in English	Name in Samskrutam
1	*Śrīmātā*	श्रीमाता
2	*Śrīmahārājnī*	श्रीमहाराज्ञी
3	*Śrīmatsimhāsaneśvarī*	श्रीमत्सिंहासनेश्वरी
4	*Chidagnikuŋḍasambhūtā*	चिदग्निकुण्डसंभूता
5	*Devakāryasamudyatā*	देवकार्यसमुद्यता
6	*Udyadbhānusahasrābhā*	उद्यद्भानुसहस्राभा
7	*Caturbāhusamanvitā*	चतुर्बाहुसमन्विता
8	*Rāgasvarūpapāśāḍhyā*	रागस्वरूपपाशाढ्या
9	*Krodhākārānkuśojvalā*	क्रोधाकाराङ्कुशोज्वला
10	*Manorupekṣukodaŋḍā*	मनोरुपेक्षुकोदण्डा
11	*Pajnchatanmātrasāyakā*	पञ्चतन्मात्रसायका
12	*Nijārunaprabhāpūramajjad-brahmaŋḍamaŋḍalā*	निजारुणप्रभापूरमज्जद् ब्रह्माण्डमण्डला
13	*Champakāśokapunnāga sougandhi Kalasatkachā*	चम्पकाशोकपुन्नाग सौगन्धि कलसत्कचा
14	*Kuruvindamaŋiśrenīkanatkoţīra Manḍitā*	कुरुविन्दमणिश्रेणीकनत्कोटीर मण्डिता
15	*Aşţamīchandra Vibhrājadalikasthala Śobhitā*	अष्टमीचन्द्र विभ्राजदलिकस्थल शोभिता
16	*Mukhachandrakalannkābhamrug anābhiviśeṣakā*	मुखचन्द्रकलन्ङ्काभमृगनाभिविशेषका
17	*Vadanasmaramāngalyagruhator aŋachillikā*	वदनस्मरमाङ्गल्यगृहतोरणचिल्लिका
18	*Vaktralakşmī Parīvāha chalanmīnābhalochanā*	वक्त्रलक्ष्मी परीवाह चलन्मीनाभलोचना

#	Name in English	Name in Samskrutam
19	*Navachampakapuṣpābhanāsāda ṇḍavirājitā*	नवचम्पकपुष्पाभनासादण्डविराजिता
20	*Tārākāntitiraskāri Nāsābharaṇabhāsurā*	ताराकान्तितिरस्कारि नासाभरणभासुरा
21	*Kadambamanjarīklupta karṇapūramanoharā*	कदम्बमंजरीक्लृप्तकर्णपूरमनोहरा
22	*Tāṭankayugalībhūtatapanodupa maṇḍalā*	ताटङ्कयुगलीभूततपनोडुपमण्डला
23	*Padmarāgaśilādarśaparibhāvikap olabhūḥ*	पद्मरागशिलादर्शपरिभाविकपोलभूः
24	*Navavidrumabimba Śrīnyakkāridaśanaccadā*	नवविद्रुमबिम्ब श्रीन्यक्कारिदशनच्छदा
25	*Śuddhavidyānkurākāradvija panktidwayojjwalā*	शुद्धविद्याङ्कुराकारद्विज पक्तिद्वयोावला
26	*Karpūravīṭikāmodasamākarṣi digantarā*	कर्पूरवीटिकामोदसमाकषि ʻदिगन्तरा
27	*Nijasallāpamādhurya Vinirbhartsitakacchapī*	निजसल्लापमाधुर्य विनिर्भर्त्सितकच्छपी
28	*Mandasmitaprabhāpūramajjat kāmeśamānasā*	मन्दस्मितप्रभापूरमज्जत कामेशमानसा
29	*Anākalitasādruśyachibukaśrī virājitā*	अनाकलितसादृश्यचिबुकश्री विराजिता
30	*Kāmeśabaddhamāngalyasūtraśo bhitakandharā*	कामेशबद्धमाङ्गल्यसूत्रशोभित कन्धरा
31	*Kanakāngadakeyūrakamanīya bhujānvitā*	कनकाङ्गदकेयूरकमनीय भुजान्विता
32	*Ratnagraiveyachintākalola muktāphalānvitā*	रत्नग्रैवेयचिन्ताकलोल मुक्ताफलान्विता
33	*Kāmeśvarapremaratnamaṇiprath ipaṇastanī*	कामेश्वरप्रेमरत्नमणिप्रथिपणस्तनी

#	Name in English	Name in Samskrutam
34	*Nābhyālavālaromālilatāphala kuchadvayī*	नाभ्यालवालरोमालिलताफल कुचद्वयी
35	*Lakṣyaromalatādhāra tāsamunneyamadhyamā*	लक्ष्यरोमलताधारतासमुन्नेयमध्यमा
36	*Stanabhāradalanmadhya paţţabandhavalitrayā*	स्तनभारदलन्मध्यपट्टबन्ध वलित्रया
37	*Aruŋārunakousumbhavastra bhāsvatkaţītaţī*	अरुणारुणकौसुम्भवस्त्र भास्वत्कटीतटी
38	*Ratnakimkiŋikāramyaraśanā dāmabhūṣitā*	रत्नकिंकिणिकारम्यरशना दामभूषिता
39	*Kāmeśajnātasoubhāgyamārdavor udvayānvitā*	कामेशज्ञातसौभाग्यमार्दवोरु द्वयान्विता
40	*Mānikyamukuţākārajānudvaya virājitā*	माणिक्यमुकुटाकारजानुद्वयवि राजिता
41	*Indragopaparikṣiptasmara tūnābhajanghikā*	इन्द्रगोपपरिक्षिप्तस्मरतूणाभ जङ्घिका
42	*Gūḍhagulphā*	गूढगुल्फा
43	*Kūrmapruşţhajayiśnuprapa dānvitā*	कूर्मपृष्ठजयिश्णुप्रपदान्विता
44	*Nakhadīdhitisamchannana majjana Tamoguŋā*	नखदीधितिसंछन्ननमज्जन तमोगुणा
45	*Padadvayaprabhājālaparākruta saroruhā*	पदद्वयप्रभाजालपराकृत सरोरुहा
46	*Sijnjānamaŋimanjīramaŋḍita Śrīpadāmbujā*	सिञ्जानमणिमंजीरमण्डित श्रीपदांबुजा
47	*Marālīmandagamanā*	मरालीमन्दगमना
48	*Mahālāvaŋyaśevadhiḥ*	महालावण्यशेवधि:
49	*Sarvāruŋā*	सर्वारुणा

#	Name in English	Name in Samskrutam
50	*Anavadyāngī*	अनवद्याङ्गी
51	*Sarvābharaŋabhūṣitā*	सर्वाभरणभूषिता
52	*Śivakāmeśvarānkasthā*	शिवकामेश्वराङ्कस्था
53	*Śivā*	शिवा
54	*Svādhīnavallabhā*	स्वाधीनवल्लभा
55	*Sumerumadhyasrungasthā*	सुमेरुमध्यश्रुङ्गस्था
56	*Śrīmannagaranāyikā*	श्रीमन्नगरनायिका
57	*Chintāmaŋigruhāntasthā*	चिन्तामणिगृहान्तस्था
58	*PajnchaBrahmasanasthitā*	पञ्चब्रह्मासनस्थिता
59	*Mahāpadmāţavīsamsthā*	महापद्माटवीसंस्था
60	*Kadambavanavāsinī*	कदंबवनवासिनी
61	*Sudhāsāgaramadhyasthā*	सुधासागरमध्यस्था
62	*Kāmākṣī*	कामाक्षी
63	*Kāmadāyinī*	कामदायिनी
64	*Devarṣigaŋasamghātastūyamānā tmavaibhavā*	देवर्षिगणसंघातस्तूयमानात्मवैभवा
65	*Bhanḍāsuravadhodyuktaśakti Senāsamanvitā*	भण्डासुरवधोद्युक्तशक्तिसेना समन्विता
66	*Sampatkarīsamārūḍhasindhuravr ajasevitā*	सम्पत्करीसमारूढसिन्धुरव्रज सेविता
67	*Aśvārūḍhādhiṣţitāśvakoţi koţibhirāvrutā*	अश्वारूढाधिष्ठिताश्वकोटि कोटिभिरावृता
68	*Chakrarājarathārūḍhasarvā yudhapariṣkrutā*	चक्रराजरथारूढसर्वायुध परिष्कृता
69	*Geyachakrarathārūḍhamantrinī parisevitā*	गेयचक्ररथारूढमन्त्रिणी परिसेविता

#	Name in English	Name in Samskrutam
70	*Kirichakrarathārūḍhadaŋḍa nāthāpuraskrutā*	किरिचक्ररथारूढदण्डनाथा पुरस्कृता
71	*Jwālāmālinikākṣipta vahniprākāramadhyagā*	ज्वालामालिनिकाक्षिप्त वह्निप्राकारमध्यगा
72	*Bhanḍasainyavadhodyuktaśakti vikramaharṣitā*	भण्डसैन्यवधोद्युक्तशक्ति विक्रमहर्षिता
73	*Nityāparākramāţopanirīkṣana samutsukā*	नित्यापराक्रमाटोपनिरीक्षण समुत्सुका
74	*Bhanḍaputravadhodyuktabālā vikramananditā*	भण्डपुत्रवधोद्युक्तबाला विक्रमनन्दिता
75	*Mantrinyambāvirachitaviṣanga vadhatoṣitā*	मन्त्रिण्यम्बाविरचितविषङ्ग वधतोषिता
76	*Viśukraprāŋaharaŋavārāhīvīrya nanditā*	विशुक्रप्राणहरणवाराहीवीर्यनंदिता
77	*Kāmeśvaramukhālokakalpita Śrīgaŋeśvarā*	कामेश्वरमुखालोककल्पित श्रीगणेश्वरा
78	*Mahāgaŋeśanirbhinnavighna yantraprahaṛṣitā*	महागणेशनिर्भिन्नविघ्नयन्त्र प्रहर्षिता
79	*Bhanḍāsurendranirmuktaśastra pratyastravarṣiŋī*	भण्डासुरेन्द्रनिर्मुक्तशस्त्र प्रत्यस्त्रवर्षिणी
80	*Karāmgulinakhotpannanārāyaŋa daśakrutiḥ*	करांगुलिनखोत्पन्ननारायणदशाकृतिः
81	*Mahāpāśupatāstrāgninirdhagdhā surasainikā*	महापाशुपतास्त्राग्निनिर्धग्धा सुरसैनिका
82	*Kāmeśvarāstranirdagdhasa bhaŋḍāsuraśūnyakā*	कामेश्वरास्त्रनिर्दग्धसभण्डासुर शून्यका
83	*Bramopendramahendradi devasamstutavaibhavā*	ब्रमोपेन्द्रमहेन्द्रदिदेवसंस्तुतवैभवा

#	Name in English	Name in Samskrutam
84	*Haranetrāgnisamdagdhakāmasa mjīvanouṣadhiḥ*	हरनेत्राग्निसंदग्धकामसंजीवनौषधि:
85	*Śrīmadvāgbhavakūţaikasvarūpa mukhapamkajā*	श्रीमद्वाग्भवकूटैकस्वरूपमुखपंकजा
86	*Kanţhādhakaţiparyantamadhyak ūţasvarūpiŋī*	कण्ठाधकटिपर्यन्तमध्यकूटस्व रूपिणी
87	*Śaktikūţaikatāpannakatyadhobhā gadhāriŋī*	शक्तिकूटैकतापन्नकट्यधोभागधारिणी
88	*Mūlamantratmikā*	मूलमन्त्रात्मिका
89	*Mūlakūţatrayakalebarā*	मूलकूटत्रयकलेबरा
90	*Kulāmrutaikarasikā*	कुलामृतैकरसिका
91	*Kulasanketapālinī*	कुलसङ्केतपालिनी
92	*Kulānganā*	कुलाङ्गना
93	*Kulāntasthā*	कुलान्तस्था
94	*Koulinī*	कौलिनी
95	*Kulayoginī*	कुलयोगिनी
96	*Akulā*	अकुला
97	*Samayāntasthā*	समयान्तस्था
98	*Samayācāratatparā*	समयाचारतत्परा
99	*Mūlādhāraikanilayā*	मूलाधारैकनिलया
100	*Brahmagranthivibhedinī*	ब्रह्मग्रन्थिविभेदिनी
101	*Maŋipūrāntaruditā*	मणिपूरान्तरुदिता
102	*Viṣŋugranthivibhedinī*	विष्णुग्रन्थिविभेदिनी
103	*Āgnāchakrantarālasthā*	आज्ञाचक्रान्तरालस्था
104	*Rudragranthivibhedinī*	रुद्रग्रन्थिविभेदिनी
105	*Sahasrārāmbujārūḍhā*	सहस्राराम्बुजारूढा

#	Name in English	Name in Samskrutam
106	*Sudhāsārābhivarṣiŋī*	सुधासाराभिवर्षिणी
107	*Taḍillatāsamaruchiḥ*	तडिल्लतासमरुचि:
108	*Ṣaţchakroparisamsthitā*	षट्चक्रोपरिसंस्थिता
109	*Mahāsaktiḥ*	महासक्ति:
110	*Kunḍalinī*	कुन्डलिनी
111	*Bisatantutanīyasī*	बिसतन्तुतनीयसी
112	*Bhavānī*	भवानी
113	*Bhāvanāgamyā*	भावनागम्या
114	*Bhavāraŋyakuţhārikā*	भवारण्यकुठारिका
115	*Bhadrapriyā*	भद्रप्रिया
116	*Bhadramūrttiḥ*	भद्रमूर्त्ति:
117	*Bhaktasoubhāgyadāyinī*	भक्तसौभाग्यदायिनी
118	*Bhaktipriyā*	भक्तिप्रिया
119	*Bhaktigamyā*	भक्तिगम्या
120	*Bhaktivaśyā*	भक्तिवश्या
121	*Bhayāpahā*	भयापहा
122	*Śāmbhavī*	शाम्भवी
123	*Śāradārādhyā*	शारदाराध्या
124	*Śarvāŋī*	शर्वाणी
125	*Śarmadāyinī*	शर्मदायिनी
126	*Śānkarī*	शान्करी
127	*Śrīkarī*	श्रीकरी
128	*Sādhvī*	साध्वी
129	*Śaracchandranibhānanā*	शरच्चन्द्रनिभानना
130	*Śātodarī*	शातोदरी

#	Name in English	Name in Samskrutam
131	*Śāntimatī*	शान्तिमती
132	*Nirādhārā*	निराधारा
133	*Niranjanā*	निरन्जना
134	*Nirlepā*	निर्लेपा
135	*Nirmalā*	निर्मला
136	*Nityā*	नित्या
137	*Nirākārā*	निराकारा
138	*Nirākulā*	निराकुला
139	*Nirguŋā*	निर्गुणा
140	*Niśkalā*	निश्कला
141	*Śāntā*	शान्ता
142	*Niśkāmā*	निश्कामा
143	*Nirupaplavā*	निरुपप्लवा
144	*Nityamuktā*	नित्यमुक्ता
145	*Nirvikārā*	निर्विकारा
146	*Niṣprapajnchā*	निष्प्रपञ्चा
147	*Nirāśrayā*	निराश्रया
148	*Nityaśuddhā*	नित्यशुद्धा
149	*Nityabuddhā*	नित्यबुद्धा
150	*Niravadyā*	निरवद्या
151	*Nirantarā*	निरन्तरा
152	*Niṣkāraŋā*	निष्कारणा
153	*Niṣkalamkā*	निष्कलंका
154	*Nirupādhiḥ*	निरुपाधि:
155	*Nirīśvarā*	निरीश्वरा

#	Name in English	Name in Samskrutam
156	*Nīrāgā*	नीरागा
157	*Rāgamathanī*	रागमथनी
158	*Nirmadā*	निर्मदा
159	*Madanāśinī*	मदनाशिनी
160	*Niścintā*	निश्चिन्ता
161	*Nirahamkārā*	निरहंकारा
162	*Nirmohā*	निर्मोहा
163	*Mohanāśinī*	मोहनाशिनी
164	*Nirmamā*	निर्ममा
165	*Mamatāhantrī*	ममताहन्त्री
166	*Niṣpāpā*	निष्पापा
167	*Pāpanāśinī*	पापनाशिनी
168	*Niṣkrodhā*	निष्क्रोधा
169	*Krodhaśamanī*	क्रोधशमनी
170	*Nirlobhā*	निर्लोभा
171	*Lobhanāśinī*	लोभनाशिनी
172	*Niḥsamśayā*	नि:संशया
173	*Samśayaghnī*	संशयघ्नी
174	*Nirbhavā*	निर्भवा
175	*Bhavanāśinī*	भवनाशिनी
176	*Nirvikalpā*	निर्विकल्पा
177	*Nirābādhā*	निराबाधा
178	*Nirbhedā*	निर्भेदा
179	*Bhedanāśinī*	भेदनाशिनी
180	*Nirnāśā*	निर्नाशा

#	Name in English	Name in Samskrutam
181	*Mrutyumathanī*	मृत्युमथनी
182	*Niṣkriyā*	निष्क्रिया
183	*Niṣparigrahā*	निष्परिग्रहा
184	*Nistulā*	निस्तुला
185	*Nīlachikurā*	नीलचिकुरा
186	*Nirapāyā*	निरपाया
187	*Niratyayā*	निरत्यया
188	*Durlabhā*	दुर्लभा
189	*Durgamā*	दुर्गमा
190	*Durgā*	दुर्गा
191	*Duḥkhahantrī*	दुःखहन्त्री
192	*Sukhapradā*	सुखप्रदा
193	*Duşţadūrā*	दुष्टदूरा
194	*Durāchāraśamanī*	दुराचारशमनी
195	*Doṣavarjitā*	दोषवर्जिता
196	*Sarvajnā*	सर्वज्ञा
197	*Sāndrakaruŋā*	सान्द्रकरुणा
198	*Samānādhika Varjitā*	समानाधिक वर्जिता
199	*Sarvaśaktimayī*	सर्वशक्तिमयी
200	*Sarvamangalā*	सर्वमंगला
201	*Sadgatipradā*	सद्गतिप्रदा
202	*Sarveśvarī*	सर्वेश्वरी
203	*Sarvamayī*	सर्वमयी
204	*Sarvamantrasvarūpiŋī*	सर्वमन्त्रस्वरूपिणी
205	*Sarvayantrātmikā*	सर्वयन्त्रात्मिका

#	Name in English	Name in Samskrutam
206	*Sarvatantrarūpā*	सर्वतन्त्ररूपा
207	*Manonmanī*	मनोन्मनी
208	*Māheśvarī*	माहेश्वरी
209	*Mahādevī*	महादेवी
210	*Mahālakṣmī*	महालक्ष्मी
211	*Mruḍapriyā*	मृडप्रिया
212	*Mahārūpā*	महारूपा
213	*Mahāpūjyā*	महापूज्या
214	*Mahāpātakanāśinī*	महापातकनाशिनी
215	*Mahāmāyā*	महामाया
216	*Mahāsatvā*	महासत्वा
217	*Mahāśaktiḥ*	महाशक्तिः
218	*Mahāratiḥ*	महारतिः
219	*Mahābhogā*	महाभोगा
220	*Mahaiśvaryā*	महैश्वर्या
221	*Mahāvīryā*	महावीर्या
222	*Mahābalā*	महाबला
223	*Mahābuddhiḥ*	महाबुद्धिः
224	*Mahāsiddhiḥ*	महासिद्धिः
225	*Mahāyogesvareśvarī*	महायोगेस्वरेश्वरी
226	*Mahātantra*	महातन्त्रा
227	*Mahāmantra*	महामन्त्रा
228	*Mahāyantrā*	महायन्त्रा
229	*Mahāsanā*	महासना
230	*Mahāyāgakramāyādhyā*	महायागक्रमाराध्या

#	Name in English	Name in Samskrutam
231	*Mahābhairavapūjitā*	महाभैरवपूजिता
232	*Maheśvaramahākalpamahātānḍ avasākṣinī*	महेश्वरमहाकल्पमहाताण्डवसाक्षिणी
233	*Mahākāmeśamahiṣi*	महाकामेशमहिषी
234	*Mahātripurasundarī*	महात्रिपुरसुन्दरी
235	*Catuṣṣaṣţiyupacārādhyā*	चतुष्षष्टियुपचाराढ्या
236	*Catuṣṣaṣţikalāmayī*	चतुष्षष्टिकलामयी
237	*Mahācatuṣṣaṣţikoţiyoginīgaŋa sevitā*	महाचतुष्षष्टिकोटियोगिनीगनसेविता
238	*Manuvidyā*	मनुविद्या
239	*Candravidyā*	चन्द्रविद्या
240	*Candramaŋḍalamadhyagā*	चन्द्रमन्डलमध्यगा
241	*Cārurūpā*	चारुरूपा
242	*Cāruhāsā*	चारुहासा
243	*Cārucandrakalādharā*	चारुचन्द्रकलाधरा
244	*Carācarajagannāthā*	चराचरजगन्नाथा
245	*Cakrarājaniketanā*	चक्रराजनिकेतना
246	*Pārvatī*	पार्वती
247	*Padmanayanā*	पद्मनयना
248	*Padmarāgasamaprabhā*	पद्मरागसमप्रभा
249	*Panchapretāsanāsīnā*	पन्चप्रेतासनासीना
250	*Panchabrahmasvarūpiŋī*	पन्चब्रह्मस्वरूपिणी
251	*Cinmayī*	चिन्मयी
252	*Paramānandā*	परमानन्दा
253	*Vijnānaghanarūpiŋī*	विज्ञानघनरूपिणी
254	*Dhyānadhyātrughyeyarūpā*	ध्यानध्यातृध्येयरूपा

#	Name in English	Name in Samskrutam
255	*Dharmādharmavivarjitā*	धर्माधर्मविवर्जिता
256	*Viśvarūpā*	विश्वरूपा
257	*Jāgarinī*	जागरिणी
258	*Svapantī*	स्वपन्ती
259	*Taijasātmikā*	तैजसात्मिका
260	*Suptā*	सुप्ता
261	*Prajnātmikā*	प्रज्ञात्मिका
262	*Turyā*	तुर्या
263	*Sarvāvasthāvivarjitā*	सर्वावस्थाविवर्जिता
264	*Sruṣţikartrī*	सृष्टिकर्त्री
265	*Brahmarūpā*	ब्रह्मरूपा
266	*Goptrī*	गोप्त्री
267	*Govindarūpiŋī*	गोविन्दरूपिणी
268	*Samhāriŋī*	संहारिणी
269	*Rudrarūpā*	रुद्ररूपा
270	*Tirodhānakarī*	तिरोधानकरी
271	*Īśvarī*	ईश्वरी
272	*Sadāśivā*	सदाशिवा
273	*Anugrahadā*	अनुग्रहदा
274	*Panchakrutyaparāyanā*	पन्चकृत्यपरायणा
275	*Bhānumaŋḑalamadhyasthā*	भानुमन्डलमध्यस्था
276	*Bhairavī*	भैरवी
277	*Bhagamālinī*	भगमालिनी
278	*Padmāsanā*	पद्मासना
279	*Bhagavatī*	भगवती

#	Name in English	Name in Samskrutam
280	*Padmanābhasahodarī*	पद्मनाभसहोदरी
281	*Unmeṣanimiṣotpannavipannabhu vanāvalī*	उन्मेषनिमिषोत्पन्नविपन्नभुवनावली
282	*Sahasraśīrṣavadanā*	सहस्रशीर्षवदना
283	*Sahasrākṣī*	सहस्राक्षी
284	*Sahasrapāt*	सहस्रपदा
285	*Ābrahmakīţajananī*	आब्रह्मकीटजननी
286	*Varŋāśramavidhāyinī*	वर्णाश्रमविधायिनी
287	*Nijāgnārūpanigamā*	निजाज्ञारूपनिगमा
288	*Puŋyāpuŋyaphlapradā*	पुण्यापुण्यफलप्रदा
289	*Srutisīmantasindūrikruta pādābjadhūlikā*	श्रुतिसीमन्तसिन्दूरिकृतपादाब्ज धूलिका
290	*Sakalāgamasamdohaśakti samputamouktikā*	सकलागमसंदोहशुक्तिसंपुटमौक्तिका
291	*Puruṣārthapradā*	पुरुषार्थप्रदा
292	*Pūrŋā*	पूर्णा
293	*Bhoginī*	भोगिनी
294	*Bhuvaneśvarī*	भुवनेश्वरी
295	*Ambikā*	अंबिका
296	*Anādinidhanā*	अनादिनिधना
297	*Haribrahmendrasevitā*	हरिब्रह्मेन्द्रसेविता
298	*Nārāyaŋī*	नारायणी
299	*Nātharūpā*	नादरूपा
300	*Nāmarūpavivarjitā*	नामरूपविवर्जिता
301	*Hrīmkārī*	ह्रींकारी
302	*Hrīmatī*	ह्रीमती

#	Name in English	Name in Samskrutam
303	*Hrudyā*	हृद्या
304	*Heyopādeyavarjitā*	हेयोपादेयवर्जिता
305	*Rājarājārchitā*	राजराजार्चिता
306	*Rājnī*	राज्ञी
307	*Ramyā*	रम्या
308	*Rājīvalochanā*	राजीवलोचना
309	*Rajnjanī*	रञ्जनी
310	*Ramaŋī*	रमणी
311	*Rasyā*	रस्या
312	*Raŋatkinkiŋimekhalā*	रणत्किङ्किणिमेखला
313	*Ramā*	रमा
314	*Rākenduvadanā*	राकेन्दुवदना
315	*Ratirūpā*	रतिरूपा
316	*Ratipriyā*	रतिप्रिया
317	*Rakṣākarī*	रक्षाकरी
318	*Rākṣasaghnī*	राक्षसघ्नी
319	*Rāmā*	रामा
320	*Ramaŋalampatā*	रमणलम्पटा
321	*Kāmyā*	काम्या
322	*Kāmakalārūpā*	कामकलारूपा
323	*Kadambakusumapriyā*	कदम्बकुसुमप्रिया
324	*Kalyānī*	कल्याणी
325	*Jagatīkandā*	जगतीकन्दा
326	*Karuŋāsa Sāgarā*	करुणारस सागरा
327	*Kalāvatī*	कलावती

#	Name in English	Name in Samskrutam
328	*Kalālāpā*	कलालापा
329	*Kāntā*	कान्ता
330	*Kādambarīpriyā*	कादम्बरीप्रिया
331	*Varadā*	वरदा
332	*Vāmanayanā*	वामनयना
333	*Vāruŋī Madavihvalā*	वारुणी मदविह्वला
334	*Viśvādhikā*	विश्वाधिका
335	*Vedavedyā*	वेदवेद्या
336	*Vindhyāchalanivāsinī*	विन्ध्याचलनिवासिनी
337	*Vidhātrī*	विधात्री
338	*Vedajananī*	वेदजननी
339	*Vişŋumāyā*	विष्णुमाया
340	*Vilāsinī*	विलासिनी
341	*Kṣetrasvarūpā*	क्षेत्रस्वरूपा
342	*Kṣetreśī*	क्षेत्रेशी
343	*Kṣetrakṣetrajnapālinī*	क्षेत्रक्षेत्रज्ञपालिनी
344	*Kṣayavruddhivinirmuktā*	क्षयवृद्धिविनिर्मुक्ता
345	*Kṣetrapālasamarchitā*	क्षेत्रपालसमर्चिता
346	*Vijayā*	विजया
347	*Vimalā*	विमला
348	*Vandyā*	वन्द्या
349	*Vandārujanavatsalā*	वन्दारुजनवत्सला
350	*Vāgvādinī*	वाग्वादिनी
351	*Vāmakeśī*	वामकेशी
352	*Vahnimaŋḍalavāsinī*	वह्निमण्डलवासिनी

#	Name in English	Name in Samskrutam
353	*Bhaktimatkalpalatikā*	भक्तिमत्कल्पलतिका
354	*Paśupāśavimochanī*	पशुपाशविमोचनी
355	*Samhrutāśeśapāśaŋḍā*	सम्हृताशेशपाशण्डा
356	*Sadāchārapravarttikā*	सदाचारप्रवर्त्तिका
357	*Tāpatrayāgnisantaptasamāhlāda nachandrikā*	तापत्रयाग्निसन्तप्तसमाह्लादन चन्द्रिका
358	*Taruŋī*	तरुणी
359	*Tāpasārādhyā*	तापसाराध्या
360	*Tanumadhyā*	तनुमध्या
361	*Tamopahā*	तमोपहा
362	*Chitiḥ*	चितिः
363	*Tatpadalakṣyārthā*	तत्पदलक्ष्यार्था
364	*Chidekarasarūpiŋī*	चिदेकरसरूपिणी
365	*Svātmānandalavī Bhūtabrahmadyānanda Santatiḥ*	स्वात्मानन्दलवी भूतब्रह्माद्यानन्द सन्ततिः
366	*Parā*	परा
367	*Pratyakchitīrūpā*	प्रत्यक्चितीरूपा
368	*Paśyantī*	पश्यन्ती
369	*Paradevatā*	परदेवता
370	*Madhyamā*	मध्यमा
371	*Vaikharīrūpā*	वैखरीरूपा
372	*Bhakta Mānasahamsikā*	भक्त मानसहंसिका
373	*Kāmeśvaraprāŋanādī*	कामेश्वरप्राणनाडी
374	*Krutajnā*	कृतज्ञा
375	*Kāmapūjitā*	कामपूजिता

#	Name in English	Name in Samskrutam
376	*Śrungārarasasampūrŋā*	श्रृंगाररससम्पूर्णा
377	*Jayā*	जया
378	*Jālandharasthitā*	जालन्धरस्थिता
379	*Oḍyānapīţhanilayā*	ओड्याणपीठनिलया
380	*Bindumaŋḍalavāsinī*	बिन्दुमन्डलवासिनी
381	*Rahoyāgakrmārādhyā*	रहोयागक्रमाराध्या
382	*Rahastarpaŋatarpitā*	रहस्तर्पणतर्पिता
383	*Sadyaḥ Prasādinī*	सद्य: प्रसादिनी
384	*Viśvasākṣiŋī*	विश्वसाक्षिणी
385	*Sākṣivarjitā*	साक्षिवर्जिता
386	*Ṣaḍangadevatāyuktā*	षडङ्गदेवतायुक्ता
387	*Ṣāḍguŋyaparipūritā*	षाड्गुण्यपरिपूरिता
388	*Nityaklinnā*	नित्यक्लिन्ना
389	*Nirupamā*	निरुपमा
390	*Nirvāŋasukhadāyinī*	निर्वाणसुखदायिनी
391	*Nityāṣoḍaśikārūpā*	नित्याषोडशिकारूपा
392	*Śrīkanţhārdhaśarīriŋī*	श्रीकण्ठार्धशरीरिणी
393	*Prabhāvatī*	प्रभावती
394	*Prabhārūpā*	प्रभारूपा
395	*Prasiddhā*	प्रसिद्धा
396	*Parameśvarī*	परमेश्वरी
397	*Mūlaprakrutiḥ*	मूलप्रकृति:
398	*Avyaktā*	अव्यक्ता
399	*Vyaktāvyaktasvarūpiŋī*	व्यक्ताव्यक्तस्वरूपिणी
400	*Vyāpinī*	व्यापिनी

#	Name in English	Name in Samskrutam
401	*Vividhākārā*	फविविधाकारा
402	*Vidyā'vidyāsvarūpiŋī*	विद्याऽविद्यास्वरूपिणी
403	*Mahākāmeśanayanaku mudāhlādakou Mudī*	महाकामेशनयनकुमुदाह्लादकौ मुदी
404	*Bhaktahārdatamobheda bhānumadbhānusantatiḥ*	भक्तहार्दतमोभेदभानुमद्भानुसन्ततिः
405	*Śivadūtī*	शिवदूती
406	*Śivārādhyā*	शिवाराध्या
407	*Śivamūrttiḥ*	शिवमूर्त्तिः
408	*Śivamkarī*	शिवंकरी
409	*Śivapriyā*	शिवप्रिया
410	*Śivaparā*	शिवपरा
411	*Śiṣţeṣţā*	शिष्टेष्टा
412	*Śiṣţapūjitā*	शिष्टपूजिता
413	*Aprameyā*	अप्रमेया
414	*Svaprakāśā*	स्वप्रकाशा
415	*Manovāchāmagocharā*	मनोवाचामगोचरा
416	*Chichchaktiḥ*	चिच्छक्तिः
417	*Chetanārūpā*	चेतनारूपा
418	*Jadaśaktiḥ*	जडशक्तिः
419	*Jadātmikā*	जडात्मिका
420	*Gāyatrī*	गायत्री
421	*Vyāhrutiḥ*	व्याहृतिः
422	*Sandhyā*	सन्ध्या
423	*Dvijavrundaniṣevitā*	द्विजवृन्दनिषेविता
424	*Tatvāsanā*	तत्वासना

#	Name in English	Name in Samskrutam
425	*Tat*	तत्
426	*Tvam*	त्वम्
427	*Ayī*	अयी
428	*Pajnchakośāntarasthitā*	पञ्चकोशान्तरस्थिता
429	*Nissīmamahimā*	निस्सीममहिमा
430	*Nityayouvanā*	नित्ययौवना
431	*Madaśālinī*	मदशालिनी
432	*Madaghūrŋitaraktākṣī*	मदघूर्णितरक्ताक्षी
433	*Madapāţalagaŋḍabhūḥ*	मदपाटलगण्डभूः
434	*Chanḍana Drava Digdhāngī (ngā)*	चन्दन द्रव दिग्धाङ्गी (ङ्गा)
435	*Chāmpeyakusumapriyā*	चाम्पेयकुसुमप्रिया
436	*Kuśalā*	कुशला
437	*Komalākārā*	कोमलाकारा
438	*Kurukullā*	कुरुकुल्ला
439	*Kuleśvarī*	कुलेश्वरी
440	*Kulakuŋḍālayā*	कुलकुण्डालया
441	*Koulamārgatatparasevitā*	कौलमार्गतत्परसेविता
442	*Kumāragaŋanāthāmbā*	कुमारगणनाथाम्बा
443	*Tuşţiḥ*	तुष्टिः
444	*Puşţiḥ*	पुष्टिः
445	*Matiḥ*	मतिः
446	*Dhrutiḥ*	धृतिः
447	*Śāntiḥ*	शान्तिः
448	*Svastimatī*	स्वस्तिमती
449	*Kāntiḥ*	कान्तिः

#	Name in English	Name in Samskrutam
450	*Nandinī*	नन्दिनी
451	*Vighnanāśinī*	विघ्ननाशिनी
452	*Tejovatī*	तेजोवती
453	*Trinayanā*	त्रिनयना
454	*Lolākṣīkāmarūpiŋī*	लोलाक्षीकामरूपिणी
455	*Mālinī*	मालिनी
456	*Hamsinī*	हंसिनी
457	*Mātā*	माता
458	*Malayāchalavāsinī*	मलयाचलवासिनी
459	*Sumukhī*	सुमुखी
460	*Nalinī*	नलिनी
461	*Subhrūḥ*	सुभ्रूः
462	*Śobhanā*	शोभना
463	*Suranāyikā*	सुरनायिका
464	*Kālakaŋţhī*	कालकण्ठी
465	*Kāntimatī*	कान्तिमती
466	*Kṣobhiŋī*	क्षोभिणी
467	*Sūkṣmarūpiŋī*	सूक्ष्मरूपिणी
468	*Vajreśvarī*	वज्रेश्वरी
469	*VāmaDevī*	वामदेवी
470	*Vayo'vasthāvivarjitā*	वयोऽवस्थाविवर्जिता
471	*Siddheśvarī*	सिद्धेश्वरी
472	*Siddhavidyā*	सिद्धविद्या
473	*Siddhamātā*	सिद्धमाता
474	*Yaśasvinī*	यशस्विनी

#	Name in English	Name in Samskrutam
475	*Viśuddhichakra Nilayā*	विशुद्धिचक्र निलया
476	*Araktavarŋā*	आरक्तवर्णा
477	*Trilochanā*	त्रिलोचना
478	*Khaţvāngādipraharanā*	खट्वाङ्गादिप्रहरणा
479	*Vadanaikasamanvitā*	वदनैकसमन्विता
480	*Pāyasānnapriyā*	पायसान्नप्रिया
481	*Tvaksthā*	त्वक्स्था
482	*Paśulokabhayankarī*	पशुलोकभयङ्करी
483	*Amrutādimahāśaktisamvrutā*	अमृतादिमहाशक्तिसंवृता
484	*Ḍākinīśvarī*	डाकिनीश्वरी
485	*Anāhatābjanilayā*	अनाहताब्जनिलया
486	*Śyāmābhā*	श्यामाभा
487	*Vadanadvayā*	वदनद्वया
488	*Damşţrojvalā*	दंष्ट्रोज्वला
489	*Akṣamālādidharā*	अक्षमालादिधरा
490	*Rudhirasamsthitā*	रुधिरसंस्थिता
491	*Kālarātryādiśaktyoughavrutā*	कालरात्र्यादिशक्त्यौघवृता
492	*Snigdoudana Priyā*	स्निग्दौदन प्रिया
493	*Mahāvīrendravaradā*	महावीरेन्द्रवरदा
494	*Rākinyambāsvarūpiŋī*	राकिण्यम्बास्वरूपिणी
495	*Maŋipūrābjanilayā*	मणिपूराब्जनिलया
496	*Vadanatrāyasamyutā*	वदनत्रयसम्युता
497	*Vajrādikāyudhopetā*	वज्रादिकायुधोपेता
498	*Ḍāmaryādibhirāvrutā*	डामर्यादिभिरावृता
499	*Raktavarŋā*	रक्तवर्णा

#	Name in English	Name in Samskrutam
500	*Māmsaniṣţā*	माम्सनिष्टा
501	*Guḍānnaprītamānasā*	गुडान्नप्रीतमानसा
502	*Samastabhaktasukhadā*	समस्तभक्तसुखदा
503	*Lākinyambāsvarūpiŋī*	लाकिन्यम्बास्वरूपिणी
504	*Svādhiṣţānāmbujagatā*	स्वाधिष्टानाम्बुजगता
505	*Chaturvaktramanoharā*	चतुर्वक्त्रमनोहरा
506	*Śūlādhyāyudha Sampannā*	शूलाद्यायुध संपन्ना
507	*Pītavarŋā*	पीतवर्णा
508	*Atigarvitā*	अतिगर्विता
509	*Medoniṣţhā*	मेदोनिष्ठा
510	*Madhuprītā*	मधुप्रीता
511	*Bandhinyādisamanvitā*	बन्धिन्यादिसमन्विता
512	*Dadhyannāsaktahrudayā*	दध्यन्नासक्तहृदया
513	*Kākinīrūpadhārinī*	काकिनीरूपधारिणी
514	*Mūlādhārāmbujārūḍhā*	मूलाधाराम्बुजारूढा
515	*Panchavaktrā*	पन्चवक्त्रा
516	*Asthisamsthitā*	अस्थिसम्स्थिता
517	*Angkuśādipraharanā*	अङ्कुशादिप्रहरणा
518	*Varadādiniṣevitā*	वरदादिनिषेविता
519	*Mudgoudanāsaktachittā*	मुद्गौदनासक्तचित्ता
520	*Sākinyambāsvarūpiŋī*	साकिन्यम्बास्वरूपिणी
521	*Āgnāchakrabjanilayā*	आज्ञाचक्राब्जनिलया
522	*Śuklavarŋā*	शुक्लवर्णा
523	*Ṣaḍānanā*	षडानना
524	*Majjāsamsthā*	मज्जासंस्था

#	Name in English	Name in Samskrutam
525	*Hamsavatīmukhyaśakti samanvitā*	हंसवतीमुख्यशक्तिसमन्विता
526	*Haridrānnaikarasikā*	हरिद्रान्नैकरसिका
527	*Hākinīrūpadhārinī*	हाकिनीरूपधारिणी
528	*Sahasradalapadmasthā*	सहस्रदलपद्मस्था
529	*Sarvavarŋopaśobhitā*	सर्ववर्णोपशोभिता
530	*Sarvāyudhadharā*	सर्वायुधधरा
531	*Śuklasamsthitā*	शुक्लसंस्थिता
532	*Sarvatomukhī*	सर्वतोमुखी
533	*Sarvoudanaprītachittā*	सर्वौदनप्रीतचित्ता
534	*Yākinyambāsvarūpiŋī*	याकिन्यम्बास्वरूपिणी
535	*Svāhā*	स्वाहा
536	*Svadhā*	स्वधा
537	*Amatiḥ*	अमति:
538	*Medhā*	मेधा
539	*Srutiḥ*	श्रुति:
540	*Smrutiḥ*	स्मृति:
541	*Anuttamā*	अनुत्तमा
542	*Puŋyakīrttiḥ*	पुण्यकीर्त्ति:
543	*Puŋyalabhyā*	पुण्यलभ्या
544	*Puŋyaśravaŋakīrttanā*	पुण्यश्रवणकीर्त्तना
545	*Pulomajārchitā*	पुलोमजार्चिता
546	*Bandhamochanī*	बन्धमोचनी
547	*Bandhurālakā (Barbarālakā)*	बन्धुरालका (बर्बरालका)
548	*Vimarśarūpiŋī*	विमर्शरूपिणी

#	Name in English	Name in Samskrutam
549	*Vidyā*	विद्या
550	*Viyadādijagatprasūḥ*	वियदादिजगत्प्रसू:
551	*Sarvavyādhipraśamanī*	सर्वव्याधिप्रशमनी
552	*Sarvamrutyunivāriṇī*	सर्वमृत्युनिवारिणी
553	*Agragaṇyā*	अग्रगण्या
554	*Achintyarūpā*	अचिन्त्यरूपा
555	*Kalikalmaṣanāśinī*	कलिकल्मषनाशिनी
556	*Kātyāyanī*	कात्यायनी
557	*Kālahantrī*	कालहन्त्री
558	*Kamalākṣa Niṣevitā*	कमलाक्ष निषेविता
559	*Tāmbūlapūritamukhī*	ताम्बूलपूरितमुखी
560	*Dādimīkusumaprabhā*	दाडिमीकुसुमप्रभा
561	*Mrugākṣī*	मृगाक्षी
562	*Mohinī*	मोहिनी
563	*Mukhyā*	मुख्या
564	*Mruḍānī*	मृडानी
565	*Mitrarūpiṇī*	मित्ररूपिणी
566	*Nityatruptā*	नित्यतृप्ता
567	*Bhaktanidhiḥ*	भक्तनिधि:
568	*Niyantrī*	नियन्त्री
569	*Nikhilesvarī*	निखिलेस्वरी
570	*Maitryādivāsanālabhyā*	मैत्र्यादिवासनालभ्या
571	*Mahāpralayasākṣinī*	महाप्रलयसाक्षिणी
572	*Parāśaktiḥ*	पराशक्ति:
573	*Parāniṣthā*	परानिष्ठा

#	Name in English	Name in Samskrutam
574	*Prajnānaghanarūpiŋī*	प्रज्ञानघनरूपिणी
575	*Mādhvīpānālasā*	माध्वीपानालसा
576	*Mattā*	मत्ता
577	*Matrukāvarŋarūpiŋī*	मातृकावर्णरूपिणी
578	*Mahākailāsanilayā*	महाकैलासनिलया
579	*Mrunālamrududorlatā*	मृणालमृदुदोर्लता
580	*Mahanīyā*	महनीया
581	*Dayāmūrtiḥ*	दयामूर्तिः
582	*Mahāsāmrājyaśālinī*	महासाम्राज्यशालिनी
583	*Ātmavidyā*	आत्मविद्या
584	*Mahāvidyā*	महाविद्या
585	*Śrīvidyā*	श्रीविद्या
586	*Kāmasevitā*	कामसेविता
587	*Śrīṣoḍaśākṣarīvidyā*	श्रीषोडशाक्षरीविद्या
588	*Trikūţā*	त्रिकूटा
589	*Kāmakoţikā*	कामकोटिका
590	*Kaţākṣa Kinkarī Bhūtakamalākoţisevitā*	कटाक्ष किङ्करी भूतकमलाकोटिसेविता
591	*Śiraḥsthitā*	शिरःस्थिता
592	*Chandranibhā*	चन्द्रनिभा
593	*Bhālasthā*	भालस्था
594	*IndradhanuḥPrabhā*	इन्द्रधनुःप्रभा
595	*Hrudayasthā*	हृदयस्था
596	*Raviprakhyā*	रविप्रख्या
597	*Trikoŋāntaradīpikā*	त्रिकोणान्तरदीपिका

#	Name in English	Name in Samskrutam
598	*Dākṣāyanī*	दाक्षायणी
599	*Daityahantrī*	दैत्यहन्त्री
600	*Dakṣayajnavināśinī*	दक्षयज्ञविनाशिनी
601	*Darāndolitadīrghākṣī*	दरान्दोलितदीर्घाक्षी
602	*Darahāsojjavalanmukhī*	दरहासोज्ज्वलन्मुखी
603	*Gurumūrtiḥ*	गुरुमूर्तिः
604	*Guŋanidhiḥ*	गुणनिधिः
605	*Gomātā*	गोमाता
606	*Guhajanmabhūḥ*	गुहजन्मभूः
607	*Deveśī*	देवेशी
608	*Daŋḍanītisthā*	दण्डनीतिस्था
609	*Daharākāśarūpiŋī*	दहराकाशरूपिणी
610	*Pratipanmukhyarākāntatithi maŋḍalapūjitā*	प्रतिपन्मुख्यराकान्ततिथि मण्डलपूजिता
611	*Kalātmikā*	कलात्मिका
612	*Kalānāthā*	कलानाथा
613	*Kāvyālāpavinodinī*	काव्यालापविनोदिनी
614	*Sachāmararamāvāŋīsavya dakṣiŋasevitā*	सचामररमावाणीसव्यदक्षिणसेविता
615	*Ādiśaktiḥ*	आदिशक्तिः
616	*Ameyā*	अमेया
617	*Ātmā*	आत्मा
618	*Paramā*	परमा
619	*Pāvanākrutiḥ*	पावनाकृतिः
620	*Anekakoţibrahmaŋḍajananī*	अनेककोटिब्रह्माण्डजननी
621	*Divyavigrahā*	दिव्यविग्रहा

#	Name in English	Name in Samskrutam
622	*Klīmkārī*	क्लींकारी
623	*Kevalā*	केवला
624	*Guhyā*	गुह्या
625	*Kaivalyapadadāyinī*	कैवल्यपददायिनी
626	*Tripurā*	त्रिपुरा
627	*Trijagadvandyā*	त्रिजगद्वन्द्या
628	*Trimūrttiḥ*	त्रिमूर्त्तिः
629	*Tridaśeśvarī*	त्रिदशेश्वरी
630	*Tryakṣarī*	त्र्यक्षरी
631	*Divyagandhāḍhyā*	दिव्यगन्धाढ्या
632	*Sindūratilakājnchitā*	सिन्दूरतिलकाञ्चिता
633	*Umā*	उमा
634	*Śailendratanayā*	शैलेन्द्रतनया
635	*Gourī*	गौरी
636	*Gandharvasevitā*	गन्धर्वसेविता
637	*Viśvagarbhā*	विश्वगर्भा
638	*Svarŋagarbhā*	स्वर्णगर्भा
639	*Avaradā*	अवरदा
640	*Vāgadhīśvarī*	वागधीश्वरी
641	*Dhyānagamyā*	ध्यानगम्या
642	*Aparicchedyā*	अपरिच्छेद्या
643	*Jnānadā*	ज्ञानदा
644	*Jnānavigrahā*	ज्ञानविग्रहा
645	*Sarvavedāntasamvedyā*	सर्ववेदान्तसंवेद्या
646	*Satyānandasvarūpiŋī*	सत्यानन्दस्वरूपिणी

#	Name in English	Name in Samskrutam
647	*Lopāmudrārchitā*	लोपामुद्रार्चिता
648	*LīlākluptaBrahmaṇḍamaṇḍalā*	लीलाक्लुप्तब्रह्माण्डमण्डला
649	*Adruśyā*	अदृश्या
650	*Druśyarahitā*	दृश्यरहिता
651	*Vijnātrī*	विज्ञात्री
652	*Vedyavarjitā*	वेद्यवर्जिता
653	*Yoginī*	योगिनी
654	*Yogadā*	योगदा
655	*Yogyā*	योग्या
656	*Yogānandā*	योगानन्दा
657	*Yugamdharā*	युगंधरा
658	*Ichchāśaktijnānaśaktikriyāśakti svarūpiṇī*	इच्छाशक्तिज्ञानशक्तिक्रियाशक्ति स्वरूपिणी
659	*Sarvādhārā*	सर्वाधारा
660	*Supratiṣṭhā*	सुप्रतिष्ठा
661	*Sadasadrūpadhāriṇī*	सदसद्रूपधारिणी
662	*Aṣṭamūrttiḥ*	अष्टमूर्त्तिः
663	*Ajājetrī*	अजाजेत्री
664	*Lokayātrāvidhāyinī*	लोकयात्राविधायिनी
665	*Ekākinī*	एकाकिनी
666	*Bhūmarūpā*	भूमरूपा
667	*Nirdvaitā*	निर्द्वैता
668	*Dvaitavarjitā*	द्वैतवर्जिता
669	*Annadā*	अन्नदा
670	*Vasudā*	वसुदा

#	Name in English	Name in Samskrutam
671	*Vruddhā*	वृद्धा
672	*Brahmatmaikyasvarūpiŋī*	ब्रह्मात्मैक्यस्वरूपिणी
673	*Bruhatī*	बृहती
674	*Brāhmanī*	ब्राह्मणी
675	*Brāhmī*	ब्राह्मी
676	*Brahmanandā*	ब्रह्मानन्दा
677	*Balipriyā*	बलिप्रिया
678	*Bhāṣārūpā*	भाषारूपा
679	*Bruhatsenā*	बृहत्सेना
680	*Bhāvābhāvavivarjitā*	भावाभावविवर्जिता
681	*Sukhārādhyā*	सुखाराध्या
682	*Śubhakarī*	शुभकरी
683	*Śobhanā Sulabhā Gatiḥ*	शोभना सुलभा गति:
684	*Rājarājeśvarī*	राजराजेश्वरी
685	*Rājyadāyinī*	राज्यदायिनी
686	*Rājyavallabhā*	राज्यवल्लभा
687	*Rājatkrupā*	राजत्कृपा
688	*Rājapīţhaniveśitanijāśritā*	राजपीठनिवेशितनिजाश्रिता
689	*Rājyalakṣmīḥ*	राज्यलक्ष्मी:
690	*Kośanāthā*	कोशनाथा
691	*Chaturangabaleśvarī*	चतुरन्गबलेश्वरी
692	*Sāmrājyadāyinī*	साम्राज्यदायिनी
693	*Satyasandhā*	सत्यसन्धा
694	*Sāgaramekhalā*	सागरमेखला
695	*Dīkṣitā*	दीक्षिता

#	Name in English	Name in Samskrutam
696	*Daityaśamanī*	दैत्यशमनी
697	*Sarvalokavaśankarī*	सर्वलोकवशंकरी
698	*Sarvārtthadātrī*	सर्वार्त्थदात्री
699	*Sāvitrī*	सावित्री
700	*Sachchidānandarūpiŋī*	सच्चिदानन्दरूपिणी
701	*Deśakālaparichchinnā*	देशकालपरिच्छिन्ना
702	*Sarvagā*	सर्वगा
703	*Sarvamohinī*	सर्वमोहिनी
704	*Sarasvatī*	सरस्वती
705	*Śāstramayī*	शास्त्रमयी
706	*Guhāmbā*	गुहाम्बा
707	*Guhyarūpiŋī*	गुह्यरूपिणी
708	*Sarvopādhivinirmuktā*	सर्वोपाधिविनिर्मुक्ता
709	*Sadāśivapativratā*	सदाशिवपतिव्रता
710	*Sampradāyeśvarī*	सम्प्रदायेश्वरी
711	*Sādhu*	साधु
712	*Ĕ*	ई
713	*Gurumaŋḍalarūpiŋī*	गुरुमण्दलरूपिणी
714	*Kulottīrŋā*	कुलोत्तीर्णा
715	*Bhagārādhyā*	भगाराध्या
716	*Māyā*	माया
717	*Madhumatī*	मधुमती
718	*Mahī*	मही
719	*Gaŋāmbā*	गणाम्बा
720	*Guhyakārādhyā*	गुह्यकाराध्या

#	Name in English	Name in Samskrutam
721	*Komalāngī*	कोमलाङ्गी
722	*Gurupriyā*	गुरुप्रिया
723	*Svatantra*	स्वतन्त्रा
724	*Sarvatantreśī*	सर्वतन्त्रेशी
725	*Dakșiņāmūrtirūpiņī*	दक्षिणामूर्तिरूपिणी
726	*Sanakādi Samārādhyā*	सनकादि समाराध्या
727	*Śivajnnānapradāyinī*	शिवज्ञानप्रदायिनी
728	*Chitkalā*	चित्कला
729	*Anandakalikā*	आनन्दकलिका
730	*Premarūpā*	प्रेमरूपा
731	*Priyamkarī*	प्रियंकरी
732	*Nāmapārāyaņaprītā*	नामपारायणप्रीता
733	*Nandividyā*	नन्दिविद्या
734	*Naţeśvarī*	नटेश्वरी
735	*Mithyājagadadhişţhānā*	मिथ्याजगदधिष्ठाना
736	*Muktidā*	मुक्तिदा
737	*Muktirūpiņī*	मुक्तिरूपिणी
738	*Lāsyapriyā*	लास्यप्रिया
739	*Layakarī*	लयकरी
740	*Lajjā*	लज्जा
741	*Rambhādi Vanditā*	रम्भादि वन्दिता
742	*Bhavadāvasudhāvruşţiḥ*	भवदावसुधावृष्टिः
743	*Pāpāraņyadavānalā*	पापारण्यदवानला
744	*Dourbhāgyatūlavātūlā*	दौर्भाग्यतूलवातूला
745	*Jarādhvāntaraviprabhā*	जराध्वान्तरविप्रभा

#	Name in English	Name in Samskrutam
746	*Bhāgyābdhichandrikā*	भाग्याब्धिचन्द्रिका
747	*Bhaktachittakeki Ghanā Ghanā*	भक्तचित्तकेकि घना घना
748	*Rogaparvatadambholiḥ*	रोगपर्वतदम्भोलि:
749	*Mrutyudāruguţhārikā*	मृत्युदारुगुठारिका
750	*Maheśvarī*	महेश्वरी
751	*Mahākālī*	महाकाली
752	*Mahāgrāsā*	महाग्रासा
753	*Mahāśanā*	महाशना
754	*Aparnā*	अपर्णा
755	*Chaŋḍikā*	चण्डिका
756	*Chaŋḍamuŋḍāsuranişūdinī*	चण्डमुण्डासुरनिषूदिनी
757	*Kşarākşarātmikā*	क्षराक्षरात्मिका
758	*Sarvalokeśī*	सर्वलोकेशी
759	*Viśvadhāriŋī*	विश्वधारिणी
760	*Trivargadhātrī*	त्रिवर्गधात्री
761	*Subhagā*	सुभगा
762	*Tryambakā*	त्र्यम्बका
763	*Triguŋātmikā*	त्रिगुणात्मिका
764	*Svargāpavargadā*	स्वर्गापवर्गदा
765	*Śuddhā*	शुद्धा
766	*Japāpuşpa Nibhākrutiḥ*	जपापुष्प निभाकृति:
767	*Ojovatī*	ओजोवती
768	*Dyutidharā*	द्युतिधरा
769	*Yagnyarūpā*	यज्ञरूपा
770	*Priyavratā*	प्रियव्रता

#	Name in English	Name in Samskrutam
771	*Durārādhyā*	दुराराध्या
772	*Durādharṣā*	दुराधर्षा
773	*Pāţalīkusumapriyā*	पाटलीकुसुमप्रिया
774	*Mahatī*	महती
775	*Merunilayā*	मेरुनिलया
776	*Mandārakusumapriyā*	मन्दारकुसुमप्रिया
777	*Vīrārādhyā*	वीराराध्या
778	*Virāḍrūpā*	विराड्रूपा
779	*Virajā*	विरजा
780	*Viśvatomukhī*	विश्वतोमुखी
781	*Pratyagrūpā*	प्रत्यग्रूपा
782	*Parākāśā*	पराकाशा
783	*Prāŋadā*	प्राणदा
784	*Prāŋarūpiŋī*	प्राणरूपिणी
785	*Mārtāṇḍa Bhairavārādhyā*	मार्तण्ड भैरवाराध्या
786	*Mantrinīnyastarājyadhūḥ*	मन्त्रिणीन्यस्तराज्यधूः
787	*Tripureśī*	त्रिपुरेशी
788	*Jayatsenā*	जयत्सेना
789	*Nistraiguŋyā*	निस्त्रैगुण्या
790	*Parāparā*	परापरा
791	*Satyajnānānandarūpā*	सत्यज्ञानानन्दरूपा
792	*Sāmarasyaparāyaŋā*	सामरस्यपरायणा
793	*Kapardinī*	कपर्दिनी
794	*Kalāmālā*	कलामाला
795	*Kāmadhuk*	कामधुक्

#	Name in English	Name in Samskrutam
796	*Kāmarūpiŋī*	कामरूपिणी
797	*Kalānidhiḥ*	कलानिधि:
798	*Kāvyakalā*	काव्यकला
799	*Rasajnā*	रसज्ञा
800	*Rasaśevadhiḥ*	रसशेवधि:
801	*Puşţā*	पुष्टा
802	*Purātanā*	पुरातना
803	*Pūjyā*	पूज्या
804	*Puşkarā*	पुष्करा
805	*Puşkarekşaŋā*	पुष्करेक्षणा
806	*Paramjyotiḥ*	परंज्योति:
807	*Parandhāma*	परंधाम
808	*Paramānuḥ*	परमाणु:
809	*Parātparā*	परात्परा
810	*Pāśahastā*	पाशहस्ता
811	*Pāśahantrī*	पाशहन्त्री
812	*Paramantravibhedinī*	परमन्त्रविभेदिनी
813	*Mūrtā*	मूर्ता
814	*Amūrtā*	अमूर्ता
815	*Anityatruptā*	अनित्यतृप्ता
816	*Munimānasa Hamsikā*	मुनिमानस हंसिका
817	*Satyavratā*	सत्यव्रता
818	*Satyarūpā*	सत्यरूपा
819	*Sarvāntaryāmiŋī*	सर्वान्तर्यामिणी
820	*Satī*	सती

#	Name in English	Name in Samskrutam
821	*Brahmanī*	ब्रह्माणी
822	*Brahma*	ब्रह्म
823	*Jananī*	जननी
824	*Bahurūpā*	बहुरूपा
825	*Budhārchitā*	बुधार्चिता
826	*Prasavitrī*	प्रसवित्री
827	*Prachaŋḍā*	प्रचण्डा
828	*Āgnā*	आज्ञा
829	*Pratiṣţhā*	प्रतिष्ठा
830	*Prakaţākrutiḥ*	प्रकटाकृतिः
831	*Prāŋeśvarī*	प्राणेश्वरी
832	*Prāŋadātrī*	प्राणदात्री
833	*Pajnchāśatpīţharūpiŋī*	पञ्चाशत्पीठरूपिणी
834	*Viśrunkhalā*	विश्रृङ्खला
835	*Viviktasthā*	विविक्तस्था
836	*Vīramātā*	वीरमाता
837	*Viyatprasūḥ*	वियत्प्रसूः
838	*Mukundā*	मुकुन्दा
839	*Muktinilayā*	मुक्तिनिलया
840	*Mūlavigraharūpiŋī*	मूलविग्रहरूपिणी
841	*Bhāvajnā*	भावज्ञा
842	*Bhavarogaghnī*	भवरोगघ्नी
843	*Bhavachakrapravartinī*	भवचक्रप्रवर्तिनी
844	*Chanḍaḥsārā*	छन्दःसारा
845	*Śāstrasārā*	शास्त्रसारा

#	Name in English	Name in Samskrutam
846	*Mantrasārā*	मन्त्रसारा
847	*Talodarī*	तलोदरी
848	*Udārakīrtiḥ*	उदारकीर्तिः
849	*Uddhāma Vaibhavā*	उद्धाम वैभवा
850	*Varŋarūpiŋī*	वर्णरूपिणी
851	*Janma Mrutyajarā Taptajana Viśrāntidāyinī*	जन्म मृत्यजरा तप्तजन विश्रान्तिदायिनी
852	*Sarvopaniṣadudghuṣţā*	सर्वोपनिषदुद्घुष्टा
853	*Śāntyatītakalātmikā*	शान्त्यतीतकलात्मिका
854	*Gambhīrā*	गम्भीरा
855	*Gaganāntasthā*	गगनान्तस्था
856	*Garvitā*	गर्विता
857	*Gānalolupā*	गानलोलुपा
858	*Kalpanārahitā*	कल्पनारहिता
859	*Kāṣţhā*	काष्ठा
860	*Akāntā*	अकान्ता
861	*Kāntārdhavigrahā*	कान्तार्धविग्रहा
862	*Kāryakāraŋanirmuktā*	कार्यकारणनिर्मुक्ता
863	*Kāmakelitarangitā*	कामकेलितरङ्गिता
864	*Kanatkanakatāţankā*	कनत्कनकताटङ्का
865	*Līlā Vigrahadhārinī*	लीला विग्रहधारिणी
866	*Ajā*	अजा
867	*Kṣayavinirmuktā*	क्षयविनिर्मुक्ता
868	*Mugdhā*	मुग्धा
869	*Kṣipraprasādinī*	क्षिप्रप्रसादिनी

#	Name in English	Name in Samskrutam
870	*Antarmukhasamārādhyā*	अन्तर्मुखसमाराध्या
871	*Bahirmukhasudurlabhā*	बहिर्मुखसुदुर्लभा
872	*Trayī*	त्रयी
873	*Trivarganilayā*	त्रिवर्गनिलया
874	*Tristhā*	त्रिस्था
875	*Tripuramālinī*	त्रिपुरमालिनी
876	*Nirāmayā*	निरामया
877	*Nirālambā*	निरालम्बा
878	*Svātmārāmā*	स्वात्मारामा
879	*Sudhāsrutiḥ*	सुधास्रुति:
880	*Samsāra Panka Nirmagna Samuddharaŋa Paŋḍitā*	संसार पङ्क निर्मग्न समुद्धरण पण्डिता
881	*Yajnayapriyā*	यज्ञयप्रिया
882	*Yajna Kartrī*	यज्ञ कर्त्री
883	*Yajamānasvarūpiŋī*	यजमानस्वरूपिणी
884	*Dharmādhārā*	धर्माधारा
885	*Dhanādhyakṣā*	धनाध्यक्षा
886	*Dhanadhānya Vivardhinī*	धनधान्य विवर्धिनी
887	*Viprapriyā*	विप्रप्रिया
888	*Viprarūpā*	विप्ररूपा
889	*Viśvabhramaŋakāriŋī*	विश्वभ्रमणकारिणी
890	*Viśvagrāsā*	विश्वग्रासा
891	*Vidrumābhā*	विद्रुमाभा
892	*Vaiṣŋavī*	वैष्णवी
893	*Viṣŋurūpiŋī*	विष्णुरूपिणी

#	Name in English	Name in Samskrutam
894	*Ayoniḥ*	अयोनि:
895	*Yoninilayā*	योनिनिलया
896	*Kūţasthā*	कूटस्था
897	*Kularūpiŋī*	कुलरूपिणी
898	*Vīragoşţhīpriyā*	वीरगोष्ठीप्रिया
899	*Vīrā*	वीरा
900	*Naişkarmyā*	नैष्कर्म्या
901	*Nātharūpiŋī*	नादरूपिणी
902	*Vijnānakalanā*	विज्ञानकलना
903	*Kalyā*	कल्या
904	*Vidagdhā*	विदग्धा
905	*Baindavāsanā*	बैन्दवासना
906	*Tatvādhikā*	तत्वाधिका
907	*Tatvamayī*	तत्वमयी
908	*Tatvamarthasvarūpiŋī*	तत्वमर्थस्वरूपिणी
909	*Sāmagānapriyā*	सामगानप्रिया
910	*Somyā (Soumyā)*	सोम्या (सौम्या)
911	*Sadāśivakuţumbinī*	सदाशिवकुटुम्बिनी
912	*Savyāpasavyamārgasthā*	सव्यापसव्यमार्गस्था
913	*Sarvāpadvinināriŋī*	सर्वापद्विनिनारिणी
914	*Svasthā*	स्वस्था
915	*Svabhāvamadhurā*	स्वभावमधुरा
916	*Dhīrā*	धीरा
917	*Dhīrasamarchitā*	धीरसमर्चिता
918	*Chaitanyārghya Samārāadhyā*	चैतन्यार्घ्य समाराध्या

#	Name in English	Name in Samskrutam
919	*Chaitanyakusumapriyā*	चैतन्यकुसुमप्रिया
920	*Sadoditā*	सदोदिता
921	*Sadātuṣṭā*	सदातुष्टा
922	*Taruṇādityapāṭalā*	तरुणादित्यपाटला
923	*Dakṣiṇādakṣiṇārādhyā*	दक्षिणादक्षिणाराध्या
924	*Darasmeramukhāmbujā*	दरस्मेरमुखाम्बुजा
925	*Koulinī Kevalā*	कौलिनी केवला
926	*Anarghyakaivalyapadadāyinī*	अनर्घ्यकैवल्यपददायिनी
927	*Stotrapriyā*	स्तोत्रप्रिया
928	*Stutimatī*	स्तुतिमती
929	*Srutisamstutavaibhavā*	श्रृतिसंस्तुतवैभवा
930	*Manasvinī*	मनस्विनी
931	*Mānavatī*	मानवती
932	*Maheśī*	महेशी
933	*Mangalākrutiḥ*	मङ्गलाकृति:
934	*Viśvamātā*	विश्वमाता
935	*Jagaddhātrī*	जगद्धात्री
936	*Viśālākṣī*	विशालाक्षी
937	*Virāgiṇī*	विरागिणी
938	*Pragalbhā*	प्रगल्भा
939	*Paramodārā*	परमोदारा
940	*Parāmodā*	परामोदा
941	*Manomayī*	मनोमयी
942	*Vyomakeśī*	व्योमकेशी
943	*Vimānasthā*	विमानस्था

#	Name in English	Name in Samskrutam
944	*Vajriṇī*	वज्रिणी
945	*Vāmakeśvarī*	वामकेश्वरी
946	*Pajnchayajnapriyā*	पञ्चयज्ञप्रिया
947	*Pajnchapretamajnchādhiśāyinī*	पञ्चप्रेतमञ्चाधिशायिनी
948	*Pajnchamī*	पञ्चमी
949	*Pajnchabhūteśī*	पञ्चभूतेशी
950	*Pajnchasanyopachārinī*	पञ्चसङ्योपचारिणी
951	*Śāśvatī*	शाश्वती
952	*Śāśvataiśvaryā*	शाश्वतैश्वर्या
953	*Śarmadā*	शर्मदा
954	*Śambhumohinī*	शम्भुमोहिनी
955	*Dharā*	धरा
956	*Dharasutā*	धरसुता
957	*Dhanyā*	धन्या
958	*Dharmiṇī*	धर्मिणी
959	*Dharmavardhinī*	धर्मवर्धिनी
960	*Lokātītā*	लोकातीता
961	*Guṇātītā*	गुणातीता
962	*Sarvātītā*	सर्वातीता
963	*Śamātmikā*	शमात्मिका
964	*Bandhūkakusumaprakhyā*	बन्धूककुसुमप्रख्या
965	*Bālā*	बाला
966	*Līlāvinodinī*	लीलाविनोदिनी
967	*Sumangalī*	सुमङ्गली
968	*Sukhakarī*	सुखकरी

#	Name in English	Name in Samskrutam
969	*Suveṣāḍhyā*	सुवेषाढ्या
970	*Suvāsinī*	सुवासिनी
971	*Suvāsinyarchanaprītā*	सुवासिन्यर्चनप्रीता
972	*Āśobhanā*	आशोभना
973	*Śuddhamānāsā*	शुद्धमानासा
974	*Bindutarpaŋasantuşţā*	बिन्दुतर्पणसन्तुष्टा
975	*Pūrvajā*	पूर्वजा
976	*Tripurāmbikā*	त्रिपुराम्बिका
977	*Daśamudrāsamārādhyā*	दशमुद्रासमाराध्या
978	*Tripurāśrīvaśankarī*	त्रिपुराश्रीवशन्करी
979	*Jnānamudrā*	ज्ञानमुद्रा
980	*Jnānagamyā*	ज्ञानगम्या
981	*Jnānajneyasvarūpiŋī*	ज्ञानज्ञेयश्वरूपिणी
982	*Yonimudrā*	योनिमुद्रा
983	*Trikhaŋḍeśī*	त्रिखण्डेशी
984	*Triguŋā*	त्रिगुणा
985	*Ambā*	अंबा
986	*Trikoŋagā*	त्रिकोणगा
987	*Anaghā*	अनघा
988	*Adbhutachāritrā*	अद्भुतचारित्रा
989	*Vājnchitārthapradāyinī*	वाञ्छितार्थप्रदायिनी
990	*Abhyāsātiśayajnātā*	अभ्यासातिशयज्ञाता
991	*Şaḍadhvātītarūpiŋī*	षडध्वातीतरूपिणी
992	*Avyājakaruŋāmūrtiḥ*	अव्याजकरुणामूर्तिः
993	*Ajnānadhvāntadīpikā*	अज्ञानध्वान्तदीपिका

#	Name in English	Name in Samskrutam
994	*Ābālagopaviditā*	आबालगोपविदिता
995	*Sarvānullanghyaśāsanā*	सर्वानुल्लङ्घ्यशासना
996	*Śrīchakrarājanilayā*	श्रीचक्रराजनिलया
997	*Śrīmattripurasundarī*	श्रीमत्त्रिपुरसुन्दरी
998	*Śrī Śivā*	श्री शिवा
999	*Śivaśaktyaikyarūpiṇī*	शिवशक्त्यैक्यरूपिणी
1000	*Lalitāmbikā*	ललिताम्बिका

*****

Śrī Viṣṇu Sahasranāmāvali

Om Namo Narāyaṇāya

#	Name in English	Name in Samskrutam
1.	*Viśwam*	विश्वं
2.	*Viṣṇuḥ*	विष्णु:
3.	*Vaṣaṭkāraḥ*	वषट्कार:
4.	*Bhūta bhavya bhavat prabhuḥ*	भूत भव्य भवत्प्रभु:
5.	*Bhūtakṛt*	भूतकृत्
6.	*Bhūtabhṛt*	भूतभृत्
7.	*Bhāvaḥ*	भाव:
8.	*Bhūtātmā*	भूतात्मा
9.	*Bhūtabhāvanaḥ*	भूतभावन:
10.	*Pūtātma*	पूतात्म
11.	*Paramātmā*	परमात्मा
12.	*Muktānām Paramā Gatiḥ*	मुक्तानाम् परमा गति:
13.	*Avyayaḥ*	अव्यय:
14.	*Puruṣaḥ*	पुरुष:
15.	*Sākṣīḥ*	साक्षी:
16.	*Kṣetrajnaḥ*	क्षेत्रज्ञ:
17.	*Akṣaraḥ*	अक्षर:
18.	*Yogaḥ*	योग:
19.	*Yogavidāmnetraḥ*	योगविदांनेत्र:
20.	*Pradhānapuruṣeśvaraḥ*	प्रधानपुरुषेश्वर:
21.	*Nārasimhavapuḥ*	नारसिंहवपु:

#	Name in English	Name in Samskrutam
22.	*Śrīmān*	श्रीमान्
23.	*Keśavaḥ*	केशव:
24.	*Puruṣottamaḥ*	पुरुषोत्तम:
25.	*Sarvaḥ*	सर्व:
26.	*Śarvaḥ*	शर्व:
27.	*Śivaḥ*	शिव:
28.	*Sthāṇuḥ*	स्थाणु:
29.	*Bhūtādiḥ*	भूतादि:
30.	*Avyaya Nidhiḥ*	अव्यय: निधि:
31.	*Saṁbhavaḥ*	संभव:
32.	*Bhāvanaḥ*	भावन:
33.	*Bhartaḥ*	भर्ता:
34.	*Prabhavaḥ*	प्रभव:
35.	*Prabhuḥ*	प्रभु:
36.	*Ĕśvaraḥ*	ईश्वर:
37.	*Svayaṁbhūḥ*	स्वयंभू:
38.	*Śambhuḥ*	शंभु:
39.	*Ādityaḥ*	आदित्य:
40.	*Puṣkarākṣaḥ*	पुष्कराक्ष:
41.	*Mahāsvanaḥ*	महास्वन:
42.	*Anādinidhānaḥ*	अनादिनिधन:
43.	*Dhātāḥ*	धाता:
44.	*Vidhātāḥ*	विधाता:

#	Name in English	Name in Samskrutam
45.	*Dhāturuttamaḥ*	धातुरुत्तम:
46.	*Aprameyaḥ*	अप्रमेय:
47.	*Hriṣīkeśaḥ*	ह्रिषीकेश:
48.	*Padmanābhaḥ*	पद्मनाभ:
49.	*Amaraprabhuḥ*	अमरप्रभु:
50.	*Viśvakarmāḥ*	विश्वकर्मा:
51.	*Manuḥ*	मनु:
52.	*Tvaṣṭaḥ*	त्वष्ट:
53.	*Sthaviṣṭaḥ*	स्थविष्ट:
54.	*Sthavirḥ Dhṛvaḥ*	स्थविर: ध्रुव:
55.	*Agrāhyaḥ*	अग्राह्य:
56.	*Śāśvataḥ*	शाश्वत:
57.	*Kṛṣṇaḥ*	कृष्ण:
58.	*Lohitākṣaḥ*	लोहिताक्ष:
59.	*Pratardanaḥ*	प्रतर्दन:
60.	*Prabhootaḥ*	प्रभूत:
61.	*Trikakubdhāmaḥ*	त्रिककुब्धाम:
62.	*Pavitram*	पवित्रं
63.	*Maṇgalamparam*	मङ्गलंपरं
64.	*Īṣānaḥ*	ईशान:
65.	*Prāṇadaḥ*	प्राणद:
66.	*Prāṇaḥ*	प्राण:
67.	*Jyeṣṭhaḥ*	ज्येष्ठ:

#	Name in English	Name in Samskrutam
68.	*Śreṣṭaḥ*	श्रेष्टः
69.	*Prajāpatiḥ*	प्रजापतिः
70.	*Hiranyagarbhaḥ*	हिरण्यगर्भः
71.	*Bhūgarbhaḥ*	भूगर्भः
72.	*Mādhavaḥ*	माधवः
73.	*Madhusūdanaḥ*	मधुसूदनः
74.	*Īṣvaraḥ*	ईश्वरः
75.	*Vikramī*	विक्रमी
76.	*Dhanvīḥ*	धन्वीः
77.	*Medhāvīḥ*	मेधावीः
78.	*Vikramaḥ*	विक्रमः
79.	*Kramaḥ*	क्रमः
80.	*Anuttamaḥ*	अनुत्तमः
81.	*Durādharśaḥ*	दुराधर्शः
82.	*Kṛtagnaḥ*	कृतज्ञः
83.	*Kṛtiḥ*	कृतिः
84.	*Ātmavān*	आत्मवान्
85.	*Sureśaḥ*	सुरेशः
86.	*Śaraṇam*	शरणं
87.	*Śarmaḥ*	शर्मः
88.	*Viśvaretāḥ*	विश्वरेताः
89.	*Prajābhavaḥ*	प्रजाभवः
90.	*Ahaḥ*	अहः

#	Name in English	Name in Samskrutam
91.	*Saṁvatsaraḥ*	संवत्सर:
92.	*Vyālaḥ*	व्याल:
93.	*Pratyayaḥ*	प्रत्यय:
94.	*Sarvadarśanaḥ*	सर्वदर्शन:
95.	*Ajaḥ*	अज:
96.	*Sarveśvaraḥ*	सर्वेश्वर:
97.	*Siddhaḥ*	सिद्ध:
98.	*Siddhiḥ*	सिद्धि:
99.	*Sarvādiḥ*	सर्वादि:
100.	*Acyutaḥ*	अच्युत:
101.	*Vṛṣākapiḥ*	वृषाकपि:
102.	*Ameyātmā*	अमेयात्मा
103.	*Sarvayogaviniḥ Sṛtaḥ*	सर्वयोगविनि: सृत:
104.	*Vasuḥ*	वसु:
105.	*Vasumanāḥ*	वसुमना:
106.	*Satyaḥ*	सत्य:
107.	*Samātmāḥ*	समात्मा:
108.	*Sammitaḥ*	सम्मित:
109.	*Samaḥ*	सम:
110.	*Amoghaḥ*	अमोघ:
111.	*Puṇḍarīkākṣaḥ*	पुण्डरीकाक्ष:
112.	*Vṛṣakarmāḥ*	वृषकर्मा
113.	*Vṛṣākṛtiḥ*	वृषाकृति:

#	Name in English	Name in Samskrutam
114.	*Rudraḥ*	रुद्रः
115.	*Bahuśirāḥ*	बहुशिराः
116.	*Bahṛruḥ*	बह्रुरुः
117.	*Viśvayoniḥ*	विश्वयोनिः
118.	*Sucisravāḥ*	शुचिश्रवाः
119.	*Amṛtaḥ*	अमृतः
120.	*Śaśvatasthānuḥ*	शाश्वतस्थानुः
121.	*Varārohaḥ*	वरारोहः
122.	*Mahātapāḥ*	महातपाः
123.	*Sarvagaḥ*	सर्वगः
124.	*Sarvavidbhānuḥ*	सर्वविद्भानुः
125.	*Viṣvaksenaḥ*	विष्वक्सेनः
126.	*Janārdanaḥ*	जनार्दनः
127.	*Vedaḥ*	वेदः
128.	*Vedavit*	वेदवित्
129.	*Avyangaḥ*	अव्यङ्गः
130.	*Vedāngaḥ*	वेदाङ्गः
131.	*Vedavit*	वेदवित्
132.	*Kaviḥ*	कविः
133.	*Lokādhyakṣaḥ*	लोकाध्यक्षः
134.	*Surādhyakṣaḥ*	सुराध्यक्षः
135.	*Darmādhyakṣaḥ*	धर्माध्यक्षः
136.	*Kṛtākṛtaḥ*	कृताकृतः

#	Name in English	Name in Samskrutam
137.	*Caturātmā*	चतुरात्मा
138.	*Caturvyūhaḥ*	चतुर्व्यूहः
139.	*Caturdaṁṣṭraḥ*	चतुर्दम्ष्ट्रः
140.	*Caturbhujaḥ*	चतुर्भुजः
141.	*Bhrājiṣṇuḥ*	भ्राशिष्णुः
142.	*Bhojanam*	भोजनं
143.	*Bhoktāḥ*	भोक्ताः
144.	*Sahiṣṇuḥ*	सहिष्णुः
145.	*Jagadādijaḥ*	जगदादिजः
146.	*Anaghaḥ*	अनघः
147.	*Vijayaḥ*	विजयः
148.	*Jetāḥ*	जेताः
149.	*Viśvayoniḥ*	विश्वयोनिः
150.	*Punarvasuḥ*	पुनर्वसुः
151.	*Upendraḥ*	उपेन्द्रः
152.	*Vāmanaḥ*	वामनः
153.	*Prāṁśuḥ*	प्रांशुः
154.	*Amoghaḥ*	अमोघः
155.	*Śuciḥ*	शुचिः
156.	*Ūrjitaḥ*	ऊर्जितः
157.	*Atīndraḥ*	अतीन्द्रः
158.	*Saṁgrahaḥ*	संग्रहः
159.	*Sargaḥ*	सर्गः

#	Name in English	Name in Samskrutam
160.	*Dṛtātmā*	धृतात्मा
161.	*Niyamaḥ*	नियमः
162.	*Yamaḥ*	यमः
163.	*Vedyaḥ*	वेद्यः
164.	*Vaidhyaḥ*	वैध्यः
165.	*Sadāyogiḥ*	सदायोगिः
166.	*Veeraḥ*	वीरः
167.	*Mādhavaḥ*	माधवः
168.	*Madhuḥ*	मधुः
169.	*Ateendriyaḥ*	अतीन्द्रियः
170.	*Mahāmāyaḥ*	महामायः
171.	*Mahotsāhaḥ*	महोत्साहः
172.	*Mahābalaḥ*	महाबलः
173.	*Mahābuddhiḥ*	महाबुद्धिः
174.	*Mahāveerāḥ*	महावीराः
175.	*Mahāśaktiḥ*	महाशक्तिः
176.	*Mahādyutiḥ*	महाद्युतिः
177.	*Anirdeśyavapuḥ*	अनिर्देश्यवपुः
178.	*Śrimān*	श्रीमान्
179.	*Ameyatmā*	अमेयात्मा
180.	*Mahādridṛk*	महाद्रिदृक्
181.	*Maheśvāsaḥ*	महेश्वासः
182.	*Mahībartā*	महीभर्ता

#	Name in English	Name in Samskrutam
183.	*Śrīnivāsaḥ*	श्रीनिवासः
184.	*Satāngatiḥ*	सताङ्गतिः
185.	*Aniruddhaḥ*	अनिरुद्धः
186.	*Suranandaḥ*	सुरानन्दः
187.	*Govindaḥ*	गोविन्दः
188.	*Govidam Patiḥ*	गोविदाम् पतिः
189.	*Marīciḥ*	मरीचिः
190.	*Damanaḥ*	दमनः
191.	*Hamsaḥ*	हंसः
192.	*Suparṇaḥ*	सुपर्णः
193.	*Bhujagottamaḥ*	भुजगोत्तमः
194.	*Hiraṇyanābhaḥ*	हिरण्यनाभः
195.	*Sutapāḥ*	सुतपाः
196.	*Padmanābhaḥ*	पद्मनाभः
197.	*Prajapatiḥ*	प्रजापतिः
198.	*Amṛtyuḥ*	अमृत्युः
199.	*Sarvadṛk*	सर्वदृक्
200.	*Simhaḥ*	सिम्हः
201.	*Saṁdhātā*	संधाता
202.	*Sandhimān*	सन्धिमान्
203.	*Sthitaraḥ*	स्थिरः
204.	*Ajaḥ*	अजः
205.	*Durmarṣaṇaḥ*	दुर्मर्षणः

#	Name in English	Name in Samskrutam
206.	*Śastāḥ*	शास्ता:
207.	*Viṣrutātmāḥ*	विश्रुतात्मा:
208.	*Surārihāḥ*	सुरारिहा:
209.	*Guruḥ*	गुरु:
210.	*Guruttamaḥ*	गुरुतम:
211.	*Dhāma*	धाम
212.	*Satyaḥ*	सत्य:
213.	*Satyaparākramaḥ*	सत्यपराक्रम:
214.	*Nimiṣaḥ*	निमिष:
215.	*Animiṣaḥ*	अनिमिष:
216.	*Sragviḥ*	स्रग्वि:
217.	*Vācaspatirudāradhiḥ*	वाचस्पतिरुदारधि:
218.	*Agraṇīḥ*	अग्रणी:
219.	*Grāmaṇīḥ*	ग्रामणी:
220.	*Śrīmān*	श्रीमान्
221.	*Nyāyaḥ*	न्याय:
222.	*Netā*	नेता
223.	*Samīraṇaḥ*	समीरण:
224.	*Sahasramūrdhāḥ*	सहस्रमूर्धा:
225.	*Viśvātmāḥ*	विश्वात्मा:
226.	*Sahasrākṣaḥ*	सहस्राक्ष:
227.	*Sahasrapāt*	सहस्रपात्
228.	*Āvartanaḥ*	आवर्तन:

#	Name in English	Name in Samskrutam
229.	*Nivṛttātmāḥ*	निवृत्तात्मा:
230.	*Saṁvṛtaḥ*	संवृत:
231.	*Saṁpramardanaḥ*	संप्रमर्दन:
232.	*Ahaḥ Saṁvartakaḥ*	अह: संवर्तक:
233.	*Vahniḥ*	वह्नि:
234.	*Anilaḥ*	अनिल:
235.	*Dharaṇīdharaḥ*	धरणीधर:
236.	*Suprasādaḥ*	सुप्रसाद:
237.	*Prasannatmāḥ*	प्रसन्नात्मा:
238.	*Viśvadṛk*	विश्वदृक्
239.	*Viśvabhuk*	विश्वभुक्
240.	*Vibhuḥ*	विभु:
241.	*Satkartā*	सत्कर्ता
242.	*Satkṛtā*	सत्कृता
243.	*Sādhuḥ*	साधु:
244.	*Jahnuḥ*	जह्नु:
245.	*Nārāyaṇaḥ*	नारायण:
246.	*Naraḥ*	नर:
247.	*Asankhyeyaḥ*	असङ्ख्येय:
248.	*Aprameyātmā*	अप्रमेयात्मा
249.	*Viśiṣṭaḥ*	विशिष्ट:
250.	*Śiṣṭakṛt*	शिष्टकृत्
251.	*Śuciḥ*	शुचि:

#	Name in English	Name in Samskrutam
252.	*Siddhārthaḥ*	सिद्धार्थः
253.	*Siddhasankalpaḥ*	सिद्धसङ्कल्पः
254.	*Siddhidaḥ*	सिद्धिदः
255.	*Siddhisādanaḥ*	सिद्धिसाधनः
256.	*Vṛśāhi*	वृशाहि
257.	*Vṛśabhaḥ*	वृशभः
258.	*Viṣṇuḥ*	विष्णुः
259.	*Vṛṣaparvā*	वृषपर्वा
260.	*Vṛṣodaraḥ*	वृषोदरः
261.	*Vardhanaḥ*	वर्धनः
262.	*Vardhamānaḥ*	वर्धमानः
263.	*Viviktaḥ*	विविक्तः
264.	*Śṛtisāgaraḥ*	शृतिसागरः
265.	*Subujaḥ*	सुभुजः
266.	*Dhurdharaḥ*	दुर्धरः
267.	*Vāgmī*	वाग्मी
268.	*Mahendraḥ*	महेन्द्रः
269.	*Vasudaḥ*	वसुदः
270.	*Vasuḥ*	वसुः
271.	*Naikarūpaḥ*	नैकरूपः
272.	*Bṛhadrūpaḥ*	बृहद्रूपः
273.	*Śipiviṣṭaḥ*	शिपिविष्टः
274.	*Prakaṣanaḥ*	प्रकाषनः

#	Name in English	Name in Samskrutam
275.	*Ojastejodyutidharaḥ*	ओजस्तेजोद्युतिधरः
276.	*Prakāśātmā*	प्रकाशात्मा
277.	*Pratāpanaḥ*	प्रतापनः
278.	*Ruddhaḥ*	रुद्धः
279.	*Spaṣṭākṣaraḥ*	स्पष्टाक्षरः
280.	*Mantraḥ*	मन्त्रः
281.	*Chandrāmśuḥ*	चन्द्राम्शुः
282.	*Bhāskaradyutiḥ*	भास्करद्युतिः
283.	*Amṛtāmśūdbhavaḥ*	अमृताम्शुद्भवः
284.	*Bhānuḥ*	भानुः
285.	*Śaśibinduḥ*	शशिबिन्दुः
286.	*Sureśvaraḥ*	सुरेश्वरः
287.	*Ouṣadham*	औषधम्
288.	*Jagataḥ Setuḥ*	जगतः सेतुः
289.	*Satyadharmaparākramaḥ*	सत्यधर्मपराक्रमः
290.	*Bhūtabhavyabhavannāthaḥ*	भूतभव्यभवन्नाथः
291.	*Pavanaḥ*	पवनः
292.	*Pāvanaḥ*	पावनः
293.	*Analaḥ*	अनलः
294.	*Kāmahā*	कामहा
295.	*Kāmakṛt*	कामकृत्
296.	*Kāntaḥ*	कान्तः
297.	*Kāmaḥ*	कामः

#	Name in English	Name in Samskrutam
298.	*Kāmapradaḥ*	कामप्रद:
299.	*Prabhuḥ*	प्रभु:
300.	*Yugādhikṛt*	युगादिकृत्
301.	*Yugāvartaḥ*	युगावर्त:
302.	*Naikamāyaḥ*	नैकमाय:
303.	*Mahāśanaḥ*	महाशन:
304.	*Adṛśya*	अदृश्य:
305.	*Vyaktarūpaḥ*	व्यक्तरूप:
306.	*Sahasrajit*	सहस्रजित्
307.	*Anantajit*	अनन्तजित्
308.	*Iṣṭaḥ*	इष्ट:
309.	*Aviśiṣṭaḥ*	अविशिष्ट:
310.	*Śiṣṭeṣṭaḥ*	शिष्टेष्ट:
311.	*Śikhaṇḍi*	शिखण्डि
312.	*Nahuṣaḥ*	नहुष:
313.	*Vṛṣa*	वृष:
314.	*Krodhahā*	क्रोधहा
315.	*Krodhakṛtkartā*	क्रोधकृत्कर्ता
316.	*Viśvabāhuḥ*	विश्वबाहु:
317.	*Mahīdharaḥ*	महीधर:
318.	*Acyutaḥ*	अच्युत:
319.	*Prathitaḥ*	प्रथित:
320.	*Prāṇaḥ*	प्राण:

#	Name in English	Name in Samskrutam
321.	*Prāṇadaḥ*	प्राणदः
322.	*Vāsavānujaḥ*	वासवानुजः
323.	*Apāmnidhiḥ*	अपाम्निधिः
324.	*Adhiṣṭhānam*	अधिष्ठानम्
325.	*Apramattaḥ*	अप्रमत्तः
326.	*Pratiṣṭitaḥ*	प्रतिष्टितः
327.	*Skandaḥ*	स्कन्दः
328.	*Skandadaraḥ*	स्कन्ददरः
329.	*Dhuryaḥ*	धुर्यः
330.	*Varadaḥ*	वरदः
331.	*Vāyuvāhanaḥ*	वायुवाहनः
332.	*Vasudevaḥ*	वासुदेवः
333.	*Bṛhatbhānuḥ*	भृहद्भानुः
334.	*Ādidevaḥ*	आदिदेवः
335.	*Purandaraḥ*	पुरन्दरः
336.	*Aśokaḥ*	अशोकः
337.	*Tāraṇaḥ*	तारणः
338.	*Tāraḥ*	तारः
339.	*Śūraḥ*	शूरः
340.	*Śouriḥ*	शौरिः
341.	*Janeśvaraḥ*	जनेश्वरः
342.	*Anukūlaḥ*	अनुकूलः
343.	*Śatāvartaḥ*	शतावर्तः

#	Name in English	Name in Samskrutam
344.	*Padmī*	पद्मी
345.	*Padmanibekṣaṇaḥ*	पद्मनिभेक्षण:
346.	*Padmanābhaḥ*	पद्मनाभ:
347.	*Aravindākṣaḥ*	अरविन्दाक्ष:
348.	*Padmagarbhaḥ*	पद्मगर्भ:
349.	*Śarīrabhṛt*	शरीरभृत्
350.	*Maharddhiḥ*	महर्धि:
351.	*Ṛuddhaḥ*	ऋद्ध:
352.	*Vṛddhātmā*	वृद्धात्मा
353.	*Mahākṣaḥ*	महाक्ष:
354.	*Garudadvajaḥ*	गरुडध्वज:
355.	*Atulaḥ*	अतुल:
356.	*Śarabhaḥ*	शरभ:
357.	*Bhīmaḥ*	भीम:
358.	*Samayagnaḥ*	समयज्ञ:
359.	*Havirhariḥ*	हविर्हरि:
360.	*Sarvalakṣaṇalakṣaṇyaḥ*	सर्वलक्षणलक्षण्य:
361.	*Lakṣmīvan*	लक्षमीवन्
362.	*Samitinjayaḥ*	समित्तिञ्जय:
363.	*Vikṣaraḥ*	विक्षर:
364.	*Rohitaḥ*	रोहित:
365.	*Mārgaḥ*	मार्ग:
366.	*Hetuḥ*	हेतु:

#	Name in English	Name in Samskrutam
367.	*Dāmodaraḥ*	दामोदरः
368.	*Sahaḥ*	सहः
369.	*Mahīdharaḥ*	महीधरः
370.	*Mahābhāgaḥ*	महाभागः
371.	*Vegavān*	वेगवान्
372.	*Amitāśanaḥ*	अमिताशनः
373.	*Udbhavaḥ*	उद्भवः
374.	*Kṣobhaṇaḥ*	क्षोभणः
375.	*Devaḥ*	देवः
376.	*Śrīgarbhaḥ*	श्रीगर्भः
377.	*Parameśvaraḥ*	परमेश्वरः
378.	*Karaṇam*	करणम्
379.	*Kāraṇam*	कारणम्
380.	*Kartā*	कर्ता
381.	*Vikartā*	विकर्ता
382.	*Gahanaḥ*	गहनः
383.	*Guhaḥ*	गुहः
384.	*Vyavasāyaḥ*	व्यवसायः
385.	*Vyavasthānaḥ*	व्यवस्थानः
386.	*Samsthānaḥ*	सम्स्थानः
387.	*Sthānadaḥ*	स्थानदः
388.	*Dhruvaḥ*	धृवः
389.	*Pararddhiḥ*	परर्धिः

#	Name in English	Name in Samskrutam
390.	*Paramaspaṣṭa*	परमस्पष्ट:
391.	*Thuṣṭa*	तुष्ट:
392.	*Puṣṭa*	पुष्ट:
393.	*Subhekṣaṇaḥ*	शुभेक्षण:
394.	*Rāmaḥ*	राम:
395.	*Virāmaḥ*	विराम:
396.	*Virajaḥ*	विरज:
397.	*Mārgaḥ*	मार्ग:
398.	*Neyaḥ*	नेय:
399.	*Nayaḥ*	नय:
400.	*Anayaḥ*	अनय:
401.	*Vīraḥ*	वीर:
402.	*Śaktimatām śreṣṭhaḥ*	शक्तिमताम् श्रेष्ठ:
403.	*Dharmaḥ*	धर्म:
404.	*Dharma viduttamaḥ*	धर्म विदुत्तम:
405.	*Vaikunṭhaḥ*	वैकुन्ठ:
406.	*Puruṣaḥ*	पुरुष:
407.	*Prāṇaḥ*	प्राण:
408.	*Prāṇadaḥ*	प्राणद:
409.	*Praṇavaḥ*	प्रणव:
410.	*Pṛthuḥ*	पृथु:
411.	*Hiranyagarbhaḥ*	हिरण्यगर्भ:
412.	*Śatrughnaḥ*	शत्रुघ्न:

#	Name in English	Name in Samskrutam
413.	*Vyāptaḥ*	व्याप्त:
414.	*Vāyuḥ*	वायु:
415.	*Adhokṣajaḥ*	अधोक्षज:
416.	*Ṛtuḥ*	ऋतु:
417.	*Sudarśanaḥ*	सुदर्शन:
418.	*Kālaḥ*	काल:
419.	*Parameṣṭhiḥ*	परमेष्ठि:
420.	*Parigrahaḥ*	परिग्रह:
421.	*Ugraḥ*	उग्र:
422.	*Saṁvatsaraḥ*	संवत्सर:
423.	*Dakṣaḥ*	दक्ष:
424.	*Viśrāmaḥ*	विश्राम:
425.	*Viṣvadakṣiṇaḥ*	विष्वदक्षिण:
426.	*Vistāraḥ*	विस्तार:
427.	*Sthāvarasthāṇuḥ*	स्थावरस्थाणु:
428.	*Pramāṇam*	प्रमाणम्
429.	*Bījamavyayam*	बीजमव्ययम्
430.	*Arthaḥ*	अर्थ:
431.	*Anarthaḥ*	अनर्थ:
432.	*Mahākośaḥ*	महाकोश:
433.	*Mahābhogaḥ*	महाभोग:
434.	*Mahādhanaḥ*	महाधन:
435.	*Anirviṇṇaḥ*	अनिर्विण्ण:

#	Name in English	Name in Samskrutam
436.	*Sthaviṣṭhaḥ*	स्थविष्ठः
437.	*Abhūḥ*	अभूः
438.	*Dharmayūpaḥ*	धर्मयूपः
439.	*Mahāmakhaḥ*	महामखः
440.	*Nakṣatranemiḥ*	नक्षत्रनेमिः
441.	*Nakṣatrī*	नक्षत्री
442.	*Kṣamaḥ*	क्षमः
443.	*Kṣāmaḥ*	क्षामः
444.	*Samīhanaḥ*	समीहनः
445.	*Yagnaḥ*	यज्ञः
446.	*Ijyaḥ*	इज्यः
447.	*Mahejyaḥ*	महेज्यः
448.	*Kratuḥ*	क्रतुः
449.	*Satram*	सत्रम्
450.	*Satrāmgathiḥ*	सत्राङ्गतिः
451.	*Sarvadharśī*	सर्वदर्शी
452.	*Vimuktātmā*	विमुक्तात्मा
453.	*Sarvagnaḥ*	सर्वज्ञः
454.	*Jnānām uttamam*	ज्ञानानां उत्तमम्
455.	*Suvṛtaḥ*	सुव्रतः
456.	*Sumukhaḥ*	सुमुखः
457.	*Sūkṣmaḥ*	सूक्ष्मः
458.	*Sughoṣaḥ*	सुघोषः

#	Name in English	Name in Samskrutam
459.	*Sukhadaḥ*	सुखदः
460.	*Suhṛt*	सुहृत्
461.	*Manoharaḥ*	मनोहरः
462.	*Jitakrodhaḥ*	जितक्रोधः
463.	*Vīrabāhuḥ*	वीरबाहुः
464.	*Vidhāraṇaḥ*	विदारणः
465.	*Svāpanaḥ*	स्वापनः
466.	*Svavaśaḥ*	स्ववशः
467.	*Vyāpiḥ*	व्यापिः
468.	*Naikātmāḥ*	नैकात्माः
469.	*Naikakarmakṛt*	नैककर्मकृत्
470.	*Vatsaraḥ*	वत्सरः
471.	*Vatsalaḥ*	वत्सलः
472.	*Vatsī*	वत्सी
473.	*Ratnagarbhaḥ*	रत्नगर्भः
474.	*Dhaneśvaraḥ*	धनेश्वरः
475.	*Dharmagup*	धर्मगुप्
476.	*Dharmakṛt*	धर्मकृत्
477.	*Dharmī*	धर्मी
478.	*Sat*	सत्
479.	*Asat*	असत्
480.	*Kṣaram*	क्षरम
481.	*Akṣaram*	अक्षरम

#	Name in English	Name in Samskrutam
482.	*Avijnātaḥ*	अविज्ञात:
483.	*Sahasrāmśuḥ*	सहस्राम्शु:
484.	*Vidhātā*	विधाता
485.	*Kṛtalakṣaṇaḥ*	कृतलक्षण:
486.	*Gabhastinemiḥ*	गभस्तिनेमि:
487.	*Satvasthaḥ*	सत्त्वस्थ:
488.	*Simhaḥ*	सिम्ह:
489.	*Bhūtamaheśvaraḥ*	भूतमहेश्वर:
490.	*Ādidevaḥ*	आदिदेव:
491.	*Mahādevaḥ*	महादेव:
492.	*Deveśaḥ*	देवेश:
493.	*Devabṛdguruḥ*	देवभृद्गुरु:
494.	*Uttaraḥ*	उत्तर:
495.	*Gopatiḥ*	गोपति:
496.	*Goptā*	गोप्ता
497.	*Jnānagamyaḥ*	ज्ञानगम्य:
498.	*Purātanaḥ*	पुरातन:
499.	*Śarīrabhūtabhṛt*	शरीरभूतभृत्
500.	*Bhoktāḥ*	भोक्ता:
501.	*Kapīndraḥ*	कपीन्द्र:
502.	*Bhūridhakṣiṇaḥ*	भूरिदक्षिण:
503.	*Somapaḥ*	सोमप:
504.	*Amṛtapaḥ*	अमृतप:

#	Name in English	Name in Samskrutam
505.	*Somaḥ*	सोमः
506.	*Purūjit*	पुरुजित्
507.	*Purusattamaḥ*	पुरुसत्तमः
508.	*Vinayaḥ*	विनयः
509.	*Jayaḥ*	जयः
510.	*Satyasandhaḥ*	सत्यसन्धः
511.	*Dāśārhaḥ*	दाशार्हः
512.	*Sātvatāmpatiḥ*	सात्वताम्पतिः
513.	*Jīvaḥ*	जीवः
514.	*Vinayitāsākṣi*	विनयितासाक्षि
515.	*Mukundaḥ*	मुकुन्दः
516.	*Amitavikramaḥ*	अमितविक्रमः
517.	*Ambhonidhiḥ*	अम्भोनिधिः
518.	*Anantātmā*	अनन्तात्मा
519.	*Mahodadhiśayaḥ*	महोदधिशयः
520.	*Antakaḥ*	अन्तकः
521.	*Ajaḥ*	अजः
522.	*Mahārhaḥ*	महार्हः
523.	*Svābhāvyaḥ*	स्वाभाव्यः
524.	*Jitāmitraḥ*	जितामित्रः
525.	*Pramodanaḥ*	प्रमोदनः
526.	*Ānandaḥ*	आनन्दः
527.	*Nandanaḥ*	नन्दनः

#	Name in English	Name in Samskrutam
528.	*Nadaḥ*	नदः
529.	*Satyadharmā*	सत्यधर्मा
530.	*Trivikramaḥ*	त्रिविक्रमः
531.	*Maharṣikapilācāryaḥ*	महर्षिकपिलाचार्यः
532.	*Kṛtagnaḥ*	कृतज्ञः
533.	*Medinīpatiḥ*	मेदिनीपतिः
534.	*Tripadaḥ*	त्रिपदः
535.	*Tridaśādhyakṣaḥ*	त्रिदशाध्यक्षः
536.	*Mahāśṛngaḥ*	महाशृङ्गः
537.	*Kṛtāntakṛt*	कृतान्तकृत्
538.	*Mahāvarāhaḥ*	महावराहः
539.	*Govindaḥ*	गोविन्दः
540.	*Suṣeṇaḥ*	सुषेणः
541.	*Kanakāngadī*	कनकाङ्गदी
542.	*Guhyaḥ*	गुह्यः
543.	*Gabhīraḥ*	गभीरः
544.	*Gahanaḥ*	गहनः
545.	*Guptaḥ*	गुप्तः
546.	*Cakragadādharaḥ*	चक्रगदाधरः
547.	*Vedhāḥ*	वेधाः
548.	*Svāngaḥ*	स्वाङ्गः
549.	*Ajitaḥ*	अजितः
550.	*Kṛṣṇaḥ*	कृष्णः

#	Name in English	Name in Samskrutam
551.	*Dṛḍaḥ*	दृढ:
552.	*Sankarṣanocyutaḥ*	सङ्करषनोच्युत:
553.	*Varuṇaḥ*	वरुण:
554.	*Vāruṇaḥ*	वारुण:
555.	*Vṛkṣaḥ*	वृक्ष:
556.	*Puṣkarākṣaḥ*	पुष्कराक्ष:
557.	*Mahāmanāḥ*	महामना:
558.	*Bhagavān*	भगवान्
559.	*Bhagahā*	भगहा
560.	*Ānandī*	आनन्दी
561.	*Vanamālī*	वनमाली
562.	*Halāyudhaḥ*	हलायुध:
563.	*Ādityaḥ*	आदित्य:
564.	*Jyotirādityaḥ*	ज्योतिरादित्य:
565.	*Sahiṣṇuḥ*	सहिष्णु:
566.	*Gatisattamaḥ*	गतिसत्तम:
567.	*Sudhanvā*	सुधन्वा
568.	*Khaṇḍaparaśuḥ*	खण्डपरशु:
569.	*Dhāruṇaḥ*	दारुण:
570.	*Draviṇapradaḥ*	द्रविणप्रद:
571.	*Divaḥspṛk*	दिव:स्पृक्
572.	*Sarvadhṛgvyāsaḥ*	सर्वदृग्व्यास:
573.	*Vācaspatirayonijaḥ*	वाचस्पतिरयोनिज:

#	Name in English	Name in Samskrutam
574.	*Trisāmā*	त्रिसामा
575.	*Sāmagaḥ*	सामग:
576.	*Sāma*	साम
577.	*Nirvāṇam*	निर्वाणम्
578.	*Bheṣajam*	भेषजम्
579.	*Bhiṣak*	भिषक्
580.	*Sanyāskṛt*	सन्यासकृत्
581.	*Samaḥ*	सम:
582.	*Śāntaḥ*	शान्त:
583.	*Niṣṭhā*	निष्ठा
584.	*Śāntiḥ*	शान्ति:
585.	*Parāyaṇam*	परायणम्
586.	*Śubhāngaḥ*	शुभाङ्ग:
587.	*Śāntidaḥ*	शान्तिद:
588.	*Sraṣṭā*	स्रष्टा
589.	*Kumudaḥ*	कुमुद:
590.	*Kuvaleśayaḥ*	कुवलेशय:
591.	*Gohitaḥ*	गोहित:
592.	*Gopatiḥ*	गोपति:
593.	*Goptā*	गोप्ता
594.	*Vṛṣabhākṣaḥ*	वृषभाक्ष:
595.	*Vṛṣapriyaḥ*	वृषप्रिय:
596.	*Anivartī*	अनिवर्ती

#	Name in English	Name in Samskrutam
597.	*Nivṛttātmā*	निवृत्तात्मा
598.	*Saṃkṣeptā*	सम्क्षेप्ता
599.	*Kṣemakṛt*	क्षेमकृत्
600.	*Śivaḥ*	शिव:
601.	*Śrīvatsavakṣaḥ*	श्रीवत्सवक्ष:
602.	*Śrīvāsaḥ*	श्रीवास:
603.	*Śrīpatiḥ*	श्रीपति:
604.	*Śrīmatāmvaraḥ*	श्रीमताम्वर:
605.	*Śrīdaḥ*	श्रीद:
606.	*Śrīśaḥ*	श्रीश:
607.	*Śrīnivāsaḥ*	श्रीनिवास:
608.	*Śrīnidhiḥ*	श्रीनिधि:
609.	*Śrīvibhāvanaḥ*	श्रीविभावन:
610.	*Śrīdharaḥ*	श्रीधर:
611.	*Śrīkaraḥ*	श्रीकर:
612.	*Śreyaḥ*	श्रेय:
613.	*Śrīmān*	श्रीमान्
614.	*Lokatrayāśrayaḥ*	लोकत्रयाश्रय:
615.	*Svakṣaḥ*	स्वक्ष:
616.	*Svangaḥ*	स्वङ्ग:
617.	*Śatānandaḥ*	शतानन्द:
618.	*Nandiḥ*	नन्दि:
619.	*Jyotirgaṇeśvaraḥ*	ज्योतिर्गणेश्वर:

#	Name in English	Name in Samskrutam
620.	*Vijītātmā*	विजितात्मा
621.	*Avidheyātmā*	अविधेयात्मा
622.	*Satkīrtiḥ*	सत्कीर्तिः
623.	*Cinnasamśayaḥ*	चिन्नसम्शयः
624.	*Udhīrṇaḥ*	उदिर्णः
625.	*Sarvataścakṣuḥ*	सर्वतश्चक्षुः
626.	*Anīśaḥ*	अनीशः
627.	*Śāśvatasthiraḥ*	शाश्वतस्थिरः
628.	*Bhūśayaḥ*	भूशयः
629.	*Bhūṣaṇaḥ*	भूषणः
630.	*Bhūtiḥ*	भूतिः
631.	*Viśokaḥ*	विशोकः
632.	*Śokanāśanaḥ*	शोकनाशनः
633.	*Arciṣmān*	अर्चिष्मान्
634.	*Arcitaḥ*	अर्चितः
635.	*Kumbhaḥ*	कुम्भः
636.	*Viśuddhātmā*	विश्द्धात्मा
637.	*Viśodhanaḥ*	विशोधनः
638.	*Aniruddhāḥ*	अनिरुद्धाः
639.	*Apratirathaḥ*	अप्रतिरथः
640.	*Pradyumnaḥ*	प्रद्युम्नः
641.	*Amitavikramaḥ*	अमितविक्रमः
642.	*Kālaneminihā*	कालनेमिनिहा

#	Name in English	Name in Samskrutam
643.	*Vīraḥ*	वीर:
644.	*Śouriḥ*	शौरि:
645.	*Śūrajaneśvaraḥ*	शूरजनेश्वर:
646.	*Trilokatmāḥ*	त्रिलोकात्मा:
647.	*Trilokeśaḥ*	त्रिलोकेश:
648.	*Keśavaḥ*	केशव:
649.	*Keśihā*	केशिहा
650.	*Hariḥ*	हरि:
651.	*Kāmadevaḥ*	कामदेव:
652.	*Kāmapālaḥ*	कामपाल:
653.	*Kāmīḥ*	कामी:
654.	*Kāntaḥ*	कान्त:
655.	*Kṛtāgamaḥ*	कृतागम:
656.	*Anirdheśyavapuḥ*	अनिर्देश्यवपु:
657.	*Viṣṇuḥ*	विष्णु:
658.	*Vīraḥ*	वीर:
659.	*Ānantaḥ*	आनन्त:
660.	*Dhananjayaḥ*	धनञ्जय:
661.	*Brahmaṇyaḥ*	ब्रह्मण्य:
662.	*Brahmakṛt*	ब्रह्मकृत्
663.	*Brahmā*	ब्रह्मा
664.	*Brahma*	ब्रह्म
665.	*Brahmavivardhanaḥ*	ब्रह्मविवर्धन:

#	Name in English	Name in Samskrutam
666.	*Brahmavit*	ब्रह्मवित्
667.	*Brāhmaṇaḥ*	ब्राह्मण:
668.	*Brahmī*	ब्रह्मी
669.	*Brahmajnaḥ*	ब्रह्मज्ञ:
670.	*Brāhmaṇapriyaḥ*	ब्रामणप्रिय:
671.	*Mahākramaḥ*	महाक्रम:
672.	*Mahākarmaḥ*	महाकर्म:
673.	*Mahātejaḥ*	महातेज:
674.	*Mahoragaḥ*	महोरग:
675.	*Mahākratuḥ*	महाक्रतु:
676.	*Mahāyajvā*	महायज्वा
677.	*Mahāyagnaḥ*	महायज्ञ:
678.	*Mahāhaviḥ*	महाहवि:
679.	*Sthavyaḥ*	स्तव्य:
680.	*Sthavapriyaḥ*	स्तवप्रिय:
681.	*Stotram*	स्तोत्रम्
682.	*Stutiḥ*	स्तुति:
683.	*Stotrā*	स्तोत्रा
684.	*Raṇapriyaḥ*	रणप्रिय:
685.	*Pūrṇāḥ*	पूर्णा:
686.	*Pūrayitā*	पूरयिता
687.	*Puṇyaḥ*	पुण्य:
688.	*Puṇyakṛtiḥ*	पुण्यकृति:

#	Name in English	Name in Samskrutam
689.	*Anāmayaḥ*	अनामय:
690.	*Manojavaḥ*	मनोजव:
691.	*Tīrthakaraḥ*	तीर्थकर:
692.	*Vasuretāḥ*	वसुरेता:
693.	*Vasupradaḥ*	वसुप्रद:
694.	*Vasupradaḥ*	वसुप्रद:
695.	*Vāsudevaḥ*	वासुदेव:
696.	*Vasuḥ*	वसु:
697.	*Vasumnāḥ*	वसुम्ना:
698.	*Haviḥ*	हवि:
699.	*Sadgatiḥ*	सद्गति:
700.	*Satkṛtiḥ*	सत्कृति:
701.	*Sattā*	सत्ता
702.	*Sadbhūtiḥ*	सद्भूति:
703.	*Satparāyaṇaḥ*	सत्परायण:
704.	*Ṣūrasenaḥ*	षूरसेन:
705.	*Yaduśresṭhaḥ*	यदुश्रेष्ठ:
706.	*Sannivāsaḥ*	सन्निवास:
707.	*Suyāmunaḥ*	सुयामुन:
708.	*Bhūtāvāsaḥ*	भूतावास:
709.	*Vāsudevaḥ*	वासुदेव:
710.	*Sarvāsunilayaḥ*	सर्वासुनिलय:
711.	*Analaḥ*	अनल:

#	Name in English	Name in Samskrutam
712.	*Darpahā*	दर्पहा
713.	*Darpadaḥ*	दर्पदः
714.	*Dṛptaḥ*	दृप्तः
715.	*Durdharaḥ*	दुर्धरः
716.	*Aparājitaḥ*	अपराजितः
717.	*Viśvamūrtiḥ*	विश्वमूर्तिः
718.	*Mahāmūrtiḥ*	महामूर्तिः
719.	*Dīptamūrtiḥ*	दीप्तमूर्तिः
720.	*Amūrtimān*	अमूर्तिमान्
721.	*Anekamūrtiḥ*	अनेकमूर्तिः
722.	*Avyaktaḥ*	अव्यक्तः
723.	*Śatamūrtiḥ*	शतमूर्तिः
724.	*Śatānanaḥ*	शताननः
725.	*Ekaḥ*	एकः
726.	*Naikaḥ*	नैकः
727.	*Savaḥ*	सवः
728.	*Kaḥ*	कः
729.	*Kim*	किम्
730.	*Yat*	यत्
731.	*Tat*	तत्
732.	*Padamanuttamam*	पदमनुत्तमम्
733.	*Lokabandhuḥ*	लोकबन्धुः
734.	*Lokanāthā*	लोकनाथः

#	Name in English	Name in Samskrutam
735.	*Mādhavāḥ*	माधवा:
736.	*Bhakthavatsalaḥ*	भक्तवत्सल:
737.	*Suvarṇavarṇaḥ*	सुवर्णवर्ण:
738.	*Hemāngaḥ*	हेमाङ्ग:
739.	*Varāngaḥ*	वराङ्ग:
740.	*Candanāngaḥ*	चन्दनाङ्ग:
741.	*Vīrahāḥ*	वीरहा:
742.	*Viṣamaḥ*	विषम:
743.	*Śūnyaḥ*	शून्य:
744.	*Gṛtāśiḥ*	घृताशि:
745.	*Acalaḥ*	अचल:
746.	*Calaḥ*	चल:
747.	*Amānī*	अमानी
748.	*Mānadaḥ*	मानद:
749.	*Mānyāḥ*	मान्य:
750.	*Lokasvāmiḥ*	लोकस्वामि
751.	*Trilokadṛk*	त्रिलोकधृक्
752.	*Sumedhā*	सुमेधा
753.	*Medhajaḥ*	मेधज:
754.	*Dhanyaḥ*	धन्य:
755.	*Satyamedhāḥ*	सत्यमेधा:
756.	*Dharādharaḥ*	धराधर:
757.	*Tejovṛṣaḥ*	तेजोवृष:

#	Name in English	Name in Samskrutam
758.	*Dhyutidharaḥ*	द्युतिधरः
759.	*Sarvaśāstrabṛtāvaraḥ*	सर्वशास्त्रभृताम्वरः
760.	*Pragrahaḥ*	प्रग्रहः
761.	*Nigrahaḥ*	निग्रहः
762.	*Vyagraḥ*	व्यग्रः
763.	*Naikaśriṇgaḥ*	नैकश्रिण्गः
764.	*Gadāgrajaḥ*	गदाग्रजः
765.	*Caturmūrtiḥ*	चतुर्मूर्तिः
766.	*Caturbāhuḥ*	चतुर्बाहुः
767.	*Caturvyūhaḥ*	चतुर्व्यूहः
768.	*Caturgatiḥ*	चतुर्गतिः
769.	*Caturātmāḥ*	चतुरात्माः
770.	*Caturbhāvaḥ*	चतुर्भावः
771.	*Caturvedavit*	चतुर्वेदवित्
772.	*Ekapāt*	एकपात्
773.	*Samāvartaḥ*	समावर्तः
774.	*Nivṛttātmā*	अनिवृत्तात्मा
775.	*Durjyaḥ*	दुर्जयः
776.	*Duratikramaḥ*	दुरतिक्रमः
777.	*Durlabhaḥ*	दुर्लभः
778.	*Durgamaḥ*	दुर्गमः
779.	*Durgaḥ*	दुर्गः
780.	*Durāvāsaḥ*	दुरावासः

#	Name in English	Name in Samskrutam
781.	*Durārihāḥ*	दुरारिहा:
782.	*Śubhāngaḥ*	शुभाङ्ग:
783.	*Lokasārangaḥ*	लोकसारङ्ग:
784.	*Sutantuḥ*	सुतन्तु:
785.	*Tantuvardhanaḥ*	तन्तुवर्धन:
786.	*Indrakarmā*	इन्द्रकर्मा
787.	*Mahākarmā*	महाकर्मा
788.	*Kṛthakarmā*	कृतकर्मा
789.	*Kṛtāgamaḥ*	कृतागम:
790.	*Udbhavaḥ*	उद्भव:
791.	*Sundaraḥ*	सुन्दर:
792.	*Sundaḥ*	सुन्द:
793.	*Ratnanābhaḥ*	रत्ननाभ:
794.	*Sulocanaḥ*	सुलोचन:
795.	*Arkaḥ*	अर्क:
796.	*Vājasanaḥ*	वाजसन:
797.	*Śṛngī*	शृङ्गी
798.	*Jayantaḥ*	जयन्त:
799.	*Sarvavijjayi*	सर्वविज्जयि
800.	*Suvarṇabinduḥ*	सुवर्णबिन्दु:
801.	*Akṣobhyaḥ*	अक्षोभ्य:
802.	*Sarvavāghīśvareśvaraḥ*	सर्ववागीश्वरेश्वर:
803.	*Mahāhṛdaḥ*	महाहृद:

#	Name in English	Name in Samskrutam
804.	*Mahāgartaḥ*	महागर्तः
805.	*Mahābhūtaḥ*	महाभूतः
806.	*Mahānidhiḥ*	महानिधिः
807.	*Kumudaḥ*	कुमुदः
808.	*Kundaraḥ*	कुन्दरः
809.	*Kundaḥ*	कुन्दः
810.	*Parjanyaḥ*	पर्जन्यः
811.	*Pāvanaḥ*	पावनः
812.	*Anilaḥ*	अनिलः
813.	*Amṛtānśaḥ*	अमृताशः
814.	*Amṛtavapuḥ*	अमृतवपुः
815.	*Sarvagnaḥ*	सर्वज्ञः
816.	*Sarvatomukhaḥ*	सर्वतोमुखः
817.	*Sulabhaḥ*	सुलभः
818.	*Suvrataḥ*	सुव्रतः
819.	*Siddhaḥ*	सिद्धः
820.	*Śatrujit*	शत्रुजित्
821.	*Śatrutāpanaḥ*	शत्रुतापनः
822.	*Nyagrodhaḥ*	न्यग्रोधः
823.	*Udumbaraḥ*	उदुम्बरः
824.	*Aśvatthaḥ*	अश्वत्थः
825.	*Cāṇūrāndaraniṣūdanaḥ*	चाणूरान्ध्रनिषूदनः
826.	*Sahasrārciḥ*	सहस्रार्चिः

#	Name in English	Name in Samskrutam
827.	*Saptajīhvāḥ*	सप्तजिह्वा:
828.	*Saptaidhāḥ*	सप्तैधा:
829.	*Saptavāhanaḥ*	सप्तवाहन:
830.	*Amūrtiḥ*	अमूर्ति:
831.	*Anaghaḥ*	अनघ:
832.	*Acintyaḥ*	अचिन्त्य:
833.	*Bhayakṛt*	भयकृत्
834.	*Bhayanāśanaḥ*	भयनाशन:
835.	*Aṇuḥ*	अणु:
836.	*Bṛhat*	बृहत्
837.	*Kṛśaḥ*	कृश:
838.	*Sthūlaḥ*	स्थूल:
839.	*Guṇabhṛt*	गुणभृत्
840.	*Nirguṇaḥ*	निर्गुण:
841.	*Mahān*	महान्
842.	*Adhṛt*	अद्दत:
843.	*Svadhṛt*	स्वधृत:
844.	*Svāsyaḥ*	स्वास्य:
845.	*Prāgvamśaḥ*	प्राग्वम्श:
846.	*Vamśvardhanaḥ*	वम्शवर्धन:
847.	*Bhārabhṛt*	भारभृत्
848.	*Kathitaḥ*	कथित:
849.	*Yogī*	योगी

#	Name in English	Name in Samskrutam
850.	*Yogīśaḥ*	योगीशः
851.	*Sarvakāmadaḥ*	सर्वकामदः
852.	*Āśramaḥ*	आश्रमः
853.	*Śramaṇaḥ*	श्रमणः
854.	*Kṣāmaḥ*	क्षामः
855.	*Suparṇaḥ*	सुपर्णः
856.	*Vāyuvāhanaḥ*	वायुवाहनः
857.	*Dhanurdharaḥ*	धनुर्धरः
858.	*Dhanurvedaḥ*	धनुर्वेदः
859.	*Daṇḍaḥ*	दण्डः
860.	*Damayitā*	दमयिता
861.	*Damaḥ*	दमः
862.	*Aparājitaḥ*	अपराजितः
863.	*Sarvasahaḥ*	सर्वसहः
864.	*Niyantā*	नियन्ता
865.	*Aniyamaḥ*	अनियमः
866.	*Ayamaḥ*	अयमः
867.	*Satvavān*	सत्ववान्
868.	*Sātvikaḥ*	सात्त्विकः
869.	*Satyaḥ*	सत्यः
870.	*Satyadharmaparāyaṇaḥ*	सत्यधर्मपरायणः
871.	*Abhiprāyaḥ*	अभिप्रायः
872.	*Priyārhaḥ*	प्रियार्हः

#	Name in English	Name in Samskrutam
873.	*Arhaḥ*	अर्हः
874.	*Priyakṛt*	प्रियकृत्
875.	*Prītivardhanaḥ*	प्रीतिवर्धनः
876.	*Vihāyasagatiḥ*	विहायसगतिः
877.	*Jyotiḥ*	ज्योतिः
878.	*Suruciḥ*	सुरुचिः
879.	*Hutabhuk*	हुतभुक्
880.	*Vibhuḥ*	विभुः
881.	*Raviḥ*	रविः
882.	*Virocanaḥ*	विरोचनः
883.	*Sūryaḥ*	सूर्यः
884.	*Savitā*	सविता
885.	*Ravilocanaḥ*	रविलोचनः
886.	*Anantaḥ*	अनन्तः
887.	*Hutabhuk*	हुतभुक्
888.	*Bhoktāḥ*	भोक्ताः
889.	*Sukhadaḥ*	सुखदः
890.	*Naikajaḥ*	नैकजः
891.	*Agrajaḥ*	अग्रजः
892.	*Anirviṇṇaḥ*	अनिर्विण्णः
893.	*Sadāmarṣiḥ*	सदामर्षि
894.	*Lokādhiṣṭhānam*	लोकाधिष्ठानम्
895.	*Adbhutaḥ*	अद्भुतः

#	Name in English	Name in Samskrutam
896.	*Sanāt*	सनात्
897.	*Sanātanatamaḥ*	सनातनतम:
898.	*Kapilaḥ*	कपिल:
899.	*Kapiḥ*	कपि:
900.	*Apyayaḥ*	अप्यय:
901.	*Svastidaḥ*	स्वस्तिद:
902.	*Svastikṛt*	स्वस्तिकृत्
903.	*Svasti*	स्वस्ति
904.	*Svastibhuk*	स्वस्तिभुक्
905.	*Svastidakṣiṇa*	स्वस्तिदक्षिण:
906.	*Aroudhraḥ*	अरौद्र:
907.	*Kuṇḍalī*	कुण्डली
908.	*Cakrī*	चक्री
909.	*Vikramī*	विक्रमी
910.	*Ūrjitaśāsanaḥ*	ऊर्जितशासन:
911.	*Śabdātigaḥ*	शब्दातिग:
912.	*Śabdasahaḥ*	शब्दसह:
913.	*Śiśirā*	शिशिर:
914.	*Śarvarīkaraḥ*	शर्वरीकर:
915.	*Akrūraḥ*	अक्रूर:
916.	*Peśalaḥ*	पेशल:
917.	*Dhakṣaḥ*	दक्ष:
918.	*Dakṣiṇaḥ*	दक्षिण:

#	Name in English	Name in Samskrutam
919.	*Kṣamiṇāmvaraḥ*	क्षमिणांवर:
920.	*Vidvattamaḥ*	विद्वत्तम:
921.	*Vītabhayaḥ*	वीतभय:
922.	*Puṇyaśravaṇakīrtanaḥ*	पुण्यश्रवणकीर्तन:
923.	*Uttāraṇaḥ*	उत्तारण:
924.	*Duṣkṛtihā*	दुष्कृतिहा
925.	*Puṇyaḥ*	पुण्य:
926.	*Duḥsvapnanāśanaḥ*	दु:स्वप्ननाशन:
927.	*Vīrahā*	विरहा
928.	*Rakṣaṇaḥ*	रक्षण:
929.	*Santaḥ*	सन्त:
930.	*Jīvanaḥ*	जीवन:
931.	*Paryavastitaḥ*	पर्यवस्थित:
932.	*Anantarūpaḥ*	अनन्तरूप:
933.	*Anantaśrī*	अनन्तश्री:
934.	*Jitamanyuḥ*	जितमन्यु:
935.	*Bhayāpahaḥ*	भयापह:
936.	*Caturaśraḥ*	चतुरश्र:
937.	*Gabīrātmā*	गभिरात्मा
938.	*Vidiśaḥ*	विदिश:
939.	*Vyādiśaḥ*	व्यादिश:
940.	*Diśaḥ*	दिश:
941.	*Anādiḥ*	अनादि:

#	Name in English	Name in Samskrutam
942.	*Bhurbhuvaḥ*	भूर्भुवः
943.	*Lakṣmīḥ*	लक्ष्मीः
944.	*Suvīraḥ*	सुवीरः
945.	*Rucirāngadaḥ*	रुचिराङ्गदः
946.	*Jananaḥ*	जननः
947.	*Janajanmādiḥ*	जनजन्मादिः
948.	*Bhīmaḥ*	भीमः
949.	*Bhīmaparākramaḥ*	भीमपराक्रमः
950.	*Ādhārnilayaḥ*	आधारनिलयः
951.	*Adhātā*	अधाता
952.	*Puśpahāsaḥ*	पुश्पहासः
953.	*Prajāgaraḥ*	प्रजागरः
954.	*Ūrdhvagaḥ*	ऊर्ध्वगः
955.	*Satpathācāraḥ*	सत्पथाचारः
956.	*Prāṇadaḥ*	प्राणदः
957.	*Praṇavaḥ*	प्रणवः
958.	*Paṇaḥ*	पणः
959.	*Pramāṇam*	प्रमाणम्
960.	*Prānanilayaḥ*	प्राणनिलयः
961.	*Prāṇabhṛt*	प्राणभृत्
962.	*Prāṇajīvanaḥ*	प्राणजीवनः
963.	*Tattvam*	तत्त्वम्
964.	*Tattvavit*	तत्त्ववित्

#	Name in English	Name in Samskrutam
965.	*Ekātmā*	एकात्मा
966.	*Janmamṛtyujarātigaḥ*	जन्ममृत्युजरातिग:
967.	*Bhūrbhuvaḥsvastaruḥ*	भूर्भुव:स्वस्तरु:
968.	*Tāraḥ*	तार:
969.	*Savitā*	सविता
970.	*Prapitāmahaḥ*	प्रपितामह:
971.	*Yagnaḥ*	यज्ञ:
972.	*Yagnapatiḥ*	यज्ञपति:
973.	*Yajvā*	यज्वा
974.	*Yagnāngaḥ*	यज्ञाङ्ग:
975.	*Yagnavāhānā*	यज्ञवाहन:
976.	*Yagnabṛt*	यज्ञभृत्
977.	*Yagnakṛt*	यज्ञकृत्
978.	*Yagnī*	यज्ञी
979.	*Yagnabhuk*	यज्ञभुक्
980.	*Yagnasādhanaḥ*	यज्ञसाधन:
981.	*Yagnāntakṛt*	यज्ञ।न्तकृत्
982.	*Yagnaguhyam*	यज्ञगुह्यम्
983.	*Annam*	अन्नम्
984.	*Annādaḥ*	अन्नाद:
985.	*Ātmayoniḥ*	आत्मयोनि:
986.	*Svayamjātaḥ*	स्वयम्जात:
987.	*Vaikhānaḥ*	वैखान:

#	Name in English	Name in Samskrutam
988.	*Sāmagāyanaḥ*	सामगायनः
989.	*Devakīnandanaḥ*	देवकीनन्दनः
990.	*Sraṣṭā*	स्रष्टा
991.	*Kṣitiśaḥ*	क्षितिशः
992.	*Pāpanāśanaḥ*	पापनाशनः
993.	*Śanghabṛt*	शङ्घभृत्
994.	*Nandakī*	नन्दकी
995.	*Cakrī*	चक्री
996.	*Śārngadhanvā*	शार्ङ्गधन्वा
997.	*Gadādharaḥ*	गदाधरः
998.	*Rathāngapāṇiḥ*	रथाङ्गपाणिः
999.	*Akṣobhyaḥ*	अक्षोभ्यः
1000.	*Sarvapraharaṇāyudhaḥ*	सर्वप्रहरणायुधः

*****

Bibiliography

1. Śree *Lalitā* Sahasranāma – English translation of Bhāskararāya's bhāşyam by the same author.
2. Samatā – a comparison of Śrī *Lalitā* Sahasranāma with Śrī *Vişņu* Sahasranāma, Śrīmad Bhagavad *Gīta*, Soundaryalaharī and Saptaśatī – by the same author.
3. Śree *Vişņu* Sahasranāma by Swami Tapasyananda, Ramakrishna Mutt Publications
4. Śree *Śiva* Sahasranāma Bhāshyam by Anna, Ramakrishna Mutt Publications

*****

Kāyena Vācā Manasendŗyervā, Buddhiḥ Ātmavāvā Prakŗtesvabhāvāt, Karomi Yadyat Sakalam Parasmai, Śrīman Nārāyaņayeti Samarpayāmi
Om Tat Sat

I offer all that I do, To Lord *Nārāyaņa*, Whatever I do with my body, with my mind, with my brain, with my soul and on account of natural tendency!
Om that is the truth.

*****

Other books by this Author

(http://Ramamurthy.jaagruti.co.in)

#	Title	Pages	Publisher	Remarks
		Indology Related		
1.	*Śrī Lalitā Sahasranāmam*	753	CBH Publications	English translation of Śrī *Bhāskararāya's Bhāśyam*
2.	Power of *Śrī Vidyā*	78		
3.	*Samatā*	176		An exposition of Similarities in *Lalitā Sahasranāma* with *Soundaryalaharī, Saptaśatī, Viśṇu Sahasranāma* and *Śrīmad Bhagavad Gīta*
4.	*Advaita* in *Shākta*	80		
5.	*Śrī Lalitā Triśatī*	176		300 divine names of the celestial Mother – **English** translation of *Śrī Ādhi Śaṅkara*'s *Bhāśyam*
6.	Secrets of *Mahāśakti*	88		
7.	*Daśa Mahā Vidyā*	60	HH *Praṇavānunda Avadūta Saraswati Swamiji,* Ayyarmalai.	Ten cosmic forms of the Divine mother
8.	ஸ்ரீவித்யா பேதங்கள்	60		
9.	*Vaidhīka* Wedding	48	Self	
10.	வைதீகத் திருமணம்	60		
11.	ஸ்ரீ லலிதா திரிஶதி	234	HH *Rāmānanda Saraswati Swamiji,* Madurai	Tamil translation of Śrī Ādi *Śaṅkara*'s Bhāśyam
12.	ஸ்ரீகுரு பாதுகா பூஜா விதானம்	44	Bhagavān Śīrdi Sāibaba Trust, Edapalli, Kunoor	
13.	ஸ்ரீவித்யா ஶடாம்னாய மந்திரங்கள்	44		
14.	ஷண்மத மந்திரங்கள்	150	Agni Trust, Anaimalai, Pollachi	
15.	*Śrīvidya* Variances	60	Self as e-book	
16.	*Ṣanmata Mantras*	86		
17.	வேதங்கள் ஒரு பகுப்பாய்வு	280		
18.	ஸ்ரீ தேவீ ஸ்துதிகள்	131		
19.	*Ekatā*	276	ORIGINALS, Delhi.	

#	Title	Pages	Publisher	Remarks
20.	ஸ்ரீ மஹா ப்ரத்யங்கிரா தேவீ	60		
21.	*Śrī Mahā Pratyangirā Devī*	60		
22.	*Vedas* - An Analytical Perspective	260	ORIGINALS, Delhi.	
		Applied Samskrutam Based		
23.	*Paribhāṣā Stora*-s	96	CBH Publications	An exploration of *Lalitā Sahasranāma*
24.	*Śrī Cakra*, An Esoteric Approach	64		Mathematical Construction to draw *Śrī Cakra*
25.	Number System in Samskrutam	126		
26.	*Vedic* Mathematics	160		30 formulae elucidated
27.	Vedic IT	162	ORIGINALS, Delhi.	Information Technology and Samskrutam
		IT Based		
28.	Orthogonal Array	178	ORIGINALS, Delhi	A Statistical Tool for Software Testing
		Banking Based		
29.	Retail Banking	213	ORIGINALS, Delhi.	
30.	Corporate Banking	232		
31.	Dictionary of Financial Terms	215		
32.	श्री ललिता सहस्रनाम written by this author's sister, Ms. Sampoornam N	750		Hindi translation of Śrī Bhāskararāya's *Bhāśyam*

More books are on the unveil. Let *Viṣṇu*, *Śiva* and *Śakti* shower their fullest blessings on him to share more of his knowledge and experiences.

*****

www.ingramcontent.com/pod-product-compliance
Lightning Source LLC
LaVergne TN
LVHW051623080426
835511LV00016B/2142
* 9 7 8 9 3 8 2 2 3 7 1 0 5 *